Reputational Risk

FT Prentice Hall
FINANCIAL TIMES

In an increasingly competitive world, we believe it's quality of thinking that will give you the edge – an idea that opens new doors, a technique that solves a problem, or an insight that simply makes sense of it all. The more you know, the smarter and faster you can go.

That's why we work with the best minds in business and finance to bring cutting-edge thinking and best learning practice to a global market.

Under a range of leading imprints, including *Financial Times Prentice Hall*, we create world-class print publications and electronic products bringing our readers knowledge, skills and understanding which can be applied whether studying or at work.

To find out more about our business publications, or tell us about the books you'd like to find, you can visit us at **www.pearsoned.co.uk**

PEARSON
Education

Reputational Risk

How to manage for value creation

ARIF ZAMAN

FINANCIAL TIMES

An imprint of **Pearson Education**

London • New York • Toronto • Sydney • Tokyo • Singapore
Hong Kong • Cape Town • Madrid • Paris • Amsterdam • Munich • Milan

PEARSON EDUCATION LIMITED

Head Office:
Edinburgh Gate
Harlow CM20 2JE
Tel: +44 (0)1279 623623
Fax: +44 (0)1279 431059
Website: www.briefingzone.com

First published in Great Britain in 2004

© Pearson Education Limited 2004

The right of Arif Zaman to be identified as author of
this work has been asserted by him in accordance
with the Copyright, Designs and Patents Act 1988.

ISBN 0 273 66155 8

British Library Cataloguing in Publication Data
A CIP catalogue record for this book can be obtained from the British Library.

10 9 8 7 6 5 4 3 2 1

Typeset by Monolith – www.monolith.uk.com
Printed and bound in Great Britain by Ashford Colour Press Ltd, Gosport, Hants.

The Publishers' policy is to use paper manufactured from sustainable forests.

About the author

Arif Zaman is an Associate Fellow in the Corporate Responsibility team within the Sustainable Development Programme at the Royal Institute of International Affairs ('Chatham House') and a Research Fellow at Henley Management College's Centre for Corporate Reputation and Relationships. He was one of the last people to be sponsored for his MBA by British Airways and one of the few to do so not on the company's in-house MBA programme but at Henley. He received a Recognizing our People award from BA for his contribution to the revamped Code of Conduct and BA's first Social Report and Sustainability Policy. He was an inaugural recipient of The International Air Cargo Association (TIACA) industry award for two research papers produced in 1998 and subsequently used in a UN study.

Previously he was Global and Market Industry Analyst at British Airways from 1993 to 2002 where he contributed to several strategic projects at both the group and business unit level. He is currently on a year's sabbatical leave from British Airways.

Arif is on the board of the Strategic Planning Society and the Red Shift Theatre Company, the latter of which he has recently completed a term as Chair. He is also a Fellow of the Royal Asiatic Society and the Royal Society of Arts.

He is author of 'Made in Japan – Converging Trends in Corporate Responsibility and Corporate Governance' (Chatham House paper, July 2003).

He offers several perspectives:

■ working in the service sector previously based in a key customer account team but developing strategic relationships with global manufacturing companies and their supply chains;

■ not an academic but a freelance researcher at one of the world's leading research centres in corporate reputation and relationships and one of the world's leading institutes for the analysis of international issues;

■ not a communications consultant but has worked in a leading financial PR firm whose successor firm was recently named PR agency of the year;

■ not an accountant but has worked in a Big 4 bank and a commercial finance team at a leading international airline;

■ active on the boards of several leading national organizations in the non-profit sector (including a university travel bursary, a business strategy educational group and a leading theatre company);

■ British-born but with a sense of his Pakistani and Indian and Muslim identity.

Arif can be contacted at arifzaman@ftnetwork.com

Contents

Figures

Tables

Foreword

by Keith MacMillan, Director, Centre for Organization Reputation and Relationships (CORR), Chairman, Centre for Board Effectiveness (CBE), and John Madejski Professor of Business Reputation, Henley Management Centre

Each generation of managers has to come to terms with an array of new challenges. And with new challenges comes a new set of 'rules of the game'. Today the challenges are less certain and less tangible, but are nevertheless of critical importance. Many affect corporate reputation, bringing with them both opportunities and risks. It is the risks which hit the headlines. The reputations of many major companies, formerly held in high regard, now hang in tatters. Had they known how, their reputations could have been better managed. They did not appear to appreciate how strong the forces are that affect reputation.

This book is very timely. The new 'rules of the game' concerning corporate reputation are taking shape. These go well beyond corporate image or identity and are in a totally different league from public relations. The start is now corporate governance and the reform of company law, where the duties of directors and company reporting requirements explicitly deal with the imperatives of reputation. Underpinning these are the fundamentals of good management, in developing strong relationships with those stakeholders who provide current and future support for the business – customers, employees, investors and the community.

By focussing on these fundamental relationships, this book points the way to how to manage reputational risk. It is not rocket science, but if these basic points are not sufficiently in the forefront of manager's minds it will be difficult for them to avoid risk. Moreover, companies now have to report on the steps they are taking to manage risk. This book indicates that the best way for a business to report on reputational risk is to report on the strength of its stakeholder relationships. Such reports can provide other benefits. They are also good indicators of business opportunities, the other side of the coin to risk. The stronger these relationships, the greater are the opportunities to the business. And this is where the sources of future business value are really to be found.

Preface

This book is borne out of experience, research (originally for an MBA sponsored by British Airways at Henley Management College), participation in several action learning networks (such as the Social and Ethical Risk Group in 2000–2 and the Strategic Planning Society's Risk Special Interest Group, of which the author was Chair, in 2001–03) and further reflection (while a researcher at the Royal Institute of International Affairs ('Chatham House') and Henley Management College. It sets out to provide clear and relevant meaning for a term that is often and increasingly used but seldom defined: 'reputational risk'. It approaches the subject not from the perspective of a consultant (as a crisis to be managed) or an insurance adviser (as something that can be insured or planned for as a hazard) – as is too often the case – but as a corporate practitioner with two decades working in major FTSE100 companies in the service sector.

Acknowledgements

Space does not permit acknowledgment to all 24 interviewees for my MBA dissertation, who provided the catalyst for many of the ideas as well as the many people since, who have helped inform my perspective. However I am grateful to the following in particular: Professor Keith MacMillan at Henley Management College; the participating companies in the original research (Barclays Bank, British Telcom, Marks & Spencer, Reuters, Dell and Fedex); Alan Buchanan and Keith Packer at British Airways (as well as several key past and current members of BA's board and executive team); Kevin O'Toole at 'Airline Business'; Ted White at CalPERS; Steve Russell at HSBC; Ken Rushton at the FSA; Jane Nelson at the International Business Leaders Forum; Dr DeAnne Julius, Chairman of the Royal Institute of International Affairs; Dr Maleeha Lodhi, Pakistan's Ambassador to the UK; and Mr Shigeru Handa at Toyota Motor Corporation.

I would also like to thank Laurie Donaldson at Financial Times Prentice Hall for his patience, perseverance and perception.

All views expressed remain those of the author.

To Alison with much love and unending gratitude.

I also dedicate this to the memory of Bashir and Asif Zaman, Tausif and Zohra Lodhi and Asghar Khan who were not there at the end but who helped me in more ways than they will ever know along the way.

In this modern era, issues of staff morale and motivation, brand loyalty and reputational risk, and environmental sustainability are now also widely recognized as key drivers of competitive advantage.

Gordon Brown, 4 March 2003.[1]

It is hard to overstate the importance of reputation in a market economy. To be sure, a market economy requires a structure of formal rules – a law of contracts, bankruptcy statutes, a code of shareholder rights – to name but a few. But rules cannot substitute for character. In virtually all transactions, whether with customers or with colleagues, we rely on the word of those with whom we do business. If we could not do so, goods and services could not be exchanged efficiently. Even when followed to the letter, rules guide only a small number of the day-to-day decisions required of corporate management. The rest are governed by whatever personal code of values corporate managers bring to the table.

Alan Greenspan, 8 May 2003.[2]

1   *http://www.hm-treasury.gov.uk/newsroom_and_speeches/press/2003/press_33_03.cfm*
2   *http://www.federalreserve.gov/boarddocs/speeches/2003/20030508/default.htm*

Executive summary

As this book went to press, British Airways experienced a rare bout of wildcat industrial action which left its reputation reeling. Though further action was averted, in many ways the incident captures much of the essence of what can happen when reputations sour, with customers especially, but also with employees and shareholders. Without analysing what happened, it highlighted the fragility of reputation. BA will recover (within a week, 95 per cent of staff polled on the corporate intranet – which many customer service staff use – said that the relationship between management and staff will improve as a result of the issues highlighted by the recent dispute) but few can claim any reputational gain. Certainly not the customers who were stranded at Heathrow during the holiday peak, the management that was so visibly caught out by the sudden nature of the action, the employees who walked out (who acted at best hastily, at worst irresponsibly), the unions (who were so uncoordinated in their initial response and seemingly so disconnected from their members' feelings that official channels were initially ignored) and even the shareholders who attended the company's AGM 72 hours before the action was taken, oblivious of the ticking time bomb. In the midst of the chaos one group perhaps saw some reputational gain though in the scheme of things this was understandably overshadowed by the tales of woe. When the cargo employees came to the support of the turmoil in the passenger terminals and helped with baggage handling in the nearby cargo facility, it prompted at least one major UK retailer and key cargo customer to comment on their commitment during a crisis.

This book sets out a holistic view of reputational risk and cases such as this are not a primary focus. There are plenty of primers on crisis management but there is little available that attempts to link reputational risk with value creation. For that to happen, the starting point must be corporate governance and Turnbull in particular. This book argues that for value to be realized, reputation needs to be seen as much more than the amount of column inches that PR departments and their advisers monitor. At its core it is about the character of the business and is what key stakeholders expect in terms of corporate behaviour. The risk arises when key stakeholders make comparisons with what they expect and what they experience but the key point is that this can be positive as well as negative. There is much for companies to do but so much that can be done if reputation is recognized and treated as the intangible asset that it so patently is. Moreover a focus on reputational risk for value creation can be a powerful way of understanding how to manage the business which connects to peoples' feelings and attitudes as well as actions. Arguably a service company has an in-built advantage here.

When the CEO of Zurich Financial Services departed after providing four profit warnings, it was clear that he had lost the trust of shareholders. Negative surprises thrill no-one and employees and shareholders are not exempt too. This book looks closely at each key stakeholder group to understand why and how stakeholder expectations are changing with time, attention and trust in short supply – and, crucially, how boards and management can begin to respond.

All this needs to put in a global context and a penultimate chapter attempts to do so. Ethical and social risk is a sub-set of reputational risk, not the other way round. Economic *durability* (from positive customer, employee and shareholder relationships) and environmental *sustainability* (and social responsibility) together provide the bedrocks for future *viability*. That is also a reality in which all the actors in BA's ugly experience – or any company's immediate crisis – also have a shared stake whether they know it or not.

Why reputation management is not enough

WHAT YOU MUST KNOW BEFORE YOU START

1 What is lacking in current approaches to reputation?

2 How does reputation link to corporate governance?

3 Why is the context changing for reputational risk?

4 How are the drivers of corporate brand equity changing?

5 How does this impact stakeholder expectations?

6 Why is emotional logic perhaps the most critical business driver?

7 What are the scarcities of time, attention and trust?

8 What is the social values shift?

9 Why is social capital a crucial building block of reputational risk (and reputational opportunity)?

10 What are the key changing ideas that underpin an integrative approach to understanding reputational risk?

It is ten years since *Financial Times Prentice Hall* first published *Reputational Risk Management*. In that period much has changed – and much has not. The Turnbull Committee on Internal Control (1999) brought the focus on reputation out of the marketing arena and into the heart of the discussion about ownership and value creation. However, much of the current material on reputation (in books, conference presentations or consultants' sales pitches) tends to concentrate exclusively on 'reputation management'. Too often this is completely synonymous with two areas which have negative connotations (for which author consultants are doubtless available to advise) and are more about value destruction than value creation:

■ crisis management

■ loss prevention.

Reputational up-side means that reputation risk can also be seen in terms of opportunities to be seized and value to be created. Innovative companies view risk through the lens of opportunity rather than just internal control and compliance, i.e. they see *risk* as both up-side and downside, as an opportunity platform as well as a safety net. Implicit in this is moving from a reactive to a more proactive approach.

WHY SHOULD I BE READING THIS?

This book will set out the need for a much more integrated approach and emerges out of international research which cuts across corporate silos, academic disciplines and national boundaries. In fact the biggest reputational risk that a company may face is to deny that it has one.

3

Current approaches to reputation are neither 'strategic' nor integrated. Often missing is a superficial and weak understanding of either *reputation* or *risk* (and often both). Why? There are two reasons why, one obvious, the other less so:

1 The use of both terms by so many people across functions and disciplines.

2 The way in which the meaning of language changes over time. Both 9/11 (highlighting both the political/safety aspects of risk) and Enron/Andersen (highlighting the fragility of reputation when trust is lost) show how events can give lead to new twists on familiar words.

Post-Enron, regulators have stressed that if:

> *the basic goal for directors should be the success of the company in the collective best interests of shareholders, directors should also recognise the company's need to foster relationships with its employees, customers and suppliers,* its need to maintain its business reputation, *and its need to consider the company's impact on the community and the working environment.*
>
> Companies Bill, Cm553–11, July 2002.

This touches on three elements that are integrally and increasingly linked (*see* Figure 1.1) and, when combined with understanding stakeholder expectations, form the key to unlocking the meaning of reputational risk for an international publicly quoted company – whether for the fund manager, board director or public regulator.

Fig. 1.1 Understanding stakeholder expectations

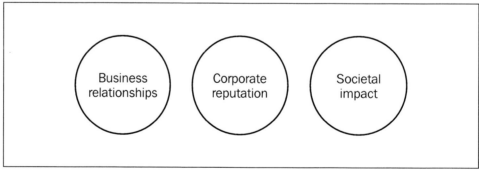

Today no company concerned with value creation for its key stakeholders can ignore – or have knowledge gaps – in these areas.

A strong, positive reputation:

- attracts staff, customers, suppliers and investors
- helps retain, staff, customers, suppliers and investors

- makes all stakeholders more forgiving

- may support higher margins

- may encourage employees to work harder

- supports share price

- increases strategic options (e.g. alliances)

- helps influence government and the media

- provides a basis for competitive advantage.

TURNBULL: A KEY REPORT, OFTEN MISUNDERSTOOD

Turnbull (1999) remains the most considered view on reputational risk within the policy arena. After Cadbury and Higgs, it is perhaps the most well-known corporate governance report. Prepared by a working party of the Institute of Chartered Accountants in England and Wales and endorsed by the London Stock Exchange, the Turnbull Report (*Internal Control: Guidance for Directors on the Combined Code*, 1999) aimed to reflect best business practice by adopting a risk-based approach to designing, operating and maintaining a sound system of internal control. For the first time, a major report on corporate governance explicitly cited risks to reputation *as a board priority*. Significantly, Sarbanes-Oxley in requiring stronger US corporate governance disclosure also emphasized a greater focus on risk management.

What Turnbull actually said was that 'significant risks could relate to reputation and business probity issues'. The key words are 'significant risks', i.e. those risks that have been identified by the senior management as being potentially damaging to the achievement of the company's objectives. It then went on to point out that boards needed to make:

> *specific arrangements for management monitoring and reporting on risk and control matters of particular importance ... which could include, for example, actual or suspected fraud and other illegal or irregular acts, or matters that could adversely affect the company's reputation or financial position.*
>
> Turnbull Report, 1999.

Most companies still see this view of reputation in a very narrow sense – about branding, public relations and managing the spin machine. Very few have approached Turnbull's comments on reputation as being about corporate behaviour – which is of course what corporate reputation actually depends on. Ironically, this is exactly what the Turnbull Committee intended in the first place.

The main authors of the Turnbull Committee have since acknowledged that 'many companies now find *reputation risk a central cause of concern*' which they need to identify and manage in the same way as they have previously managed more traditional forms of risk. They then added three caveats which have largely gone unnoticed:

1 *Control should be embedded in the culture and processes of the business.* Cumbersome risk databases can be a distraction from the primary goal of getting each person in the organization to be aware of, and manage, crucial risks related to the tasks that person performs.	*Implication*: Companies need to acknowledge that risk assurance starts and ends with corporate behaviour and not with elaborate risk registers developed with risk consultants. While corporate cultures will differ, an atmosphere in which people have and exhibit trust and respect should be universal.
2 *All employees have some responsibility for internal control.* Collectively, they should have the necessary knowledge, skills, information and authority to operate and monitor the internal control system.	*Implication*: Companies need to avoid believing that reputational risk is the exclusive province of people attending secretive board meetings or an outcome of discussions with its PR advisers. Especially in a service business, failing to deliver every day on customer expectations, can quickly erode a reputation for service quality.
3 *Communication between different levels of the organization and across departments plays a pivotal role.*	*Implication*: Silo thinking is not consistent with taking an integrated view of risk. Communication needs to be two-way, down-up as well as top-down and flow across departments. This is obviously linked to an atmosphere of trust and respect which is a precondition for open communication.

REPUTATION MANAGEMENT OR REPUTATIONAL RISK?

European risk managers see reputational risk as the biggest future threat to business. The need to understand what reputational risk is and how it can be managed to sustain value is also permeating to the public sector. Not-for-profit organizations are also grappling with new guidelines which are encouraging them to consider soft as well as hard risks, including reputational ones. This is significant as public regulators could themselves be taking a lead if corporate understanding of the issues looks to lag, on the back of competing priorities in a weaker economic environment. From 2002, every UK government department has had to indicate what its key risks, including reputation, are and what processes they have in place for managing them in line with Turnbull.

In uncertain times marked by higher volatility, a redefinition of risk is needed as companies make strategic choices when adjusting to new customer realities. This is also necessary as companies respond to challenges that are both unforeseen like 9/11 *and* arguably predictable, such as the emergence of corporate governance post-Enron as a mainstream business issue.

At the same time, several large, high profile and established companies have found by experience that if they lose the trust of a particular group of stakeholders, the costs can be very high, enduring beyond the economic life of a tangible asset. They have seen, even if they do not fully understand, that brand equity is a function of relationships and that its changing drivers can impact sustained shareholder value in three ways:

1 Access to capital.

2 Long-term profitability.

3 Cash flow.

In 2002, Greenspan noted that 'the proportion of our GDP that results from the use of conceptual, as distinct from physical, assets has been growing'. He also suggested that physical assets retain a good portion of their value even if the reputation of management is destroyed, while intangible assets may lose value rapidly.[1] The loss in value affects companies in different ways: 'in today's world where ideas are increasingly displacing the physical in the production of economic value, competition for *reputation* becomes a significant driving force (Fombrun, 2001).[2] The reality is that, in his words, 'service providers can offer only their reputations' – though this also affects companies like Shell and Unilever that have been trying in recent years to emphasize the service aspects of their production. What does this mean?

7

At the core is responding to expectations of increased transparency while building trust, through connecting with the attitudes, feelings and experiences of employees, customers and shareholders. This itself reflects a fundamental shift in what people perceive as value and a growing awareness that customers trust brands that listen. It also reflects a concerted effort to engage employees through the corporate brand and explicitly recognizes that motivated people are fundamental to the delivery of the customer proposition and ultimately a company's financial returns. This is especially true in an increasingly service-orientated economy. People may be a company's greatest asset but unless they are visibly invested in, this becomes a dangerously empty phrase.

However, people are not robots. The anti-brand backlash is partly a reflection that audiences are becoming increasingly effective at 'deconstructing' messages that, sometimes cynically, attempt to influence their behaviour. Traditional communication approaches are pushing companies into churning, frictionless markets, without loyalty or goodwill. The reputational fall-out in the financial services sector from pensions mis-selling in the UK is just one example of how customer loyalty cannot be taken for granted. The days of mindless corporate spin may be over.

This is more than an academic point. A social values shift, which growing evidence suggests cuts across all key stakeholder groups, has one clear message for boards: communication with customers, employees and shareholders needs to be seen as inherently dynamic, constantly evolving and visibly built on mutual respect and trust. Nothing less will do. Where does this leave us?

- Managing reputational risk and balancing stakeholder expectations is firmly on the board agenda and is becoming a priority for the executive leadership team.
- Value creation will increasingly depend first on a proper understanding by companies of what reputational risk really means (in language they can understand and through examples to which they can relate).

A strategy to protect and manage reputation follows from this.

WHAT DRIVES WHAT STAKEHOLDERS EXPECT OF CORPORATE BRANDS?

When looking at reputation and risk there is not enough focus on the changing drivers of corporate brand equity and how they impact stakeholder expectations. This is key to understanding what reputational risk is, why it matters and how it connects to value. In fact the challenge of balancing stakeholder expectations becomes more important as globalization increases. Moreover as one head of international audit of a FTSE 100 company told an audience days before the Bali bombing in 2002, stakeholder management assumed a more complex meaning after 9/11.

Driver 1: Emotions: the single most important business driver?

Practitioners and researchers alike have, traditionally, ignored or misunderstood the importance of feelings or emotions in management (*see* Figure 1.2). Managers are more inclined to emphasize rational or intellectual processes. Shell's reputational fall-out over Nigeria and Brent Spar in the late 1990s was fundamentally attributed by a senior Shell manager to an inability to recognize, let alone understand how emotions matter to people. As it was put to this author: 'rational and emotional elements of decision-making matter and are not mutually exclusive'. In a presentation to the BA Executive team on the company's re-branding after the modification of its tailfin global images, the context was clearly set out: 'in the absence of economic difference emotional logic will become the single most important business driver'.

Fig. 1.2 Changing drivers of corporate brand equity

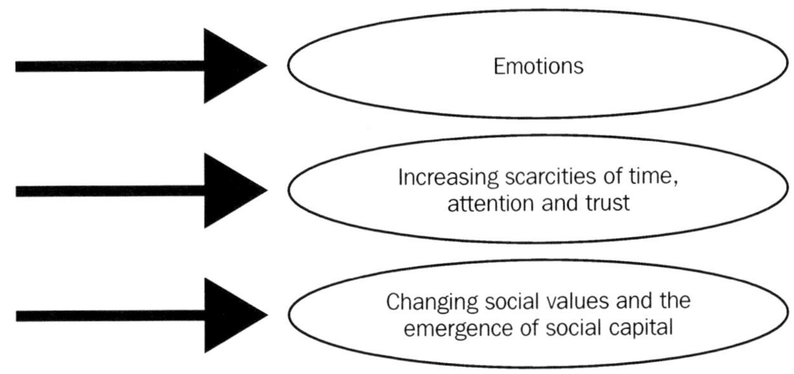

What this means is that it is important to know what organizational processes are visible and what are hidden in order to understand how decisions are really made. The key message is that psychological factors too play a part in business development (*see* Figure 1.3).

One of the most telling ways of seeing the impact of 'psychological issues' on economic value and people's expectations was in the performance of the US economy after 9/11.

Fig. 1.3 **Organizational processes**

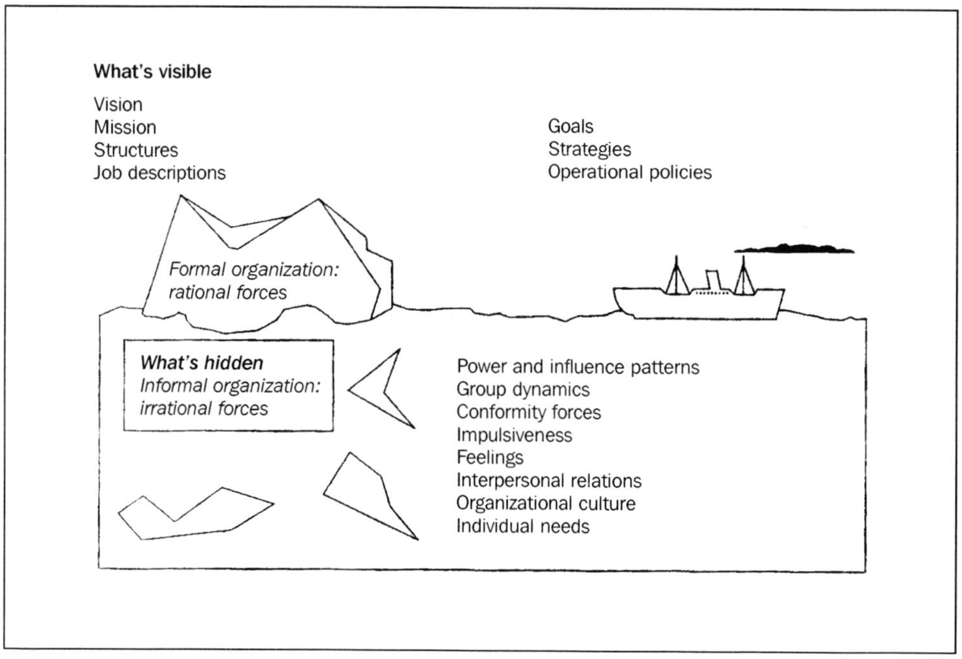
What's visible
Vision
Mission
Structures
Job descriptions
Goals
Strategies
Operational policies
Formal organization: rational forces
What's hidden
Informal organization: irrational forces
Power and influence patterns
Group dynamics
Conformity forces
Impulsiveness
Feelings
Interpersonal relations
Organizational culture
Individual needs

Source: de Vries, 2001.

Both Boeing and British Airways saw this first-hand.

- Boeing's chief economist, Bill Swann, has tracked the movement of GDP with the Conference Board's leading index of consumer confidence (*see* Figure 1.4).
- In the weeks that followed 9/11, and while coming to terms with a new international security regime, British Airways very quickly identified some of the factors at the centre of the situation (fear and anxiety from both terrorism and a weak economy) – and was consistent and clear in communicating so, whether to employees or investors (*see* Figure 1.5).

Fig. 1.4 **US consumer confidence and economic growth after 9/11**

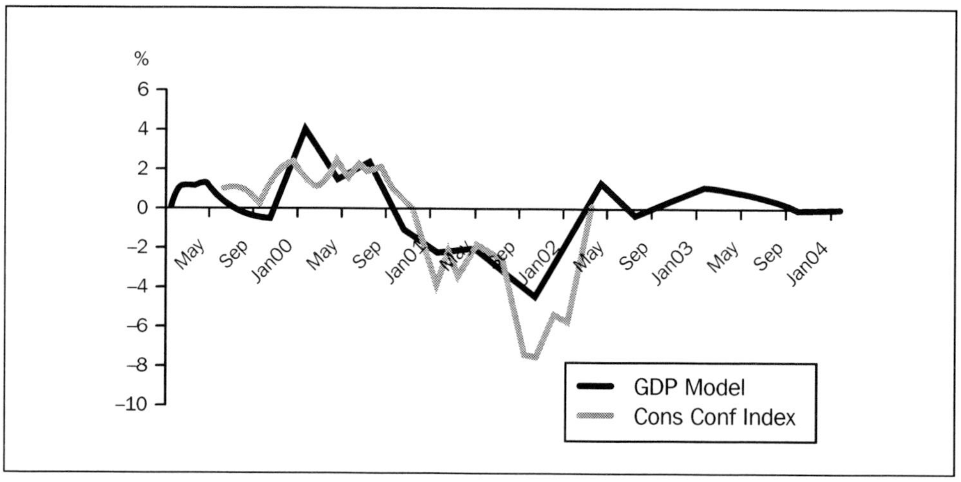
%
6
4
2
0
–2
–4
–6
–8
–10
May
Sep
Jan00
May
Sep
Jan01
May
Sep
Jan02
May
Sep
Jan03
May
Sep
Jan04
GDP Model
Cons Conf Index

Source: Boeing, 2002.

Fig. 1.5   BA communicates fear to its stakeholders after 9/11

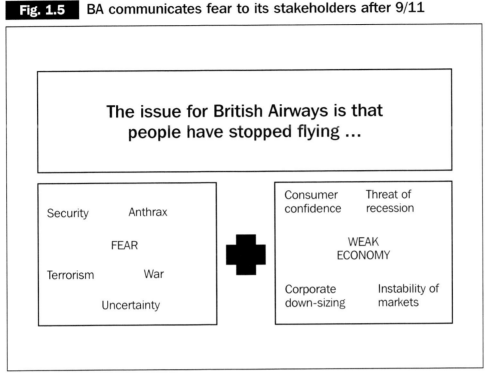

The issue for British Airways is that people have stopped flying ...

Security   Anthrax

FEAR

Terrorism   War

Uncertainty

Consumer   Threat of
confidence   recession

WEAK
ECONOMY

Corporate   Instability of
down-sizing   markets

Source: British Airways, 2001.

Do soft factors matter in economic performance? Post 9/11 research by an economics Nobel Laureate show how emotional factors can impact consumer behaviour and attitudes.

Case study 1.1

US consumer behaviour after 9/11

The resilience of the US economy was extraordinary following 9/11. This is an extremely important issue because consumer behaviour has been a key support for the US economy since 9/11 yet the consumer sector was supposedly vulnerable, as individuals suffered the most direct consequences of the surprise attack.

Income alone obviously drives consumer spending but it cannot tell the whole story. Picture the scene in the days and weeks after the 9/11 attack:

■ airports were closed

■ related travel-tourism businesses lacked customers

■ people embraced family members and stayed close to home.

Low income levels in October 2001 cannot explain the high volume of spending that month or stronger performance afterwards in the lead-in and after the usually busy Christmas shopping season.

What happened was that consumers were eventually:

■ reassured by the US military response to spend for the longer-run and by greater strictness of security standards

- enticed into the market sectors for cars, electrical appliances and property by very attractive interest rates
- influenced by the economic effects of much higher military spending
- influenced by reductions in taxation and by tax rebates.

These factors overwhelmed the negative wealth effects, increased unemployment, and announcements by many of impending 'recession'.

The key point is that people's expectations are subjective and this directly impacts market movements of strategic variables in an economic context.

Source: Nobel Laureate, Laurence Klein, to DRI-WEFA Economic Outlook Conference May 2002.

In its semi-annual economic assessment in 2003, Jean-Philippe Cotis, the OECD's chief economist, acknowledged that 'worries about oil prices, anxieties in the face of war, fear of terrorism and epidemics, loss of confidence in international governance' all comprised a 'list of the so-called geopolitical and psychological factors'.

The key message: companies need to focus on both rational and emotional components to achieve results and align individual behaviours with their goals and strategy.

Fig. 1.6 Balancing the emotional and rational aspects

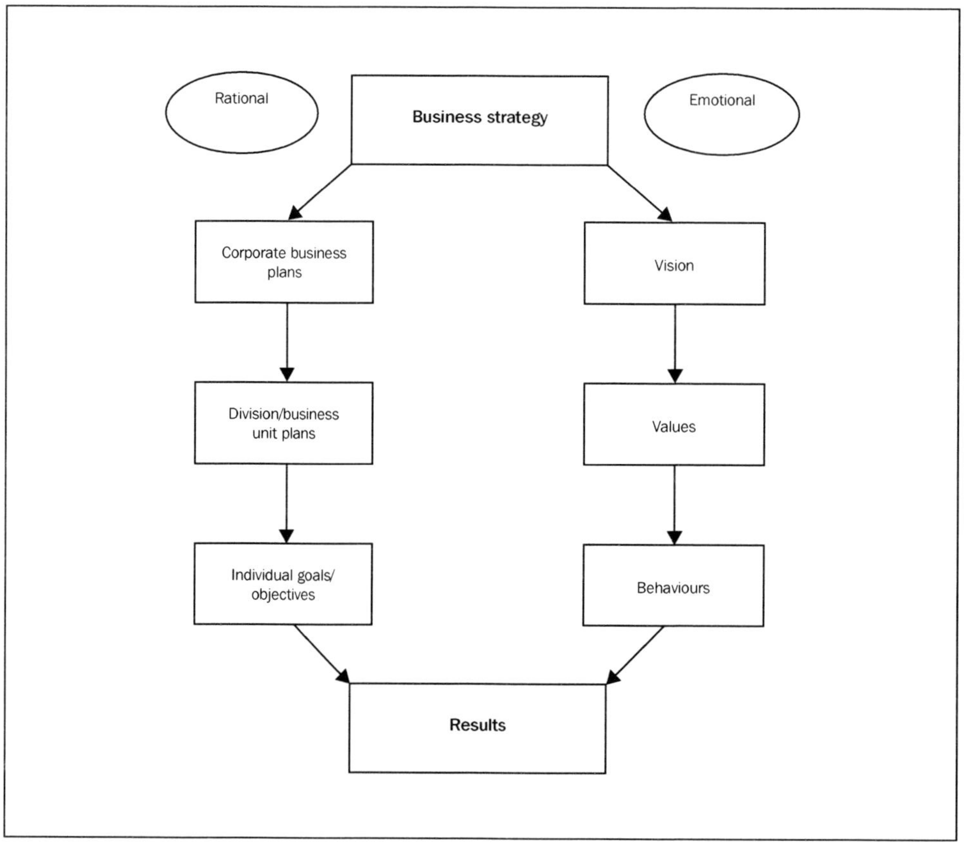

Source: Higgs and Dulewicz, 1999.

In focusing on both rational and emotional components, communication is the key. This is more than effective public relations but is much more about how companies and individuals behave. Before Enron's collapse, one fund manager of a leading FTSE 100 pension fund chose to avoid any exposure to the company precisely because managers would not back up earnings growth performance with adequate disclosure. We now know that one reason for Enron's opacity was fraud on a massive scale. The behaviour of Enron's management to this FTSE fund manager did not build trust. In fact her own reputation rose when Enron fell.

In a benchmarking study led by customer service staff at British Airways, communication was seen to be about creating the right 'emotional environment' and key to maintaining effective relationships with stakeholders.

Relationships are:

- Trusting
- Respectful
- Truthful
- Caring
- Humorous
- Leadership/followership
- Professional

= Effective Communication

Source: BA.

How does all this connect to corporate reputation? Emotional factors influence reputation-building as Table 1.1 suggests.

Table 1.1 Emotions and reputation

Emotions in organizations: key concepts	Reputation dimension	Company example
Emotion and feeling are often negative and changing, subject to interpersonal, group and political influence.	Reputation with policy-makers.	Reuters use of term 'terrorist' and reaction from US media after 11 September.[3]
History matters – individuals, groups and organizations have	Re-branding an established	British Airways' attempt to re-brand its tailfins in world images

Emotions in organizations: key concepts	Reputation dimension	Company example
'memories', emotional backcloths which shape the 'what' and 'how' of present feeling and emotional expression.	corporate brand.	backfired partly due to a perception (especially by front-line staff and premium customers) that this was an unnecessary attempt to erase BA's heritage as, still, a British carrier.
Emotional worlds often blur the distinction between 'the public' and the 'private', 'work' and 'home'; the domains can interact.	Internal and external reputation.	Senior managers at Barclays Global Capital, one of Europe's largest institutional investors, losing their jobs after news emerged of a £44,000 round of fine wines at Gordon Ramsay's Restaurant.[4]
Situations matter – feelings and emotions vary in relation to their organizational context.	Reputation and relationship (social capital).	Marks & Spencer's new restaurant at Baker Street is designed to encourage more informal codes of behaviour which are to be taken up, at the new premises at Paddington.[5]
Wider structures (e.g. economic and security-related) frame our experiences which leads to certain feelings and emotions.	Reputation and crisis management.	Marsh lost over 200 staff at the World Trade Center and many who survived were refusing to work in tall buildings or central New York for weeks after 9/11.

Table 1.2 Psychology and reputation: Making the link

Key questions that psychologists ask	Area	Suggested dimension for reputation management
What gets into our minds?	Perception.	*Focus*: single-minded focus helps to get corporate brands into people's minds.
What stays in the mind?	Learning and memory.	*Distinctiveness*: occupying an 'empty niche' makes it easier for corporate brands to stay in the mind.
How do we use it in the mind?	Thinking, reasoning and communicating.	*Consistency*: aligned communications of the corporate brand facilitates its further use in the mind.
Why do we do what we do?	Motivation and emotion.	
How do we influence each other?	Social psychology.	

Driver 2: Time, attention and trust: Increasingly scarce

Stakeholder expectations are driven by the scarcities of *time, attention* and *trust*. This is increasingly true across all key stakeholder groups – customers, employees and shareholders. Moreover it clearly determines how these groups behave and what they expect. Although each scarcity is separate and distinct, they are also inextricably linked. Shortages of time inevitably result in reduced spans of attention and this in turn makes investors less patient, employees more anxious and consumers less trusting. The last relationship – of people as customers – for any commercial business will always be paramount. This means first that consumers are either unwilling or unable to invest sufficient time in developing a close relationship with suppliers. Second, time pressures make them less tolerant of any delay or errors on the part of their suppliers. Finally the intense competition means they are continually being tempted by better offers from rival companies.

Fig. 1.7 Soul of the stakeholder

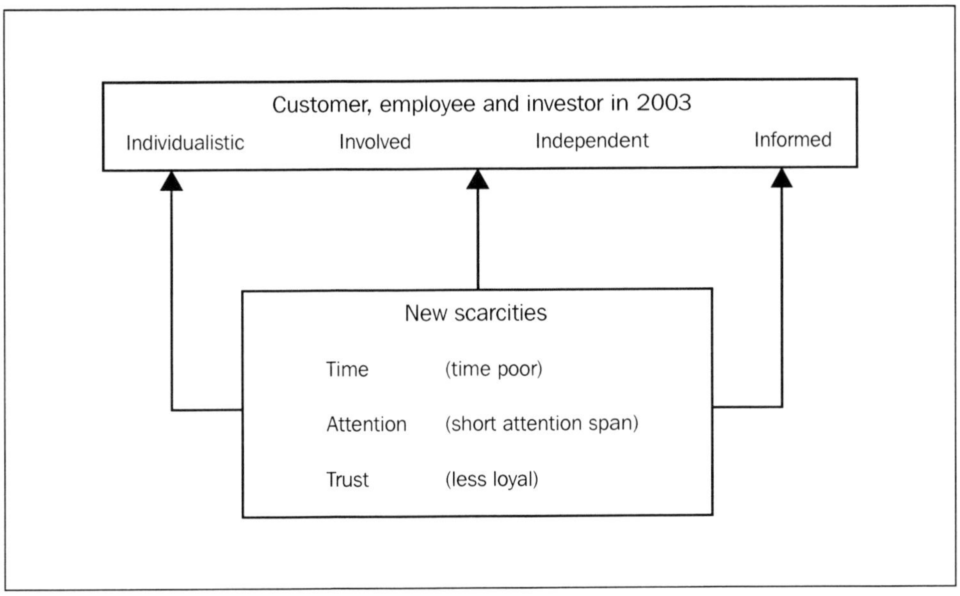

Source: Adapted from Lewis and Bridger, 2000.

This is more than anecdotal and is supported by a range of evidence.

Table 1.3 Evidence that we are time-poor

So much to do	■ more time is spent on shopping for basics: including travel, this has risen from 40 minutes a day in 1961 to 80 minutes in 2000
	■ a third of Americans, who work the longest hours in the world (*Source:* ILO), enjoy fewer than 6 hours sleep a night
	■ 80 per cent of business executives regard their workplace as stressful while 40 per cent described it as extremely stressful every day

- 94 per cent of managers do not believe the situation will improve (*Source*: American National Sleep Foundation, 2001)
- according to the LSE and Policy Studies Institute fewer than one in two workers have any control over their hours. However, 54 per cent of those who decide their own working hours are completely or very satisfied with their job compared to 42 per cent of employees whose hours are decided by their employer. Among younger workers the numbers are even higher. 80 per cent of so-called Generation Xers feel they would be more likely to stay in their jobs if their employers allowed for a balance and this rises to 93 per cent among those aged 18–25. Over the 1990s full-time men's hours rose from 45.3 to 47 per week and full-time women's hours rose from 40 to 43 hours per week. Overtime hours in particular are up, especially unpaid overtime, with full-time women now putting in more unpaid overtime than full-time men – up from 18 per cent of full-time women workers to 47 per cent over the last 10 years. (*Source*: Industrial Society, 2001)

Living in the fast lane	- email has reduced still further the time taken between origination, dissemination and assimilation - abridgement services that filter corporate messages have mushroomed: the UK's fastest growing news magazines with circulation rising at 50 per cent pa. (*The Week*) has no correspondents and no specialists but its 20 staff act as filters.
Shopping around the clock	- video cassettes, DVDs and digital TV enable viewers not only to choose which programmes they want to watch but when they watch them - research from Shell in the UK found that [in 1999] 17 million people shop at night and 30 per cent of those aged between 18 and 24 who buy in a main grocery shop, go in the evening.
Multitasking	- commuters and business travellers occupy flight and train time preparing reports on their laptops - new consumers prefer to have all the products and services they require gathered into so-called 'need pools' under one roof.
Getting it yesterday	- product cycles have now speeded up to the point of overlap with several generations existing simultaneously - everything from processing films and selling shares is now available in a high speed format - 'just-in-time' strategy is now the basis not just of manufacturing but of service companies - increasingly magazines, books and TV programmes are created against such tight deadlines that the quality and accuracy of the information on offer are undermined, making already cynical new consumers even more sceptical about its value.

Evidence that we are attention poor

Consumers are inundated with a myriad of marketing messages and offerings they need to filter and qualify. The mass of corporate data is growing at an astounding pace: in mid-2002 the world's total yearly production of print, film, optical and magnetic content needed 1.5 billion gigabytes of storage, the equivalent of 250 megabytes per person for each man, woman and child on earth. The rapidly falling price of mass storage makes it possible to maintain that information in digital form but the major question is what to do with it all?

The attention span of the US President is eight seconds[6] providing a particular challenge for crafting a message in policy briefs. Five out of ten investors either skim or do not read annual reports, and the average investor spends less than 15 minutes reading a report.[7]

Attention scarcity leads to basic two problems.	■ How to attract and keep the attention of employees, consumers, shareholders, potential employees and others. ■ How to parcel out their own attention in the face of overwhelming options.
Symptoms of attention scarcity.	■ An increased likelihood of missing key information when making decisions. ■ Diminished time for reflection on anything but simple information transactions such as e-mail and voice mail. ■ Difficulty holding others' attention (for instance, having to increase the glitziness of presentations and the number of messages to get and keep attention). ■ Decreased ability to focus when necessary.

Applied to stakeholder groups this becomes easier to see. Whether capturing attention among fund mangers as 'buy' opportunities in a market downturn, differentiating a product offering in an increasingly commoditized market-place or ensuring employees give sufficient attention to new guidelines on business integrity issued on the corporate intranet, the battle for attention is a daily reality. For all the emergence of fear and anxiety in mindsets post 9/11 and Enron can only lessen attention spans.

In order to reduce information overflow people apply mental shortcuts. Trust is one such shortcut and can act as a means of reducing complexity and information.

Case study 1.2

IBM seeks to build trust through greater disclosure

Situation

IBM shares fell 9 per cent in February 2002 after investors raised questions about its accounting practices and demanded greater accounting disclosure.

Action

To help readers navigate the financial section and provide perspective on the company's business model, IBM introduced a 'road map' in the opening of its 2001 annual report. IBM also expanded several sections of the report to achieve greater disclosure of its accounting practices. For instance, IBM added to and revised several sections of the report, including 'Management Discussion and Analysis', 'Expense and Other Income', 'Retirement-Related Benefits' and 'Debt and Equity'. In addition to expanding several sections, IBM also provided greater detail, used clearer language and inserted a graph to describe the company's capital structure and illustrate that most of IBM's debt is used to fund its global finance business. IBM revealed that it will discuss benchmarks for the current year in a new 'Focus Items for 2002' section.

IBM also created an online report that contained identical content, but used more animation to dramatize the company's message, including narrative metaphors. For instance, the chapter entitled 'Comebacks' presented an image of a boxer.

Result

Although IBM has yet to see the impact of its expanded annual report, it hopes its attempts at greater disclosure will appease investors. The positive reception in which the markets generally viewed the major sale of its hard-drive business to Hitachi was a possible indication of reputational up-side from greater openness.

Scarcities of trust

A scarcity of trust matters most of all as it directly links with reputation (more on how this link works in practice in Chapter 2).

First, the demand side. Fresh business challenges are demanding higher levels of trust across *all* stakeholders (*see* Figure 1.8).

Next the supply side. The World Economic Forum's 2003 meeting in Davos took as its theme that of 'Building Trust'. In a global public opinion survey, it found that 48 per cent of people express 'little or no trust' in global companies, with 52 per cent expressing similar scepticism about large national businesses. Interestingly trust is even low when it comes to non-goverment organizations (NGOs), trade unions and media organizations.

Fig. 1.8 Business challenges

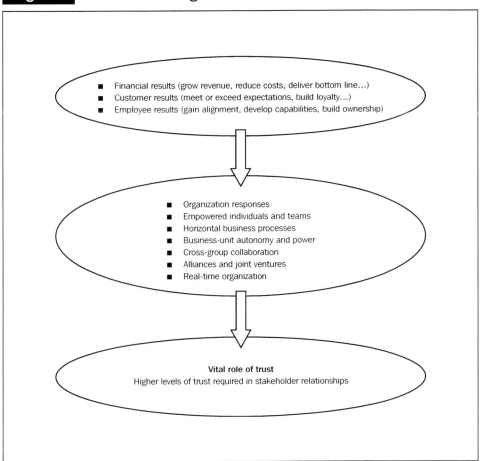

- Financial results (grow revenue, reduce costs, deliver bottom line...)
- Customer results (meet or exceed expectations, build loyalty...)
- Employee results (gain alignment, develop capabilities, build ownership)

- Organization responses
- Empowered individuals and teams
- Horizontal business processes
- Business-unit autonomy and power
- Cross-group collaboration
- Alliances and joint ventures
- Real-time organization

Vital role of trust
Higher levels of trust required in stakeholder relationships

Source: Shaw, 1997.

Fig. 1.9 Trust in leaders

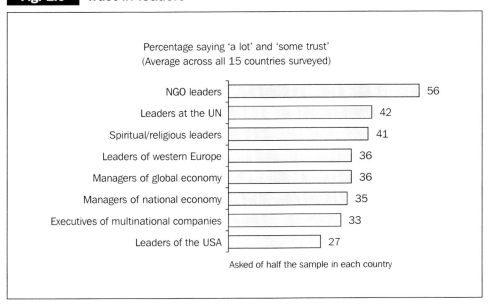

Percentage saying 'a lot' and 'some trust'
(Average across all 15 countries surveyed)

NGO leaders	56
Leaders at the UN	42
Spiritual/religious leaders	41
Leaders of western Europe	36
Managers of global economy	36
Managers of national economy	35
Executives of multinational companies	33
Leaders of the USA	27

Asked of half the sample in each country

Source: World Economic Forum, 2003.

Trust in business executives is low. A catalogue of high profile business cases suggests why (*see* Table 1.4). The fact that many were held on pedestals to be exemplars of strong reputations (with many high on reputation league tables in *Fortune* magazine and the MBA classroom) only amplified the reputational risk. At the root of these cases was that trust was broken because CEOs' pronouncements were not aligned with their actual behaviour. It was not that CEOs were not, in the vernacular, 'walking the talk' so much as 'walking the walk'. Moreover in most of these cases, for many investors, customers as well as employees, these individuals came to embody the company. Corporate and individual identity became one. This has been described as 'the irrational quest for charismatic CEOs' (Khurana, 2002).

Table 1.4 High/low reputations

Executive/company	CEOs' actions and words
Former Tyco CEO, Dennis Kozlowski.	Resigned as CEO in June 2002 after being charged with tax evasion relating to the purchase of valuable paintings. He has pleaded innocent to those charges, as well as charges that he helped loot Tyco of about $600 million. Tyco contributed $4 million to establish a Chair in corporate governance at Cambridge University which some shareholders are reportedly claiming back. Lawyers for Kozlowski allege that company loans (used to finance personal property purchases and lavish parties) were fully approved by Tyco's Board and auditors (PwC).
	'Most of us made it to the chief executive position because of a particularly high degree of responsibility ... We are offended most by the perception that we would waste the resources of a company that is a major part of our life and livelihood, and that we would be happy with directors who would permit that waste ... So as a CEO I want a strong, competent board.' Dennis Kozlowski, 2002
Former GE CEO, Jack Welch.	Papers filed on 5 September 2002 in the divorce of John F. Welch Jr., the former CEO of General Electric, by his wife contended that GE covered enormous living costs for them while he led the company and would continue to do so, for him, for the rest of his life. The SEC later probed Welch's employment and retirement agreements days after Welch altered the deal, giving up access to corporate apartments and company jets.
	'One thing I learned during my years as CEO is that perception matters. And in these times when public confidence and trust have been shaken, I've learned the hard way that perception matters more than ever.' Jack Welch, 2002
Global Crossing Chairman, Gary Winnick.	In January 2002, Global Crossing filed for Chapter 11 bankruptcy protection, listing assets of $22.4 billion and debts totalling $12.4 billion, the fourth largest bankruptcy in US history. The company has

been accused of employing misleading transactions and accounting methods which gave the appearance that the company was generating hundreds of millions of dollars in sales and cash revenues that did not actually exist. Winnick, the company's founder and chairman, cashed in $735 million of stock over four years, while receiving $10 million in salary/bonuses, consulting fees and aircraft ownership interest. In October 2002, he pledged $25 million to employees who lost money in the company's $401(k) retirement plan.

'You can't take the money with you. The only legacy I'm going to leave this planet with is my name.'

Gary Winnick, 2002

Former WorldCom CEO, Bernard Ebbers.

Ebbers was sued by New York State Attorney General Eliot Spitzer, who alleged in September that Ebbers and four other telecom executives improperly profited from hot initial public stock offerings given by Salomon Smith Barney in return for investment banking business. On 27 June 2002 the SEC charged WorldCom with 'massive accounting fraud'. The civil complaint charges WorldCom with violating anti-fraud and reporting provisions of the federal securities law. In November 2002, WorldCom was in the final phase of talks to settle fraud charges by the SEC, which would impose a fine on the company and exact promises not to violate securities laws in the future.

'You'll see people who in the early days ... took their life savings and trusted this company with their money. And I have an awesome responsibility to those people to make sure that they're done right.'

Bernard Ebbers, 2002

Source: www.corporatelibrary.com

The collapse of Enron, the indictment of its former auditor Arthur Andersen, and publicity for SEC probes of mainstream companies like Xerox and several technology and telecoms companies, has visibly jolted the confidence of buy- and sell-side investors in the usefulness, accuracy and even legality of corporate data. The number of public companies with revenues over $100 million that corrected accounting errors in SEC filings through restatements rose from 120 in 1997 to 270 by 2001, according to one study.[8]

It is difficult to measure the precise economic impact of trust. However, one official estimate sheds some light on the economic cost of loss of trust.

Focus: the economic cost of loss of trust

Using a model developed by the US Federal Reserve, economists from the Brookings Institution estimate that the effect of the current market slump caused by lowered investor confidence will have a broader impact on the economy by dampening consumer spending and business investment. Specifically it will result in:

- a protracted 17 per cent decline in share prices due to investor concerns over fraud and earnings mis-statements.
- a 0.34 per cent reduction in the GDP until the middle of 2003.

This translates into:

- $35 billion in lost production over 12 months.
- $62 billion over the next two years.
- $166 billion over the next decade.

'Part of the problem stems from the public perception that the scandal is situated at the centre rather than the periphery of the system. It hinges on companies mis-reporting their earnings, thereby skewing the price-earnings ratio, a measure which is at the core of most decisions investors make about where and when to invest.'[9]

The key word is perception, i.e. what people think to be the case based on how they feel.

Case study 1.3

Breakdown of trust at Merrill Lynch

One of the most high profile cases was at Merrill Lynch where its allegedly independent analysts misled investors by hyping stocks of firms they had a lucrative investment-banking relationship with, while privately denigrating them. This cost the company $100 million and led to changes to research standards and analyst compensation. As New York State Attorney General Eliot Spitzer said it represented 'a shocking betrayal of trust by one of Wall Street's most trusted names ... Even a 1–1, Merrill Lynch's highest investment rating, could not be trusted'.[10]

Merrill Lynch's reputation had already suffered when, at the end of 2001, it agreed to settle with Unilever in the Carol Gilley case. This was brought in London over charges of fund mismanagement by the (hitherto) widely respected city fund manager, Carol Gilley, whose reputation had been made in the 1990s while at Mercury Asset Management.

Within weeks of this case ending, the New York State Attorney General's office found that the firm's stock ratings were biased and distorted in an attempt to secure and maintain lucrative contracts for investment banking services. As a result, the firm often disseminated misleading information that helped its corporate clients but harmed individual investors.

There was a major breakdown in the supposed separation between the banking and research divisions at Merrill Lynch. In fact, analysts at Merrill Lynch helped recruit new investment banking clients and were paid to do so. The public, however, was led to believe that research analysts were independent, and that the firm's rating system would assist them in making critical investment decisions.

As part of a quid pro quo between the firm and its investment banking clients, Merrill Lynch analysts skewed stock ratings, giving favourable coverage to preferred clients, even when those stocks were dubious investments. This problem and other conflicts of interest were revealed by internal e-mail communications obtained during the investigation by the Attorney General's office. This showed analysts privately disparaging companies while publicly recommending their stocks, that the problems at Merrill Lynch went far beyond a single analyst or research unit and how individual investors were harmed.[11]

In May 2002 Merrill Lynch reached a deal with New York Attorney General Eliot Spitzer to settle accusations of conflicts of interest in stock research which included a $100 million fine and procedural changes.[12]

Key lessons:

1 There seemed to be no effective checks in place to identify and address rogue behaviour by investment analysts.

2 A contemptible attitude towards clients was all the more galling given Merrill Lynch's positioning in the market-place as a top-end investment adviser.

3 The problem seemed endemic with the firm's Chinese Walls, with some institutional and corporate clients seen to be full of holes. This was a time bomb waiting to explode but a corporate culture which sanctioned and arguably encouraged such behaviour finally led to fundamental change which had to come from the top.

4 Merrill Lynch's reputational risks could have been minimized if management had taken more decisive action earlier – and, given that this behaviour was not confined to one firm in the sector, may even have allowed Merrill Lynch to turn reputational risk into reputational opportunity. The short-term margin gains on the stock trades discouraged such behaviour. In that situation management action is crucial, to show vision, leadership – and integrity.

Loss of trust is not a wholly US phenomenon or one affecting large customers. It is also present in European financial markets and small investors. This is seen most strikingly perhaps in Germany with the collapse in popular shares like Deutsche Telekom and Deutsche Post (the latter fined £300 million by the EU for anti-competitive practices). As the Society for the Protection of Small Shareholders noted:

> *... the German shareholder culture is dead. They have lost their trust in the people who run these companies. It will be a long time before they come back.*

Small investor flight is evident in the number of shareholders dropping by 20 per cent (at the height of the Telekom-inspired boom, 9 per cent of the German population held shares against less than 7 per cent now).[13]

The Internet complicates the trust picture as one member of the studio audience in the 2002 Reith Lectures pointed out:

I'm a media researcher at the University of Luton. I read a report some time last year about a person who received a financial tip in an internet chat room and acted on the tip and made a lot of money, so he tried to track down who gave him the tip and it turned out to be a fourteen-year-old. He was a financial tipster, his friend was also posing as a surgeon and offering information, and another friend was posing as a pastor offering moral guidance. So what happens to trust when you have a technology such as the Internet that de-centres institutional validity?

Customers' new scrutiny of brands could be seen as part of a cycle of ups and downs reflecting their ongoing relationship with companies. However, while this cycle has indeed existed for some time, the current downturn in consumer sentiment is arguably of a fundamentally different origin than those of the past. Whereas, in the past, dissatisfaction with companies was generally a function of failed products or unmet service promises, today's anti-corporate sentiment also seems driven much more by consumers' frustrations with the excessive marketing of corporate brands.

It is unclear how resilient corporate reputations and traditional brand investments will be in a market of sceptical customers who are not merely resisting paying a premium for brands but who are growing hostile toward those brands for the marketing machinery they represent. This is also reflected in popular culture with many films featuring story-lines based on an individual's fight against bureaucracy, greed and autocratic behaviour by those who represent a commercial operation, for example in the Oscar winning film *Erin Brockovich*. An anti-corporate view is also prevalent in the most popular books (*see* Figure 1.10) which are inexpensive (compared to most books by CEOs or their consultants) and popular (judged by the number of mainly, favourable, reviews on amazon). A company may measure its reputation, for example, by the number of case studies it has in business schools, helped by its PR consultants, but these titles, which are definitely not about spin, arguably affect perception more – especially if reputation with customers is poor.

In response some major corporate brands such as Coca-Cola have suggested an emerging 'return to first principles' – i.e. a re-focus on the true distinctiveness of offerings and the deployment of resources into areas that create genuine utility and therefore, differentiation. In other words a narrowing of the gap between brand values and corporate values – which is often where the risk lies.

Fig. 1.10 UK's top selling business books (June 2002)

	Title	Author	Price	Date	Number of reviews on amazon.co.uk
1	*Fast Food Nation*	Eric Scholisser	£5.59	April 2002	52
2	*No Logo*	Naomi Klein	£6.29	January 2001	52
3	*Boo Hoo: A Dot Com Story*	Ernst Malmsten et al.	£6.39	June 2002	14
4	*The New Rulers of the World*	John Pilger	£10.00	June 2002	15
5	*Silent Takeover*	Noreena Hertz	£6.39	June 2002	27
6	*The World We're In*	Will Hutton	£12.59	May 2002	10

Driver 3: Changing social values and the emergence of social capital

Changing social values

Linked to a scarcity of trust is the growing and compelling evidence of a shift in social values that is directly affecting expectations of corporate behaviour on which corporate reputations at their core depend. An explosion of social expectations is happening while more and more people are defining themselves as consumers rather than workers.

■ There is a worldwide shift from economic growth issues to lifestyle values. As economies grow, living standards improve and people grow less attached to large institutions. This shift in social values is leading to changing stakeholder expectations.

■ Historical values shifts generally follow a three-stage process of gradual decay, a tipping point when new values abruptly replace the old, followed by the gelling of the new order. If the 1980s were characterized by marketing focus (on product proliferation and branding), the 1990s with customer focus (on building bespoke customer relationships), the early twenty-first century has given way to an enlightened focus (in which there is greater stakeholder inclusion with ethics as part of the brand package).

Generation Y embodies the demanding audience of the future and yet surprisingly little is known about them. No generation since their Baby Boom parents represents as large a demographic bulge or will have as great an impact on meeting their expectations than Generation Y. This group (60 million strong in the US alone, born from 1979 to 1994 and representing the largest surge in the US workforce since 72 million boomers hit the market) has grown up in a post-vinyl LP age of mobile communications, 3D video games, cable stations and high-speed Internet access. Generation Y have been playing with digital toys since the age of three. Raised with a joystick, remote or mouse in hand, Generation Y consumers are always one click away from taking a brand interaction one level deeper – or switching allegiance to a competitor's product. They want to know they can trust products and services but also knowledge and relationships. Moreover they will force their definition of trust into the employment contract.

As a result of their 'power-user' media savvy, Generation Y tends to be cynical of, if not immune to, traditional brand marketing tactics. By the time they come of buying-power age, their finely honed media filters will screen out most commercial attempts for their attention. Already, many long-time youth-oriented brands, such as Virgin, Coke, Levi Strauss and Nike, are struggling to remain credibly on-message and relevant with Generation Y.

The paradox is that Generation Y people are more comfortable with the givens of high technology, diversity and uncertainty. To this will now be living/trying to make sense of the images of 9/11 and corporate irresponsibility typified by Anderson, Enron et al.

What are the implications for business for international companies? The Coca-Cola Company, the marketing-led organization, has arguably best mastered the difficult job of maximizing returns on brand investments in its target market over the years with campaigns and slogans to its name as memorable as 'It's the Real Thing' and 'I'd Like to Buy the World a Coke.' However, it too is grappling with a new generation of consumer that is perhaps its most difficult to understand yet, let alone develop a brand positioning around. Coca-Cola have recognized, in their words that 'remaining silent is not an option anymore and that societal stakeholders have more credibility than business (at least in Europe)'.

As companies wrestle with increasingly fragmented ethnic, gender and demographic audiences, they are challenged by rapidly evolving and changing world customer behaviour. Moreover new generation consumers' life experiences are nothing like those of their predecessors and formative experiences of Generation Y consumers are much more violent.

Conveying coherent corporate messages to this increasingly diverse and demanding audience is far more difficult than it was in the past. As a result, corporate attempts to build reputations and ensure the returns on their service/product – brand investments are continuously being tested.

Fig. 1.11 Coca-Cola

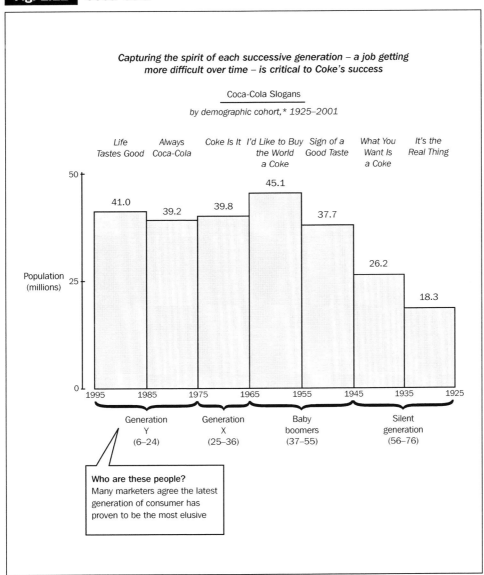

Source: Marketing Leadership Council, 2001.

Case study 1.4

Reputational up-side at British Airways after 9/11

One innovative response which connected to the social values shift was seen at British Airways where part of the business response to the financial situation post 11 September was to offer staff the opportunity to work part time or take unpaid leave while maintaining full pension contributions and so avoid compulsory redundancies. At one point up to 6,000 people were on temporary unpaid leave or temporary part-time working. Many took up career breaks, voluntary work (e.g. with children's charities in Vietnam and Brazil) or pursued opportunities which were personally important to them. In one case a member of the Safety and Security team took a year out in which he developed a quality system for a major Middle East airline and then returned to BA.

Were investors interested? When many attended the Annual Investor Day and one of the investor relations team said she was taking several weeks unpaid leave ahead of final publication of the year-end result and that BA were giving her a free ticket as part of the arrangement (available to anyone taking unpaid leave for a certain period), several analysts wondered whether this was not an approach from which others could learn including their own employers.

This was one way in which BA was able to retain relationships with employees and retain talent, reduce headcount costs, maintain the support of the trade unions and enable projects of social value. It was also a tangible way in which BA matched a belief in 'volunteering as an excellent way of developing employee skills, enabling people to build up confidence in areas useful at work and widening their horizons by trying something completely different' with practical action on the ground. Words matched by actions supported by trust-related behaviours enhanced BA's reputation both internally and externally in the weeks and months after 9/11.

Emergence of social capital

Social capital has emerged as a critical resource through which information and ideas are exchanged between a company and its stakeholders. Though still an emerging idea on the corporate radar screen, it is necessary to focus on what social capital is and especially the risks inherent in it as it is a key building block to understanding reputational risk.

Social capital is the web of social relationships that influences individual behaviour and thereby affects economic growth. Reputation reflects social capital because through reputation it becomes possible to mobilize others to action. It also relies on the size of the social networks to relay and spread recognition. Reputation can turn negative if expectations from such social interaction are not met. With earnings numbers of less value given the trust deficit described earlier, social capital – and the effectiveness of a company to harness it to build a reputation, e.g. for consistency of performance and managing investor expectations – has arguably become more important than ever. Key elements are:

- *Participation in networks* Key to all uses of the concept is the notion of more or less dense interlocking networks of relationships between individuals and groups. People engage with others through a variety of lateral associations. These associations must be both voluntary and equal. Social capital cannot be generated by individuals acting on their own.

- *Reciprocity* The individual provides a service to others, or acts for the benefit of others at a personal cost but in the general expectation that this will be returned at some undefined time in the future in case of need.

- *Importance of trust* This entails a willingness to take risks in a social context based on a sense of confidence that others will respond as expected and will act in mutually supportive ways, or at least that others do not intend harm.

- *Social norms* Generally unwritten but commonly understood formulae for both determining what patterns of behaviour are expected in a given social context, and for defining what forms of behaviour are valued or socially approved.

- *Proactivity* What is implicit in much of the above categories is a sense of personal and collective efficacy. The development of social capital requires the active and willing engagement of people. This is quite different from the receipt of services, however important. Social capital refers to people as value creators, not as passive agents.

To see how this may work in practice, look at Figure 1.12 which shows a social network structure for a company and 11 of its stakeholders. Note how stakeholder 6 is socially isolated. All else being equal, that single link will have less influence on the company than the single link with stakeholder 7. Stakeholder 7 has direct links with three other stakeholders (i.e. 5, 8, 10) and once removed indirect links with another three (i.e. 3, 9, 11). If the stakeholders were all suppliers, stakeholder 7 would be in a better position to hold a higher price than stakeholder 6. Generally, the structure of the network in which a relationship is embedded is a good predictor of the power, influence and similarity patterns that will be observed in the relationship.

Fig. 1.12 **Social network structure**

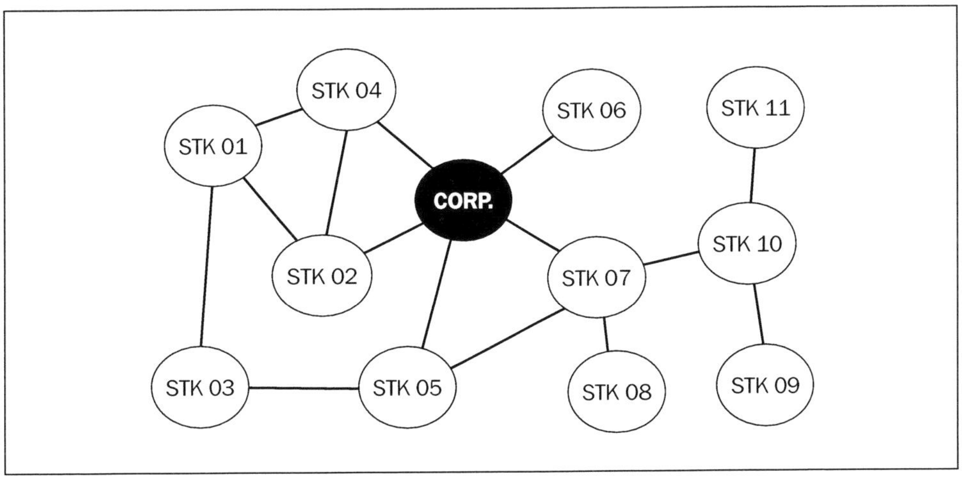

Source: Wheeler, 2001.

However, social capital carries risks. It can also be a liability depending on the situation and whose goals are being considered. Trust-based relationships with business partners or suppliers can, for example, provide the firm with resources while lowering risks and costs of opportunism. However, those same close relationships can also lead to malfeasance. If managers trust suppliers without adequate knowledge of their business processes or trustworthiness, suppliers may take advantage or may perform poorly.

Positive stakeholder relationships can be both the cause and consequence of business success. As an example, as a company builds a reputation among its peers for fair dealing and reliability in keeping promises, that reputation itself becomes a prized asset useful for sustaining its current alliances and forming future ones. The reputation and the trust are built upon a form of social capital. The social capital is embedded in the relationships that the company has established with its business partners.

Moreover social capital is an external as well as internal concept, i.e. it is concerned with relationships with customers and investors as well as employees and the community.

Table 1.5 Stakeholder relationships effect on business success

Source of competitive advantage		Factors needed to build social capital		Potential risks
Desired business outcomes	Focal capability	Interpersonal	Organizational	
Innovation	Ability of employees to access new ideas and information.	■ employees part of active external networks ■ employees and business partners trust each other ■ they have developed shared language and mental models.	■ organization supports cross boundary information sharing ■ rewards for risk taking ■ hiring from existing professional networks ■ ethics policy in place, understood and generally supported by cultural norms.	■ loss of employees to competitors ■ loss of advantage due to release of sensitive information ■ excessive focus on tools (e.g. intranet) rather than content (generation).
Innovation	Ability of employees to work collaboratively with others to create value for the organization.	■ cross-functional teams encouraged; time for informal interaction ■ employees trust each other and the company ■ enough shared language and meaning to get conversations started.	■ organization emphasizes learning/ continuous improvement not hierarchy and silos ■ rewards given for teamwork and informal networking ■ company puts money/ effort into training/ human capital (e.g.	■ groupthink ■ reduction in critical thinking ■ lower productivity ■ higher costs ■ not seeing/accepting growing overlaps in stakeholder identities ■ shared norms and beliefs can, if left unchecked, increase

Source of competitive advantage		Factors needed to build social capital		Potential risks
Desired business outcomes	*Focal capability*	*Interpersonal*	*Organizational*	
			management development centres at HQ and overseas).	hierarchical barriers.
Geographical expansion of markets	Ability to identify and take advantage of new markets.	■ cross-boundary networks created with non-traditional groups ■ managers have trust-building skills, cultural sensitivity and knowledge.	■ resources and time available for partnership development ■ communication systems in place ■ tolerance for risk taking ■ cultural sensitivity and knowledge.	■ conflicts with dissimilar business partners ■ lower productivity ■ higher costs ■ weak understanding of social context outside of home/western markets.
Enhancement of (corporate) brand value	Ability to establish a strong emotional connection with customers (and employees).	■ company creates marketing strategy that connects with value aligned customers ■ behaviour matches rhetoric ■ brand advocacy (e.g. outside work in informal situations).	■ resources for direct marketing with control mechanisms in place ■ values driven culture ■ commitment to excellence in quality and service as a baseline customer requirement, not as a differentiator.	■ loss of customers who do not share/ understand values.
Local community support/social licence to operate	Ability to manage social risk and make a valuable contribution to the community.	■ managers establish networks with opinion leaders ■ employee practices match rhetoric ■ behaviour of managers builds trust ■ shared understanding created.	■ company invests in community ■ local hiring/sourcing policy ■ manages environmental and other community risks proactively ■ pragmatic approach to down-sizing/ termination.	■ over-dependency of community ■ distortion of internal community economic relations ■ over-reliance on external CSR consultants/NGOs.
Sustained business partnerships	Ability to respond quickly and effectively to changing partner requirements.	■ sustained contact ■ trust ■ negotiated meaning/agreements.	■ communication systems in place ■ trust building routines and practices encouraged ■ ethics policy in place and generally supported by cultural norms.	■ lack of competition allows inefficiency to develop ■ excessive focus on short-term/tactical objectives at cost of allowing insufficient time for longer-term/ strategic objectives.

Source of competitive advantage		Factors needed to build social capital		Potential risks
Desired business outcomes	Focal capability	Interpersonal	Organizational	
Recruitment and retention of most talented employees	Ability to attract and retain high quality employees.	■ proactive networks created with positive prospects ■ company and managers build trust/reputation.	■ strong commitment to individual learning and personal development of employees ■ motivating compensation, incentives and rewards.	■ workforce more challenging and demanding in times of crisis.
Reduced conflict with unions	Ability to manage relationships with unions to minimize labour disruption.	■ opportunities created for dialogue between management and union ■ managers and employees strive for 'win–win' outcomes ■ shared understanding developed for key terms and concepts.	■ company provides desirable compensation and benefits ■ corporate culture supports open communication ■ key management representatives (CEO, Director of HR, etc.) have rank and file credibility.	■ higher labour costs ■ over-dependency on unions for communication ■ lack of engagement with unions on policy development (e.g. on social issues).
Customer loyalty	■ Ability to anticipate changing customer wants ■ Ability to engage customers in value creation.	■ employee behaviour builds trust ■ managers have leadership skills.	■ company creates networks that are valuable for customers ■ company gathers and shares information of value to all ■ communication systems in place (e.g. data bases to contact customers, websites).	Lack of strategic account management.

Changing ideas/disciplines

Understanding and then managing reputational risk requires the ability to think deeply as well as broadly. There are several areas of corporate focus when approaching the subject that are seldom considered together. One reason for this is the way most companies operate or are structured where corporate cultures are often able to act against thinking across silos, functions and sectors. The fact that this threatens the political powerbase of some organizational cliques may be another factor.

Such a list is not designed to prolong or over-complicate decision making but to ensure that when approaching issues of reputational risk, a balanced perspective is taken. In the pages ahead references will be made to each of these areas (and real-life examples among others). Together they comprise many of the building blocks of reputational risk and in particular suggest how value is created by taking an integrative and non-silo based approach. Above all, there is a need to focus on risk and opportunity.

Table 1.6 Building blocks for managing reputational risk for value creation

Focus not only on this	But also remember this	Illustrated by	Real-life example (in text)
1 Corporate governance structures.	Leadership, behaviours accountability.	Approach to corporate responsibility.	Marks & Spencer
2 Risk.	Opportunity.	Analyst irresponsibility.	Merrill Lynch
3 Branding.	Corporate brand equity.	Corporate brand leverage in partner relationships.	Reuters
4 Shareholders.	Customers, employees and communities.	Directors' responsibilities.	Changes announced to UK company law.
5 Corporate culture.	National cultures.	Market entry and development.	Dell (in China).
6 Tangibles/hard factors.	Intangibles/soft factors.	■ approach to risk assessment (M&S) ■ approach to customer value (BA).	■ Marks & Spencer ■ BA.
7 Content of internal communications.	Appropriate delivery channel.	Maintaining morale when under press attack.	FedEx.
8 Current trends/ focus on today.	Heritage/ remembering yesterday.	Respect for corporate ethos/ experience/mature workers.	BA (tailfins saga).
9 Corporate responsibility/ external reputation.	Individual responsibilities/ internal reputation.	Behaviours.	Barclays Bank.
10 Value.	Values.	Responsible down-sizing.	BA post 9/11 restructuring programme.

Need for integration, coherence, alignment and a holistic approach to reputation *and* risk.

EXECUTIVE SUMMARY

1   Business relationships, corporate reputation and societal impact are integrally and increasingly linked and, together with understanding stakeholder expectations, form the key to unlocking the meaning of reputational risk. We need to understand better the dynamic links between different risks which are themselves increasing in breadth and depth.

2   Loss of reputation is now the greatest risk facing most large publicly quoted companies and awareness of its importance is fast spreading to the public sector. The increasing complexity, competitiveness and internationalization of markets, coupled with a greater focus on issues of corporate responsibility, have placed the effective management both of business risk and financial risk at the very centre of a company's operations. Companies have found by experience that if they lose the trust of a particular group of stakeholders, the costs can be very high, enduring beyond the economic life of a tangible asset. Innovative companies view risk through the lens of opportunity rather than just internal control and compliance, i.e. they see risk as both up-side and downside.

3   Emotional logic is now emerging as the single most important business driver in the absence of economic difference. Acknowledging the influence of emotions on judgement, decision making and risk perception can also illuminate our understanding of reputation and corporate brands. At the core is responding to expectations while building trust through connecting with the attitudes, feelings and experiences of employees, customers and shareholders. However, audiences are becoming increasingly effective at 'deconstructing' messages that attempt to influence their behaviour. This coincides with a shift in social values across stakeholder groups.

4   Stakeholder expectations are driven by scarcities of time, attention and trust which directly drive people's behaviour and expectations. In order to reduce information overflow people apply mental shortcuts. Trust is one such a mental shortcut and can act as a means of reducing complexity and information.

5   There is a lack of trust constraining business performance due to espoused but not practised values and a lack of role modelling by senior management.

6   A shift in social values is directly affecting expectations of corporate behaviour. Shifting workplace values are affecting individual attitudes seen, for example, in greater sensitivity to work/life balance issues.

7   Social capital has emerged as a critical resource through which information and ideas are exchanged between a company and its stakeholders. However, it is necessary to acknowledge its risks as well as opportunities and also that it is about relationships with customers and investors as well as employees and the community.

8 Understanding and then managing reputational risk requires the ability to think deep as well as broad. There are several ideas that often form areas of corporate focus when approaching the subject but they are seldom considered together.

Key message

Scarcities of time, attention and trust affect people's expectations of corporate behaviour on which reputation depends. Not understanding that these drive stakeholders' decision-making processes is a reputational risk in itself.

What you must ask of your team/staff/consultants

1 What exactly are our motives for supporting corporate responsibility (e.g. major initiatives such as culture change, customer insight/NGO 'noise' or PR gloss)?

2 What matters more in building trust when trust is scarce – your service/ product or corporate brand?

3 How do your team/staff (especially those in front-line customer contact roles) feel about what we stand for (our values)?

4 Do our internal structures, processes and systems help us to manage time and attention?

5 Are our segmentations of employees, customers and shareholders helping/ hindering our communications? When were they last reviewed and by whom?

6 Are the right people inside the organization making the links between the building blocks of reputational risk?

7 How do we ensure we reflect as well as act (team awaydays, outside visitors/ speakers, secondments, etc.)? In particular how do we transfer strategic knowledge into companies when there is a need to avoid distracting or demotivating the core business?

What you must do today

1 *Re-read* Turnbull and find the references to reputation.

2 *Ask* your company secretary when was the last time a board member directly/ indirectly cited these and why.

3 *Monitor* and be abreast of developments relating to the Company Law White Paper – and ensure your people contribute to policy development by engaging with the review process.

4 *Look* at your biggest reputational issue (risk/opportunity) from the perspective of emotion – how does the chair of the audit committee on the board, key members of the executive team, your biggest institutional investor, your most valued business customer and your most talented colleague feel about it, e.g. excited, confident, relieved, anxious or horrified? If you have no idea, does that worry you?

5 *Think* of the most useful thing you learnt/made you reflect at work today. Did it come from a formal communication (e-mail) or an informal encounter (e.g. lift chat)?

Related websites

DTI   *http://www.dti.gov.uk/companiesbill/index.htm*

ICAEW   *http://www.icaew.co.uk*

Turnbull   *http://www.icaew.co.uk/cbp/index.cfm?aub=tb21_6242*

Marketing Leadership Council   *http://www.marketingleadershipcouncil.com*

Notes

1 Lev, Baruch (2002) *Intangibles: Management Measurement and Reporting.* Washington DC: Brookings University.

2 Comments to a Harvard audience in 2000, FRB website.

3 *Wall Street Journal* (2001) 'Media study terms such as "terrorist" in news reports'. 27 September.

4 *Financial Times* (2002) 25 February.

5 Visit to Marks and Spencer HQ at Baker Street, June 2001.

6 Henley Learning Partnership meeting with the Cabinet Office, 2002.

7 Clayton, John (2002) 'How to lie with formatting'. Harvard Management Communication Letter in Marketing Leadership Council *Trends in Annual Report Print Reduction.* July.

8 Huron Consulting Group cited in *The Oakland Tribune,* 7 August 2002.

9 Australian Financial Review, 19 August 2002.

10 *http://www.oag.state.ny.us/press/2002/apr/apr08b_02.html*

11 *http://www.oag.state.ny.us/press/2002/apr/apr08b_02.html*

12 *Financial Times* (2002) 'NY fines Merrill for conflicts of interest', 21 May.

13 *Financial Times* (2002) 'Share fiasco scars German investors', 23 June.

References

American National Sleep Foundation (2001) *http://www.sleepfoundation.org*

Companies Bill, Cm553–11 (2002) Modernising Company Law: Draft Clauses. HMSO, July.

de Vries, Manfred Kets (2001) *The Leadership Mystique*. London: Financial Times Prentice Hall.

Fombrun, Charles (2001) 'The value to be found in corporate reputation' in *Mastering Management 2.0*. London: Pearson Education.

Higgs, Malcolm and Dulewicz, Victor (1999) *Making Sense of Emotional Intelligence*. Windsor: NFER-Nelson.

Industrial Society (2001) *http://www.theworkfoundation.com*

Khurana, Rakesh (2002) *Searching for a Corporate Saviour: the Irrational Quest for Charismatic CEOs*. Princeton: Princeton University Press.

Lewis, David and Bridger, David (2000) *The Soul of the New Consumer*. London: Nicholas Brearley Publishing.

Marketing and Leadership Council (2001) *Brand Investments Under Fire*. Washington: Corporate Executive Board.

Shaw, Robert Bruce (1997) *Trust in the Balance*. San Francisco: Jossey-Bass Publishers.

Turnbull Report (1999) *Internal Control: Guidance for Directors on the Combined Code*. London: ICAEW.

Wheeler, David (2001) *Measuring the Business Value of Stakeholder Relationships*. The Centre for Innovation in Management, Simon Fraser University and the Haub Program in Business and Sustainability. York: Schulich School of Business, York University.

World Economic Forum (2003) 'Declining public trust foremost a leadership problem', 14 January.

2

Reputation

WHAT YOU MUST KNOW BEFORE YOU START

1 Why and how are intangible assets growing both in the economy and for companies – and what are the associated risks?

2 What intangible assets are central to managing reputational risk?

3 What is corporate reputation?

4 What are the risks attached to corporate branding?

5 What is the difference between corporate and organizational identity and why do both matter?

6 How are stakeholders converging?

7 What are the central components of trust and how does this fit into business relationships?

8 Why are the odds tilted towards distrust?

9 What are reputational agents and how do they work?

10 How can the media and NGOs act as reputational agents?

GROWTH OF INTANGIBLES

Reputation is an intangible asset. To understand how reputation is changing what is first needed is a brief understanding of what intangible assets are and why they are increasing in importance.

In the economy

As part of the change in UK company law, the DTI noted that asset structures are changing, and becoming increasingly 'soft', in the sense that a significant proportion of the value, or capacity, of a business is to be found in intangibles, rather than in tangible assets such as buildings and machinery. This was echoed in Federal Chairman Alan Greenspan's comments to a Harvard audience in 2000, when he noted that 'the share of output that is conceptual rather than physical continues to grow'.[1] What this means, he suggested, is that

> ... *in today's world where ideas are increasingly displacing the physical in the production of economic value, competition for* reputation *becomes a significant driving force. Manufactured goods often can be evaluated before the completion of a transaction. Service providers, on the other hand, can offer only their reputations.*
>
> Fombrun, 2001.

41

In April 2003, in response to recent 'revelations of corporate malfeasance', Greenspan reminded a contemporary audience of the historic links between competition, integrity, reputation and value:

> *Most bankers competed vigorously for* reputation. *Those bankers who had a history of redeeming their bank notes in specie, at par, were able to issue substantial quantities of notes, effectively financing their balance sheets with zero-interest debt. J.P. Morgan marshalled immense* power *on Wall Street in large part because his reputation for* fulfilling his promises *was exemplary.*[2]

This makes several connections which are often overlooked.

1 Reputation has value and is something companies compete for.

2 History matters – reputation can be formed over space and time.

3 Reputation can bolster power.

4 Delivery and performance are key – in this case the fulfilling of promises enabled low gearing to grow the business.

However, while companies are increasingly service-oriented, this also affects manufacturing companies too. A DTI report on *Manufacturing Strategy* (2002) noted that:

> *as manufacturers look to reorganize their operations, perhaps diversifying horizontally into related products and services, their brand – their* reputation *– will become an increasingly powerful tool in winning and retaining customers. In other words the service offered through aspects such as product development, quality assurance, liaison and delivery performance is often more valued than the actual manufacturing.*

Rise of the service economy

An economic reality

■ in the UK the service sector accounts for 70 per cent of total output and industry 28 per cent

■ in the US services account for 70 per cent of 1999 GDP and total employment, and manufacturing for just 18 per cent

■ services account for more than two-thirds share in all the OECD countries.

A large and growing percentage of most companies' total market value is comprised of intangible assets such as reputation, brand equity, strategic positioning, alliances, knowledge and human capital. In fact intangibles could be a better predictor of long-term performance.

Fig. 2.1 Intangibles – a more robust indicator of long-term performance

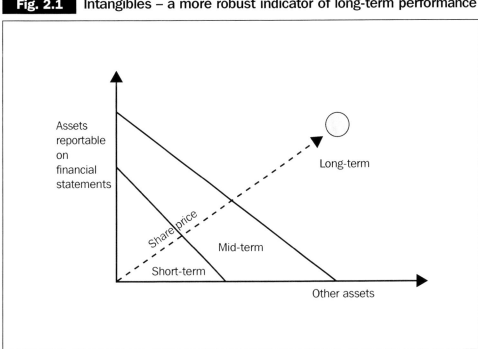

From 'service sector' to 'service logic' – and how this links with value

Today it is less meaningful to talk of services as a particular sector in society than of a service logic. Two examples come from the rapid growth of 'experience shopping' where Waterstones in late 1980s London, and a plethora of cappuccino bars a decade later, transformed the experience of book selling and coffee purchase for urban dwellers into such a process of customer value that people were happy to trade their time for comfort, ambience and convenience. This shift of emphasis from *production* to *use*, from *output* to *input*, from the *past* to the *future*, has four implications.

1   It immediately widens the scope of what an offering is.
2   It widens the scope of what kinds of characteristics a company needs to build into its offerings.
3   It focuses on what competences are required of the company.
4   Fundamentally, it also shifts the emphasis from the transaction to a more long-term relationship with the customer.

Implications for analysing risk

This also has real implications when assessing risk. When product offerings were seen as 'outputs' the risk of use was on the side of the consumer, whereas the risks normally assumed by the provider were those relating to the production process and the technical functioning of the product (for example product guarantees). With offerings increasingly leading into the future, risks are also related to utilization and value creation in the future. Thus the risks of today's businesses are highly related to the *behaviours* of individuals and companies. There is in fact at work a refocusing of risk in the economy.

Fig. 2.2 Risk after 9/11 and Enron

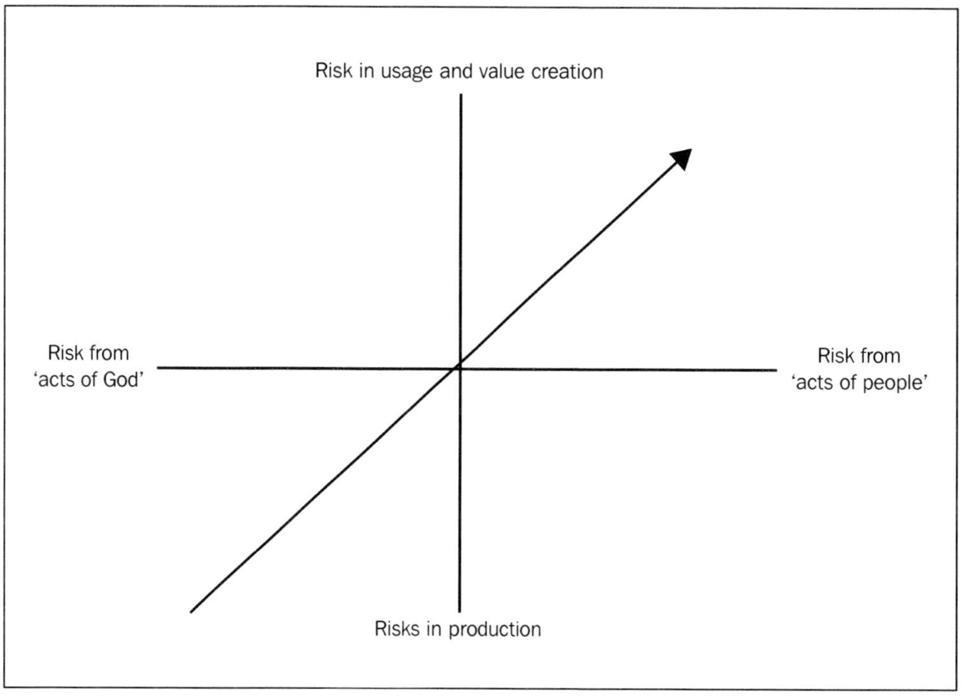

Source: Normann, 2001.

The key message is that risk assessment and risk management today must be based on more than traditional actuarial competences and insurance logic.

But exactly what intangible assets?

In a culmination of a two-year inquiry involving a cross-section of stakeholders, the DTI (2001) identified seven intangible value streams that require investment and maintenance in order to sustain current and future business prospects:

1 Relationships

2 Knowledge

3 Leadership and communication

4 Culture and values

5 Reputation and trust

6 Skills and competencies

7 Processes and systems.

'These areas comprise the intangible raw materials that talented people use to collaborate with each other in order to achieve goals, solve problems and seize opportunities.' This report emphasizes the importance of understanding the top five in relation to reputational risk as they will determine the bottom two (which are also covered in this report). In that sense they will also balance much of the traditional focus from consultants and many risk (and communication) professionals on the last two.

Table 2.1 Intangible assets and reputational risk

Intangible asset	Why relevant for reputational risk
Reputation and trust	Reputation and trust are at the heart of expectations by stakeholders of corporate behaviour.
Relationships	Effective relationships are key to identifying, assessing as well as managing reputational risk whether at the executive team level or at the front-line customer interface.
Culture and values	■ reputational risk is not managed because consultants are brought in or because the CEO says it is important ■ reputational risks relate to behaviour – both individual (values) and corporate (culture).
Leadership and communication	Reputational risk is a board issue but ensuring it is understood relies on communication that is both clear and honest.
Knowledge	■ external awareness of how employees, customers and shareholders perceive the organization is key to reputational risk ■ knowledge derives both from the application of tools and techniques (e.g. being developed at Henley) but also effective market insight/intelligence (i.e. environmental scanning, filtering, analysis and communication to decision makers).

Assets derived from strong business relationships may in fact represent the bulk of stakeholder value. But why would consumers want a relationship if they cannot even obtain satisfaction from a transaction – with many call centres and their impersonal and patience-testing automated response-routing being a case in point? The key point, however, is that the shift is underway from managing production to managing relationships. Relationships and transactions are not an either/or. Relationships transcend and frame transactions.

45

Intangible assets carry their own particular risks for companies. Not recognizing inherent value is itself a risk. In a presentation weeks after Bob Ayling's departure as CEO, BA acknowledged that 'intangible assets can create substantial new value through focus and utilization but that without treating them as such, value could easily be destroyed'.

CORPORATE REPUTATION

To understand reputational risk, one must first understand reputation and understand risk.

The problem however is that most material on reputation seldom pauses to spell out what it is and what is known about it (from credible research rather than polemic). Further, there tends to be little rigorous analysis of two of its central components – trust (identified in the DTI report) or business relationships (the importance of which has been highlighted in recent research with boards and senior managers at Henley). This is a serious omission.

What is it?

Various definitions have been suggested:

- A collective representation of a company's past actions and results that describes the company's ability to deliver valued outcomes to multiple stakeholders (Fombrun, 2001).

- The shared values of the company by its stakeholders that drive the trust, confidence and support an organization can expect from the reputation held by a person (Dowling, 2001).

- How each stakeholder group experiences the company's brand through its operations and conduct in everyday situations. How close these experiences are to what those same groups expect the company to do in the same situations. The difference between them is a measure of corporate reputation. Thus:

Reputation = Experiences – Expectations[3]

Based on their work with boards and senior managers over many years, researchers at Henley Management College have developed a framework which usefully focuses on three key elements:

- Experiences
- Feelings
- Behaviours.

Figure 2.3 shows how they see the inter-relationship.

Fig. 2.3 Relationship model

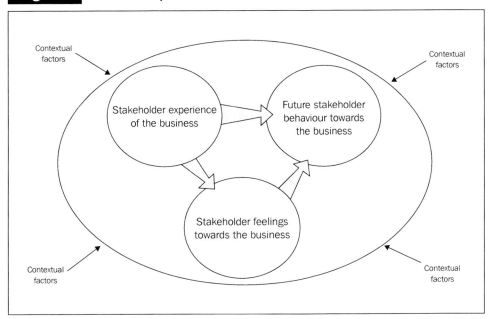

Source: MacMillan, Money and Downing, 2002.

Fig. 2.4 Business relationship model

Business behaviour and reputation	A business's reputation is built upon the relationships it has with its stakeholders. Important relationship issues include the various kinds of benefits (tangible and intangible) offered to stakeholders and how stakeholders judge the past behaviour of the business.
Stakeholder trust and commitment	These lie at the core of effective relationships. These attitudes incorporate views of a business's reliability and dependability and whether these are likely to endure in an uncertain world. They also indicate whether stakeholders are willing to put effort into maintaining their relationships with the organization.
Long-term supportive relationships	These provide the basis for increasing the resources available to the organization, extending the scope of interactions with stakeholders, generating collaborative and innovative opportunities, seeking constructive solutions to problems and resolving potential conflicts.

Source: MacMillan, Money and Downing, 2002.

All these definitions provide key elements (such as delivery against expectations through people's experiences) but the one used here is as follows:

> Corporate reputation is how key stakeholders perceive that your company or its employees behaves.

This implies a short and simple focus on *key stakeholders*, any gap in *perception* (which is where the risk can exist) – whether this comes from emotion, attitude or experience – and, crucially, *corporate behaviour*. It also links corporate and individual reputation, whether this applies to the CEO or the front-line customer service employee. As the deputy director at the DTI's Strategy Directorate put it to this author 'perception is a determinant of behaviour – both individual and corporate'. Individuals are never too small to be meaningfully involved. Companies are not faceless monoliths, leviathans or globalization monsters; they are made up of people who have values, or should be.

What do we know about how it operates?

- it is emotional as well as rational
- it depends critically on consistency of delivery
- it is about delivering to expectations at a minimum
- it is dynamic
- in a service business, the most important factors are those that directly impact the customer such as quality of the product and service which *are* perception.

Corporate reputation is also influenced by:

- the way a company communicates
- its behaviours and expression of its values
- general business performance
- relationships with its business partners
- the roots of the organization
- the media (though this is more complex than often described with residual perceptions and emotion and factors often playing a role).
- the children of opinion formers (to their parents).

There are five principles for managing relationships with resource holders (*see* Table 2.2).

Table 2.2 Five principles for managing relationships with resource holders

Principle	Key elements	Real-life example
1 Distinctiveness	Success in building reputation occurs when companies own an 'empty niche'.	BP's green positioning which aims to be one of the world's most environmentally friendly companies.
2 Focus	Reputations tend to improve when companies focus on a core theme.	Johnson and Johnson is ranked highly on public trust with trustworthiness a focus of its communications. Its advertising single-mindedly portrays J&J as nurturing and caring with babies invariably featured (despite baby products representing less than a tenth of the company's portfolio).
3 Consistency	■ companies should be consistent in actions and communications with all resource holders ■ companies with weaker reputations suffer from maintaining compartmentalized relationships where initiatives across functions are not orchestrated and integrated.	At General Motors overlapping and conflicting communications emanate from the level of individual brands, stifling the development of stakeholder loyalty to the whole company.
4 Identity	■ trying to manipulate external images by relying on advertising and public relations will fail, if this is disconnected from the company's identity ■ strong reputations are built from authentic representations of the company to its stakeholders.	British Airways' attempted re-branding exercise in 1997, though beloved (and devised) by external marketing consultants, was 'doomed to fail' in the words of one executive board member, coming as it did amidst a record drop in morale on the back of a damaging strike and what many perceived as an abrasive management style which appeared at odds with what employees and customers in particular had come to expect from BA – and on which it had built a solid reputation earlier under Colin Marshall.

Principle	Key elements	Real-life example
5 Transparency	■ companies disclose more information and are more willing to engage stakeholders in dialogue ■ communications increase the probability that a company is perceived as genuine and credible and so attracts support from stakeholders.	Enron's poor record in transparency and disclosure prior to the SEC investigation in October 2001 did not help its reputation when wider questions of business integrity came to a head.

Source: Fombrun, 2001, with company examples on BA and Enron added.

A major contribution to our understanding of the nature of corporate reputation comes from the largest international research project to date (the Global Reputation Quotient, 2002) which polled not just CEOs or investment analysts (the usual target for league tables) but ordinary members of the public. It represents the first and most comprehensive research across countries and sectors to date. Key findings are:

1 Corporate reputation is based mostly upon non-rational, emotional factors, and/or an incidental experience with one important evaluative aspect of the company.

2 Age and history may confer an aura of prestige that may compensate for poor performance or service of arguable quality (though if historic or legacy judgements are important, it is unclear how these weigh against current perceptions and how far back these go).

3 People lost trust because of (alleged) delivery of substandard products, misleading information and exaggerated expectations (e.g. World Online's unsuccessful stock market flotation).

4 Effective management of corporate image and reputation in an international setting requires a deeper understanding of the processes and the mechanisms of reputation building across nations.

Reasons for a weak corporate reputation were found to be:

■ poor performance directly connected to products and/or services

■ poor performance with respect to achievement of relevant company aims (such as a perceived general lack of success) or with regard to relations with various stakeholders and especially with employees

- value conflicts or violation of specific values (such as social values), PR crises and fundamental ideological rejection ('ideologically bad companies').

What else do we know about how reputation works?

- *Reputation develops over time through repeated interactions* As Andy Warhol said, 'repetition is reputation'. Corporate reputation is the consensus of perceptions about how a firm will behave in any given situation based on what people know about it. However, corporate reputation is not about being liked. It is about how predictable a company is in its behaviour and the likelihood that a company will meet expectations as a minimum. As researchers at Henley have found, this has two sides:

Past trust-related behaviours of the business	Includes perceptions about whether an organization has kept its past commitments, been honest and not taken excessive advantage of stakeholders in the past.
Future trust-related behaviours of stakeholders	As a consequence of having trust in a business a stakeholder will, for example, give the business the 'benefit of the doubt' in situations where the performance or integrity of the business is criticized or called into question.

- *Reputation is multifaceted* In addition to a general corporate reputation, a company can have action-specific reputations, e.g. for social responsibility, pricing aggressiveness and product quality.

- *Reputations are subjective* Current and potential customers rather than the company, are the true owners of corporate reputation. These customers construct in their minds the beliefs, feelings and attitudes that affect their opinions of a company. Thus corporate reputations are subjective as they are derived from consumers' personal experiences and knowledge, are influenced by indirect sources and are potentially inaccurate.

- *Reputations are also socially determined* Reputations are built and communicated throughout social networks, where groups of loosely connected members regularly exchange information about others. Corporate reputation is built *and* destroyed by people within networks who regularly gather and share information about the reputations of companies. This statement is especially true when information is socially interesting and relevant to a particular group.

Experiences of flight delays exchanged at business meetings damages BA's reputation despite the fact that it may have the best record for punctuality of any European airline.

- *Reputations depend on whether the evaluation is in absolute or comparison terms* The favourability of corporate reputation is applied in two ways. It is used to answer two fundamental questions:

  1 How well is this company performing (addressed whenever consumers form opinions about a company's behaviour in its own right)?

  2 How much better does this company perform relative than other companies?

- *Reputations are built over time and change slowly* Consistency in what people observe matters. Delivering on promises and repeated follow-through over time and across situations signals to others how a company tends to behave and strengthens the corporate reputation.

- Corporate reputation is likely to shift when:

  1 There is a change in the company itself or one of its important attributes (e.g. change in leadership with a new CEO, especially in a corporate service branded company such as an airline)

  2 The company aligns itself with another company whose reputation is more or less favourable along some dimension or attribute

  3 Reputation fades due to the passage of time, limited exposure or visibility of a company

  4 The reputations of separate entities become confused or indistinguishable in the mind of consumers – which is very likely to occur in very competitive situations or when there is little product differentiation.

Key point: business is now at Point 4 where accelerating competition and commodification are the norm.

Corporate branding, corporate identity and organizational identity

Corporate branding, corporate identity and organizational identity (and their associated risks) are seldom considered together. To understand the mechanics of reputational risk they need to be.

Products and services have become increasingly indistinguishable. One consequence is the massive investment in corporate brands – Consignia, Exel, Accenture and MO2 to name a few. Despite the enhanced importance of the corporate brand in sectors such as financial services, such investment carries risks. Companies like Virgin, for example, have discovered the risks of such a corporate brand when service issues negatively impact performance when extended to markets that are far removed from their original franchise when operating trains or energy companies. One of the best examples was when a Virgin train delayed John Prescott for a Labour Party rally when he was Transport Secretary.

With research continuing to show that people are not familiar with the sub-brand concept and consumers still immensely confused by who offers what and what a sub-brand signifies, the corporate brand continues to be a focus for relationship building both outside and inside the organization. In fact it could be argued that corporate (or 'master' branding) should be the default brand architecture option if this leads to a focus on a company's entire value proposition for its key stakeholders rather than a single product's functionality.

But how does this relate to value? One link with value is through fostering innovation. While there is increasing interest in developing a perceived corporate reputation for innovation, reputation impacts product innovation. Consumers who perceive a company to have a high reputation for product innovation tend to be more loyal to that company, more excited by its product introductions and more tolerant of an occasional product failure than less innovative competitors. Moreover employee perceptions of a high company reputation for product innovation lead to more organizational commitment, excitement toward work – and increased performance expectations.

Case study 2.1

Building reputation through innovation: corporate venturing

In a knowledge-based competitive environment, companies must mobilize and motivate their employees' latent entrepreneurial talent, encourage them to bring forward innovative ideas and then see them through to launch. At the same time, firms must avoid distracting or demotivating the core business. A key element of this is the management of personal risk and reward systems which can build and bind internal and external reputation. 'Corporate venturing' can nurture creativity and innovation, develop an entrepreneurial culture and create new stakeholder value.

Corporate venturing is a formal, direct relationship, usually between a larger and an independent smaller company in which both contribute financial management or technical resources, sharing risks and rewards for mutual growth.

Recent research at Henley has investigated the experiences of corporate venture managers from large international companies, in promoting innovation, entrepreneurial spirit and creating value for their organizations. It identified a number of ways reward management can facilitate this help, for example by stimulating the bringing forward of new ideas and motivating the new business development team. Of critical importance are intrinsic rewards, such as challenge and excitement, throughout the venturing process. While monetary rewards increase as the new business nears launch, they are never the sole motivator. Critical success factors for companies pursuing corporate ventures include:

- actively managing the expectations of all of those taking part
- focusing on creating space – organizational, psychological and physical – where intrinsic motivators can flourish

- recognizing the differing individual needs, attitudes, aspirations and contributions of those taking part

- using failure as a learning opportunity for both the organization and the individual

- acknowledging the need to include a broad range of stakeholders including venture team members, the incubator team and external partners

- linking incentives to key new business development goals rather than the mainstream business metrics

- releasing incentives in coordination with the new venture process, not the mainstream organization's systems

- allowing for different rewards at different phases of the venturing process.

Despite putting an innovation process in place, people often complain about 'false positives' where projects are allowed to proceed without sufficient validation, and 'false negatives' where promising projects are killed too early, often because they cannot compete on equal terms with the core business. Why? Research at Henley in 2003 identified various success factors that transcend sector differences. These include:

- Relentless focus on solving a customer problem: Lower cost, greater convenience or product/service enhancements are key motivators, but other less obvious propositions such as reassurance can also be powerful. For example, the founders of HomeServe, an unregulated subsidiary of South Staffordshire Water, recognized that customers' *fear* of suffering an expensive plumbing emergency at short notice, meant that they over-estimated the likelihood of one actually occurring, an incongruity that provided a source of value.

- Relevant and quantifiable assets and skills to contribute: One of the most common reasons for companies to establish venturing units as part of their innovation strategy is the desire to harvest the value of assets and skills in new ways. A common pitfall is over-confidence about the relevance of their assets and skills for application in new businesses.

- Internal and external networking: Networking is critical. Internal networking not only gets the company interested in the first place, it also enables the team to guide the project through the corporate turbulence – ensuring things actually happen.

However, venturing can destroy value.

The connection with reputation: FedEx at the height of the internet bubble
One corporate venture failure which had the potential to become a significant reputational risk for FedEx was its $550 million investment in 'Zapmail' in 1998 – basically fax machines at FedEx offices. Zapmail reflected a view – not inconceivable by some at the height of the Internet boom – that customers (in the US at least) would eventually abandon overnight delivery of documents in favour of electronic document transfer. Zapmail never made a return on FedEx's investment and it reportedly lost millions of dollars with management criticized for backing the venture far too long after the market-place had rejected the concept. The repositioning of FedEx as an Internet/new economy company at the same time with starry-eyed investors who were then prepared to reward dot-coms with exaggerated valuations also amplified the reputational risk.

A linked idea to the corporate brand is that of corporate identity that can act as a central force that motivates employees and that enables the formation of a strong corporate brand that brings about stakeholder loyalty. While marketing consultants brought in to develop a company's corporate identity often believe that with sufficient and effective promotion any corporate identity symbols can be made to work, there is a darker side. Reputational risks and the potential for such an exercise to cause a negative reaction among even key stakeholders – such as front-line customer service staff and high-value customers – are seldom acknowledged (including sometimes by non-executives on the board). A changing corporate identity also carries risks.

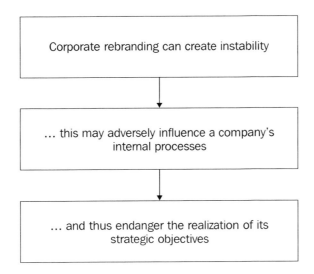

Case study 2.2

Re-branding British Airways in 1998

BA's re-branding shortly after Bob Ayling became CEO involved new images being developed in secretive meetings over two years in the late 1990s. These were eventually unveiled to many staff when they were invited to walk through an installation in a temporary caravan-like structure and emerge the other side committed and convinced that this was progress, no matter how artistically attractive the images were. Interestingly, in a meeting of city analysts, major customers and internal staff (commercial finance analysts) two years later, many present felt that a much more consensual approach was necessary. In a different context admittedly, this was precisely the approach taken when BA restructured post 9/11 which has not prevented the ability to make hard decisions (such as Concorde's retirement) without alienating key stakeholders.

Key message: corporate identify is a reflection of corporate strategy – and this includes a strategy for your people.

What is often overlooked – and perhaps was in the case of BA in 1998 – is that corporate identity is also about an organization's social context. Corporate reputation is also about organizational as well as corporate identity. If corporate identity is about the logo, slogan or livery, organizational identify consists of the many ways in which members of an organization perceive, feel and think of themselves as an organization. Stories and corporate folklore are all part of this, especially in a service-based company where people have such a central role.

Where does all this leave companies trying to understand the DNA of corporate reputation and in particular corporate identity? Identity is simply about:

There are two key questions every company should ask:

1 What does a company want a reputation for?
2 Whom does a company want a reputation with?

Reputation for what?

A key question is reputation for what? The Reputation Quotient (RQ) was developed by the Reputation Institute and Harris Interactive based on various pillars of reputation and consists of 20 attributes that drive corporate reputation (*see* Figure 2.5). Quantitative analysis supports the view that emotions and trust are key influencers of reputation.

The term 'admiration' is often associated with *Fortune* magazine's annual survey of the most admired companies. However, this assumes that all facets of reputation are equally relevant and that reputation has no independent value except as a sum of its attributes. *Fortune* and other surveys that purport to 'rank reputation' can present a myopic view that may not be a wholly accurate assessment of reputation. Indeed this problem is amply shown by how Enron rated on *Fortune*'s lists in 2001, shortly before its collapse.

Fig. 2.5 Emotions and trust as key influencers of reputation

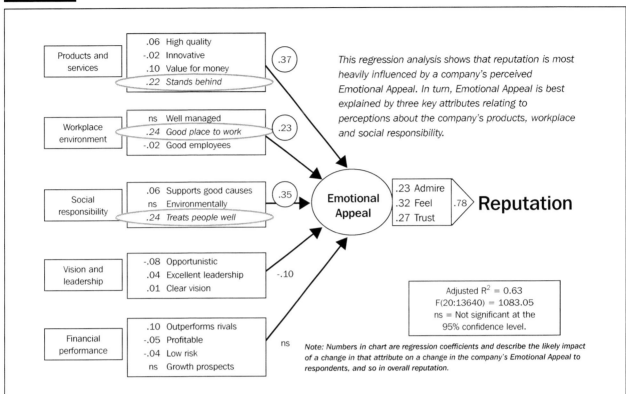

Source: The Reputation Institute, 2002

Rank	Fortune *list*
7	*Fortune 500*
16	Global 500
22	Best companies to work for
31	100 Fastest-growing companies

Companies believe they are clear about what they have a reputation for. But what do they really *want* a reputation for? For consistently reporting growing profit margins and then having to explain a sudden drop which shakes investors in a nervous market who ditch the stock? Or as a company known to investors as being boring but reliable in their financial performance and, among the leaders in their sector for their clear communications and transparency? There can be other illustrations of the point but a real-life example shows how an organization that is clear about what it wants a reputation for is able to deliver value to its stakeholders and grow. The fact that it is from the public sector does not weaken its relevance for the corporate boardroom, which at times is too hasty to see the non-plc experience as totally irrelevant.

Case study 2.3

Red Shift Theatre Company

Red Shift Theatre Company is one of the UK's leading touring theatre companies and is known for bringing classics of European literature to the stage in an accessible way. This is achieved both by how they design the product (present the play) and how they deliver the product (where they tour, which is very extensive and to many small-scale venues). It has developed into a mainstay of the UK small- to medium-scale performing arts sector and established a strong reputation for quality productions. It has differentiated its offering in a competitive market helping it to survive longer, relative to its peer group. It has been able to do this because it has demonstrated to the Arts Council, from whom it receives funding, that it has a consistent quality of artistic product that it has the confidence of venues and audiences – consistently.

Throughout its 21-year history it has always been clear about what it wanted a reputation for: a commitment to story, character and social context, expressed through a rich combination of spoken and visual language.

Red Shift's output has never compromised on this focus which has provided a common point of connection whether for its board, employees, audience, venues or funders. It nonetheless recognizes that it needs to periodically review what drives its reputation, especially as new members join the board or in major discussions with its funders so as to ensure common understanding, establish buy-in and help drive the company forward. It is also clear about its key intangible assets – reputation, relationships and knowledge – which also relate to its key risks.

Reputation with whom?

Identifying key elements of corporate reputation implies the next key question: reputation with whom? Given that corporate reputation is an evaluation of an organization's resources and capabilities by a clearly defined audience, we need to understand how this plays out to each key stakeholder group.

Table 2.3 Corporate reputation in relation to an organization's key stakeholders

Stakeholder	Character traits	Images
Employees	1 Generate trust 2 Empower 3 Instil pride.	Trustworthiness
Investors	1 Show profitability 2 Maintain stability 3 Have growth prospects.	Credibility

Stakeholder	Character traits	Images
Customers	1 Cultivate product quality 2 Provide customer service.	Reliability
Community	1 Serve the community 2 Green the environment.	Responsibility

Source: Fombrun, 1996.

The boxes in Table 2.3 are merging so that trust matters to all stakeholder and community issues matter to an increasing number of investors in the 'ethical funds' segment. How does all this link to business performance?

When its reputation was at its lowest with its customers, employees and investors, British Airways conducted its own research into stakeholder value with the Judge Institute at Cambridge in the late 1990s. The research had several starting points:

■ employee morale is closely related to customer satisfaction which in turn drives financial performance

■ higher morale can also be linked into financial performance via *inter alia* increased productivity, lower levels of absence, lower staff turnover.

The key drivers of both employee morale and customer satisfaction were identified to understand how these elements could be best influenced.

The strong link between service, customer satisfaction and employee morale provided evidence that employee morale is key in delivering high levels of service for BA's customers. Moreover staff perceptions of customer morale reflect very accurately the reality of what customers themselves express in research. This indicates that staff are potentially a critical source of knowledge in gauging customer perceptions, especially in a service business like BA where 'every contact counts'.

Table 2.4 Stakeholder value: key messages

1 Employee morale is key in delivering high levels of customer satisfaction which in turn links closely to the financial performance of the company.

2 There is a clear time lag between decline in morale and subsequent decline in customer satisfaction. Focusing on management practices and work relationships and leadership can influence employee morale.

3 There is clear time-lag between changes in customer satisfaction and financial performance – this creates a potential opportunity to redress trends in customer satisfaction prior to changes to financials. Customer satisfaction is strongly influenced by customer service.

4 Staff (particularly customer facing) are relatively in tune with customer perceptions – this offers an opportunity to involve staff more closely in customer-related issues.

Source: BA, 2000.

For some companies such as BA, BT and Marks & Spencer the difference between the brand and the corporate brand is wafer thin. Companies like these really have only one brand (their corporate brand) underpinned by several products.

Stakeholder convergence

For privatized companies such as BT and BA – where employee ownership is some 70 per cent, the employee – shareholder connect may seem more obvious. However, this is not confined to privatized companies with high employee ownership but is also true in companies competing in dynamic sectors like Marks & Spencer, Barclays, Reuters and, in the US, FedEx and Dell.

Customers and shareholders, particularly the beneficiaries of the institutional shareholders of large publicly held corporations, are increasingly one and the same. In the US, pension-fund beneficiaries now in effect own as much as 26 per cent of the outstanding stock in America's public companies with another 8 per cent through other mechanisms such as employee stock ownership plans.

The key point is this: people are becoming more aware of their role, influence and power in multiple-stakeholder guises. The scarcities of time, attention and trust are felt across the stakeholder spectrum and there will be more common denominators that colour their expectations of companies and how they behave. Increasingly the distinction between recipients of messages by external and internal stakeholders is being muddied by the amount of overlap between these groups.

Employees, especially in national heritage service brand companies such as Reuters and FedEx, view their organizations partly through the lens of how it is represented to them in their other roles – whether as investors, customers or even citizens. These operate both on an individual level (reading share tips on their companies in the financial press) but also through interactions with other people and the cultivation of social capital. How?

Conversations about people's travel, shopping or financial experiences whether on the football terrace, at the parents meeting or at the dinner party play back to employees' perceptions of how companies in these sectors are represented (whether at BA, Marks & Spencer or Barclays). In other words, employees can carry impressions of corporate identity into their organizational lives and compare them to their understanding of organizational identity as it derives from their own direct experience. They will make comparisons between corporate and organizational identity as a natural consequence. If there is a gap, which is supported/reinforced by how they feel (emotions) and what they think (attitudes), reputational risks can grow.

The other dimension to this is that journalists and investment analysts are customers of banks, airlines and shops too and high profile companies in these sectors will resonate more with these people instinctively and intuitively – so companies like the ones mentioned above may need to work additionally hard to maintain and improve their reputation. Stakeholders thus have overlapping and interlocking relationships.

One interesting example of this is in Japan where there has been an explosive growth in socially responsible ('ethical') funds. Unlike in the west, there is a heavy concentration of strong consumer corporate brands in these funds.

Table 2.5 Sector weightings in *Asahi Life*'s 'Wing of Tomorrow' fund

			Selected companies – and well-known international corporate brands		
Rank	Sector	%	Rank	Company	%
1	(consumer) electronics	32.7	1	Matsushita	3.1
2	chemical	8.7	3	Sony	3.0
3	automotive	7.0	4	Canon	2.9
4	food	5.6	5	Pioneer	2.8
5	textile	5.2	6	Ito-Yokado (includes '7–11')	2.7
6	other	4.8	7	Sharp	2.5
7	pharmaceutical	3.9	16	Nissan Motor	2.0
8	gas	3.7	17	Nikon	1.9
9	retail	3.5	19	TDK	1.9
10	machinery	3.3	20	NEC	1.9
			23	Honda	1.8
			28	Toyota	1.6

Source: Asahi Life, December 2002.

This – together with a number of high profile scandals (with companies like Tokyo Electric Power) – has meant that corporate responsibility in Japan has been strongly associated with relationships with customers, as individuals make judgements about companies in relation to their *experience* as customers but in their *behaviour* as investors.

The key implication for companies is that stakeholder groups are not separate but overlap and are linked. They need to be seen as having common concerns and voices. This can be seen through the concept of transparency. No longer just the concern of shareholders, but also customers (in pricing) and employees (in selection and career progression).

REPUTATION, TRUST AND BUSINESS RELATIONSHIPS

The DTI Report on Intangible Assets (2001) reported the following findings on *reputation and trust*.

What companies told us

1   *Reputation and trust may be linked to direct experience or third hand reporting. Essentially we are looking at past track record and future confidence based on contextual experiences.*

2   *Image and brand are important, but in essence the value of this intangible is very much to do with people and context. All of the following can influence perceptions: the way in which an organization manages its relationships and knowledge, its leadership and quality of communication, its attractiveness as a place to work for or as an organization to do business with.*

3   *Skills and competencies, processes and systems likewise reinforce the need to think about the importance of not simply thinking about areas in isolation, but in terms of the way in which they interact with each other. The degree of overlap between areas is important just as the relationship and competitive context is important.*

4   *A good reputation together with trust in the brand inspires loyalty and tends to attract new relationships, knowledge and talent. It is a vital ingredient for attracting financial resources and will certainly influence the value of a business if it comes up for sale because of its important link to future prospects.*

5   *Reputation is built up over time by the behaviours of people in the organization and the quality of products and services, but activities need to be brand enhancing and increasingly organizations are taking care to*

associate themselves with partners that share similar values. Successful companies invest significant time and effort into brand improvement, they also seek to recognize, understand and guard against factors that could potentially undermine this effort. Adopting such an approach can significantly enhance your company's ability to reach and communicate its full growth potential.

Key finding

Reputation and trust may be influenced by the first impression given by people and by tangible assets, like look and location of property, the capacity of equipment or by a long list of intellectual property. In the long term, however, image and brand are sustained by things like empathy with needs, reliability, quality, security, uniqueness, responsiveness, friendliness and so on, in other words things that help to make the overall relationship experience something to be valued.

Source: DTI, 2001.

It concluded that:

a successful company is one that looks constantly to build on its existing relationships, be they external (customers, suppliers or anyone else whose ideas and cooperation may assist in meeting goals and solving problems) or internal (different functions and their teams working together to seize opportunities and create value). Understanding how to identify, develop, organize and sustain an appropriate network of relationships that bring new ways of working, ideas and opportunities plays a key role in the quest for competitive advantage.

It is clear that this thinking is being carried through to the changes to company law being drafted in the UK.

But if trust is so central to reputational risk, what exactly is trust and what do we know about it? What in fact is trust's DNA? This may seem semantics to some but actually goes to the heart of understanding the dynamics of reputational risk as it allows a more grounded analysis of the key elements of *expectations* and *behaviour*.

Trust is concerned with stakeholder expectations about how a business will behave in the future. It means that despite the future being uncertain, the business will keep its commitments (both implicit and explicit); neither coerce nor seek to disadvantage people; and communicate openly and honestly in a timely manner. Trust has more to do with dependability, reliability and faith in an uncertain future. Central to stakeholder expectations are behaviours that build, develop or destroy trust. Dependability it could be argued relies on familiarity. However, people often confuse trust with familiarity which in any case is neither a necessary or a sufficient condition for trust. Feeling familiar may provide grounds for trust but it alone does not deliver trust.

- familiarity is not a sufficient reason to suppose that anyone actually cares about you or shares your values

- familiarity says nothing about whether a person or company is sincere or trustworthy

- familiarity is no assurance of competence, a crucial element in building trust. This is a major shortcoming of MORI type polls of corporate reputation which rely on people's familiarity and equates this with trust. Railtrack provides a telling example of how familiarity does not necessarily lead to trust.

Trust grows when we rely on others who, over time, fulfil our expectations. It fades and turns into distrust when those on whom we rely fail to meet our expectations. So what can management actually do?

Specific guidance is given later in the chapters on customer, employees and shareholders. At this point it is enough to recognize that there is an important leadership role to create an environment in which expectations are understood, shared and generally met. In other words, expectations must be met – or revised so that they can be met – if trust is to be sustained.

Do shareholders care? Craig Mackenzie is Head of Investor Responsibility at the investment arm of the Halifax and Bank of Scotland Group (HBOS) and vice chair of 'FTSE 4 Good'. He argues that people have a wide variety of moral expectations about behaviour. He identifies several high-level examples (behaviours) that companies may wish to consider:

Table 2.6 Examples of moral expectations

Honesty	People expect others not to lie to them, to tell the truth, to avoid deception, concealment or manipulation of relevant facts.
Fairness	People expect others to be fair, to avoid discriminating between stakeholders of a similar kind (employees of different colours or genders, customers of different kinds), people expect others to treat similar people equally.
Care	People expect others to avoid doing substantial harm to others, or at least to take due care to do no harm, or to warn others should their actions risk harm.
Rights	People expect others to respect people's rights.
Responsibility	People expect others to be accountable for their actions, to take responsibility for harm they do.

Source: Social and Ethical Risk Group, 2001.

There are also a number of features of moral expectations that are relevant to the management of the risks they cause for companies.

Table 2.7 Features of moral expectations

Difference of opinion	■ While many broad moral expectations are almost universal, there is normally a wide variety of difference at the level of detailed interpretation – between different stakeholder groups, between different cultures, between men and women, between unionized and non-unionized employees etc. ■ There is, therefore, no substitute for companies but to seek to understand in broad terms what their important stakeholders' expectations are.
Change	■ Expectations change over time. ■ New expectations emerge (for example, the expectation that clothing retailers should take responsibility by what is done by their third-world suppliers), old ones fade away.
The importance of perception	■ Expectations are based on perception. People react not on any underlying reality about whether someone has lied, for example, but on their perception of whether a lie has been made. ■ Companies can correct misperceptions, but by then it might be too late. This means that companies must work hard to understand how stakeholders perceive their activities. It is no good for a company to believe a product is safe, if its customers perceive it to be dangerous.
Moral truth	■ If your goal is to maintain a good relationship with stakeholders it is less important to be morally 'right' (according to some moral philosophy, religious authority or the CEO's personal conscience), than it is to act in a way that meets your stakeholders' moral expectations whatever they may be. ■ Many companies make the mistake of ignoring stakeholders whose views they consider to be unjustified, 'woolly' or just plain 'wrong'. Being right is not a sufficient basis for good management of ethical risks in business. ■ This does not mean that companies cannot express moral views, but they must understand how those views will be interpreted by stakeholders.
The importance of intentions	■ Many expectations are not simply about how people should act, but about they think and feel, both before and after their action. ■ Killing someone intentionally is murder, killing someone unintentionally is not. Murdering someone and then feeling instant and terrible remorse is normally treated more favourably than murdering someone in cold blood and without remorse. ■ Companies must not only act well, but they must intend to act well, and they must show remorse when they fail to do so.

Source: Social and Ethical Risk Group, 2001.

How can companies respond to all this? They need to hone in on the DNA of trust to understand how they can build reputation and create value.

The DNA of trust

The trust equation:

$$T = C + R + I$$

Where

T = trustworthiness

C = credibility

R = reliability

I = intimacy

Source: Adapted from Maister et al., 2002.

These are seen by customers, employees and shareholders in different spheres.

Component	*Sphere*
Credibility	Words
Reliability	Actions
Intimacy	Emotions

Key points:

Credibility

■ Corporate credibility is the believability of its intentions and communications at a particular moment in time. It is whether a company can be relied on to do what it says it will do.

■ A lack of credibility leads consumers to question the validity of claims by a company, making consumers less likely to buy its products. Conversely, high credibility enhances brand equity.

Reliability

■ Reliability is the one component of the trust equation that has an explicit action orientation.

■ It links words and deeds, intention and action. It is this action orientation that distinguishes reliability from credibility.

- It is the repeated experience of links between promises and action.

- Reliability also has an emotional aspect in the sense that we unconsciously form opinions about someone's reliability by the extent to which they seem to anticipate our own habits and expectations.

Case study 2.4

Reliability at Fedex as a trust-enhancer

The reputation of Fedex with customers for reliability comes not just from effective advertising and the obvious 'technical' aspect of their service offerings but from a range of characteristics which are consistent and reinforce credibility.

- first ring-responses on their 1-800 number

- a voicemail interface is as painless as possible

- an agent answering the phone who is clearly knowledgeable and energetic

- consistent look and feel of their packaging

- way the zip-strip always tears off the same way

- consistent use of paint, livery and corporate identity on the trucks

- uniforms that distinguish them from other carriers

- easy-to-use and accurate 'tracking' system

- fact that the delivery driver turnover is low

- from the driver consistently leaving your package in the same place (the place you want it left).

Consistency is one form of reliability. However, consistency alone is not enough to create reliability. It must also be consistency in terms of the customer's preferences, not just the providers. Consistency is also a form of integrity and several types of consistency are important to the development and maintenance of trust.

Intimacy

- Intimacy is driven by emotional honesty, a willingness to expand the bounds of acceptable topics, while maintaining mutual respect and by respecting boundaries.

- Greater intimacy means that fewer subjects are barred from the discussion.

Distrust

It is easier to lose trust than to gain trust because of the operation of tendencies to believe trust-lowering information and because there is more trust-lowering information available. When it comes to winning trust, the playing field is not level. It is tilted towards distrust for these, not always obvious, reasons:

■ Negative (trust-building) events are more visible and noticeable than positive (trust-building) events. Negative events often take the form of specific, well-defined incidents such as lies, accidents, discoveries of errors or other mismanagement. Positive events, while sometimes visible, more often are fuzzy or distinct. When events are invisible or poorly defined, they carry little weight in shaping our attitudes and opinions.

■ When events do come to our attention, negative-trust destroying events carry much greater weight than positive events. The importance of trust is at least in part related to the frequency (or rarity) of trust-destroying incidents. In systems where we are concerned about low-probability/high consequence events, problematic events will decrease them.

■ Sources of bad (trust-destroying) news tend to be seen as more credible than sources of good news. Regulators tend to respond, in this sense, like the public.

■ Distrust, once initiated, tends to reinforce and perpetuate distrust. This occurs in two ways. First, distrust tends to inhibit the kinds of personal contacts and experiences that are necessary to overcome distrust. By avoiding others whose motives or actions we distrust, we never get to see if these people are competent, well-meaning and trustworthy. Second, initial trust or distrust colours our interpretation of events, thus reinforcing our prior beliefs.

REPUTATIONAL AGENTS

Reputational risks do not happen in isolation. They interact with processes that are psychological (our emotions), social (our networks) and cultural (our environment). It is this interaction that underpins how we experience risk, whether hard or soft.

Pressures on companies from key stakeholders are framed by reputational agents. As the World Bank, which first coined the term, has noted:

> *they include accounting and auditing professionals, lawyers, investment bankers and analysts, credit rating agencies, consumer activists, environmentalists, and media. Keeping an eye on corporate performance and insider behaviour, these reputational agents can exert pressure on companies to disclose relevant information, improve human capital, recognize the interests of outsiders, and otherwise behave as good corporate citizens. They can also put pressure on government through their influence over public opinion.*
>
> *www.worldbank.org/html/fpd/privatesector/cg/aboutus.htm*

The influence of NGOs, especially after the riots at the Seattle WTO meeting, the growth of the media in an electronic age and the power exerted by the rating agencies in assessing corporate health (highlighted by the collapse of Enron) are all evidence of how corporate reputation is framed and shaped for key stakeholders at least in part by these agents. A similar concept (which Marks and Spencer use) are 'corporate brand editors'.

This works in various ways. Three examples:

1 *Signals*: An unusually high number of senior mangers leaving Sears plc in the early 1990s which signalled wider business performance issues to some stakeholders. Directors selling shares may be another.

2 *Ex-employees*: For example, a junior manager who leaves BA to join a major management consultancy and becomes an executive card member for a key corporate client overnight.

3 *Media*:

> *It's a bit bizarre this coming from a PR man but PR is often as much about keeping people out of the press as putting them into it.*
> Jonathan Wootliff, Edelman Communications and Director of Communications, Greenpeace International, 1995–2000.

The FT's Lex column is, by its own admission, a reputational agent. It 'does not see the media as stakeholders of the companies with which they interact' but 'as that of an agent for its readers with a mandate to try to influence events and behaviour on their behalf where they are shareholders' (Davies, 1999). As one city old hand recently noted, 'reading Lex is rather like attending a conference where the speaker on the platform is concentrating his gaze on a small group of senior – and attentive – people at the front while the rest of the audience listens with varying degrees of understanding and interest'. This is because Lex 'is talking directly and exclusively to a few thousand senior fund managers' (Golding, 2003) whose daily fare includes buying perhaps £50 million of shares in BP or selling £20 million shares in Deutsche Telekom. Lex is a key reputational agent for any major quoted company – especially one that is traded on more than one exchange.

Media visibility is not necessarily a desirable determinant of corporate reputation and can increase reputational risk over performance. Visibility in the media is all too often bad visibility: it heightens public attention, raises eyebrows and reduces the latitude managers have in making strategic decisions without interference. Subsequent investigative report and newspaper write-ups – whether positive or negative – often do little to help a company's reputation, especially with a less trusting public.

Case study 2.5

Investment analysts on the 'vicious circle' in media coverage at Marks & Spencer in early 2001

The severity and extent of Marks & Spencer's financial problems have set up something of a 'vicious circle' in media coverage. Each disappointing set of results or trading update seems to provoke a new set of fashion editorials or television profiles on what has gone wrong with M&S. Inevitably the tone of such discussion is concerned with why M&S is less successful than in the past. This tends to generate editorials that focus on what is wrong with the business, not what is right. For a fashion business, dependent on consumer perceptions, this is destructive.

An obvious answer is for M&S to launch a media counter-offensive. However, that may not make this an easy task ... [and] the sheer weight of adverse editorial means that it would be extremely expensive to counter.

Source: Schroder Salomon Smith Barney, 2001.

The importance of the media as reputational agents is increased in times of uncertainty and crisis when there is greater public appetite for newsflow. This was the case during the way in which the media were used during the military action in Afghanistan after 9/11.[4] It could even by argued that if mass media control debate, they have incentives to weaken trust.

NGOs are powered by media coverage. They enjoy a greater level of trust among the general public than global companies. In times of corporate crisis, twice as many respondents would turn to NGOs as an impartial source of information than would look to the company involved or to the news media.

EXECUTIVE SUMMARY

1   Asset structures are changing, and becoming increasingly 'soft' with a significant proportion of the value, or capacity, of a business found in intangibles assets. There is a shift from transactions to the behaviours of individuals and companies through strong business relationships which may represent the bulk of stakeholder value today. Relationships and transactions are not an either/or. Relationships transcend and frame transactions.

2   The value streams that require most 'investment and maintenance' for corporate reputation are trust, relationships, knowledge, leadership and communication, and culture and values. Not recognizing inherent value is itself a risk. Intangible assets can create substantial new value through focus and utilization but that without treating them as such, value could easily be destroyed.

3 Corporate reputation is how key stakeholders perceive that your company or its employees behave. This definition recognizes key elements, i.e. *key stakeholders*, any gap in *perception* – and, crucially, *corporate behaviour*. It also crucially links corporate and individual reputation, which for a service company, may be indistinguishable.

4 Corporate branding, corporate identity and organizational identity (and their associated risks) need to be considered together. Corporate identify is a reflection of corporate strategy and this includes a strategy for your people.

5 A key question is reputation for what? The next key question is reputation with whom?

6 People are becoming more aware of their role, influence and power in multiple stakeholder guises. Stakeholder groups are not separate but overlap and are linked. In this sense they form a hybrid and converge. More and more people around the world are defining themselves as consumers rather than workers.

7 Expectations are based on perception. Companies can correct misperceptions, but by then it might be too late. This means that companies must work hard to understand how stakeholders perceive their activities. It is no good for a company to believe a product is safe, if its customers perceive it to be dangerous.

8 It is easier to lose trust than to gain trust because of the operation of tendencies to believe trust-lowering information and because there is more trust-lowering information available.

9 The influence of NGOs (which tend to be more trusted than companies and depend on media coverage), the growth of the media and the leverage exerted by the rating agencies are all proof of how corporate reputation is framed and shaped by reputational agents or 'corporate brand editors'.

10 Media visibility is not necessarily a desirable determinant of corporate reputation.

Key message

Corporate reputation and trust rely crucially on expectations of behaviour and these are increasing framed by reputational agents.

What you must ask of your team/staff/consultants

1 What do we want a reputation for?

2 Who do we want a reputation with?

3 From what we know about corporate reputation, what are the top three things that matter from our perspective?

4   If trust is so important to us, are we absolutely sure that we know what its drivers are from the perspective of our key stakeholders and the communities that matter to us?

5   Who are the most the significant reputational agents for us and why?

What you must do today

1   *Ask* – your Head of Communications if you can get an answer today to how your top customers, investors and employees perceive your corporate brand?

2   *Ask* your Heads of Investor Relations and Sales to what extent there is an overlap between your top investors and top corporate customers?

3   *Review* the level of your employee share ownership against your financial performance – does this create more risks than opportunities if your share price performance remains weak? Do you have a clear strategy in this area?

Related websites

Brookings Institute Intangibles project:
http://www.brook.edu/dybdocroot/es/research/projects/intangibles/ic.htm
Henley Management College Centre for Reputation and Relationships:
http://www.henleymc.ac.uk/henleymc01.nsf/pages/CORR
Reputation Institute:
http://www.reputationinstitute.com

Notes

1   Greenspan, Alan (2000).

2   FRB website, emphases added: *http://www.federalreserve.gov/boarddocs/ speeches/2003/20030492default.htm*. Alan Greenspan speech 'The Reagan Legacy', The Ronald Reagan Library, CA; Simi Valley. 9 April 2003.

3   Institute of Directors and the Royal Society of Arts, National forum on the purpose and values of business, cited in Harpur, Oonagh (2001) 'Building a sustainable reputation' in *Business Ethics*. London: Economist and Profile Books.

4   Conversation with Maleeha Lodhi, when Pakistan Ambassador to the US during this period. Lodhi was the first woman newspaper editor of an Asian daily newspaper prior to her first term as Ambassador to Washington DC.

References

Asahi Life, December 2002.

British Airways (2000) Research conducted with the Judge Institute.

Dowling, Grahame (2001) *Creating Corporate Reputations – Identity, Image and Performance*. Oxford: Oxford University Press.

DTI (2001) *Creating Value from Your Intangible Assets*. London: DTI.

DTI (2002) *Manufacturing Strategy*. London: DTI.

Fombrun, Charles (1996) *Reputation: Realizing Value from the Corporate Image*. Boston: Harvard Business School Press.

Fombrun, Charles (2001) 'The value to be found in corporate reputation', in *Mastering Management 2.0*. London: Pearson Education.

MacMillan, K., Money, K.G. and Downing, S.J. (2002) Centre for Organization Reputation and Relationships (CORR), Henley Management Centre.

Normann, Richard (2001) *Reframing Business: Shaping the Prime Mover Mindset*, Chichester: John Wiley and Sons.

The Reputation Institute (2002) *http://www.reputationinstitute.com*

Schroder Saloman Smith Barney (2001) Research Note on Marks & Spencer: 'When I'm 64'. 4 April.

Social and Ethical Risk Group (2001) unpublished report, London: Shared View.

Sutcliffe, Hilary, Abrahams, David, Mackenzie, Craig, Barry, Mike, Ede, Mark, Zaman, Arif, Ransome, Jill and Craddock, James (2001) 'Social and Ethical Risk Group' unpublished report of the Working Group. London.

Risk

WHAT YOU MUST KNOW BEFORE YOU START

1 How did 9/11 change our perception of risk?

2 Why do organizations fail to anticipate the future?

3 Why is a conventional risk management approach unsuitable in understanding reputational risk?

4 Are you sure you always focus on the up-side as well as the downside in questions of risk?

5 What is your appetite for risk?

6 Do you know how human factors affect our perception of risk and influence the quality of decision making?

7 What do we really know about the impact of culture on risk?

8 Why are risks taken even when the evidence points in the other direction?

9 Why is it still hard to really discuss risk with anyone on Wall Street without thinking – at least a little bit – about 1998?

10 What do you really understand by the words 'reputational risk'?

11 How do companies identify social and ethical risk?

UNDERSTANDING UNCERTAINTY AND DEFINING RISK

Understanding uncertainty

For some, risk assumed a fresh meaning after 9/11. With civil aircraft taken over by suicide terrorists (they themselves being a relatively new phenomenon) and directed for the White House, the Pentagon and the World Trade Center, it became clear that the combination of politicians, military and business were now sinisterly equal targets in what was also the first attack on the US mainland by a foreign force since 1812. Particularly disturbing was how passenger aircraft could be transformed into missiles of mass destruction. This directly affected our perception of risk from aircraft operated by friendly and familiar airlines which most people had until then seen purely through the lens of their last business trip or holiday.

People will need to accept more and wider uncertainty not as an occasional feature of the competitive landscape but as being increasingly the norm. Conventional corporate planning and risk metrics, in which the most likely outcome is forecast and a business plan and risk-management process built to fit, struggles to cope with the unknown, especially when the risks are intangible.

The impact of 9/11 on attitudes towards risk were seen not only in the days after 9/11 which affected both 'American policy-making and above all the American pysche'[1] but also months later by US financial policy-makers who continued to see economic risk through the fear, shock and resurgent emphasis on US security interests post 9/11.

What this means, with the breakdown of trust, is a need to understand what is needed to develop strategy under conditions of uncertainty. Companies need to move from a 'make and sell' mindset to one of 'sense and respond'.

Fig. 3.1 Two ways to think about a business

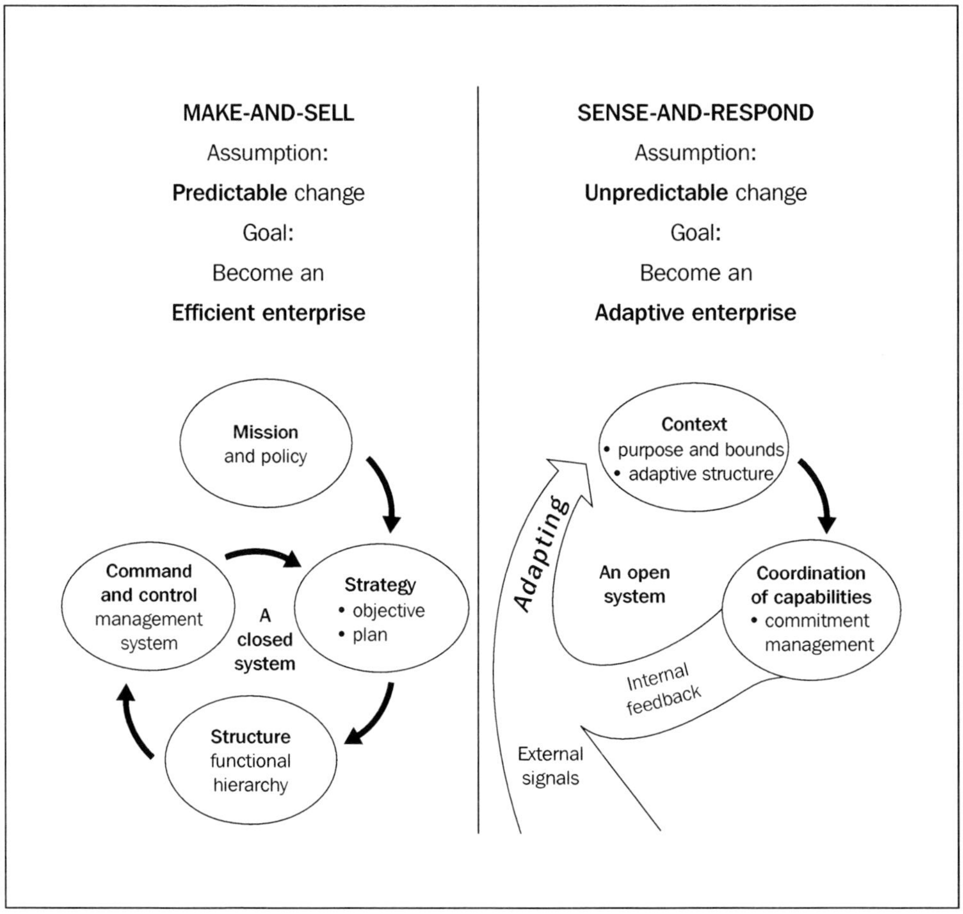

Source: Haeckel, 1999.

But *how* can companies respond?

1 By making strategic investments (for example in reputation-building areas and actions).

2 By actively monitoring various sources of uncertainty that can affect stakeholder expectations.

Environmental scanning and increased business awareness through exercises like scenario planning can help to spot 'reputational red flags'. Coming to British Airways from Shell as chief economist, DeAnne Julius used precisely this approach in the early 1990s to highlight the possible risks (in a still very inwardly focused corporate culture less than ten years after privatization) to what IATA and Boeing (among many others) saw as unlimited opportunities from Asian growth (several years before Asia's financial crisis in 1997). However, scanning emerging (reputational) issues and forecasting has limitations, as Julius herself has acknowledged.

Focus:

Why organizations fail to anticipate the future:

- losing important messages in the 'noise' unless there are 'filters' to keep out the unimportant data
- a mental model so firmly held that they cannot believe that anything different is possible
- companies believing what they want to believe where it is easy to believe something that has been developed as a result of a lot of effort and so must be a firm foundation for the future
- the experts' model is impervious to new thoughts and well able to reject any contrary view
- not understanding the company's own assumptions, which they can easily believe are facts rather than just assumptions
- putting the wrong weights on the known issues
- a culture of obedience and orthodoxy can prevent firms from asking the right questions
- over-estimating the ability of the company to deal with whatever events might arise
- failures in organizational learning – gaining knowledge *per se* is not sufficient, because not until it has been absorbed by the organization is it considered to be 'learnt'.

Four major sources of forecasting error:

1   Increasing difficulty in making assumptions about individual behaviour.
2   Changing role of government (no longer necessarily the major driver of change).
3   Problem of time-scales, which are often over-optimistic.
4   Loss of faith in our ability to produce continual progress.

The challenge becomes more pressing when companies have to manage in the white space – a large, but mostly unoccupied territory in every company where rules are vague, authority is fuzzy, budgets are non-existent, and strategies unclear – and where, as a consequence, risk and entrepreneurial activity go hand in hand.

If anticipating reputational or other crises is difficult, this underlines the importance of how effectively companies *behave* in their response while also highlighting the need for companies to increase the likelihood of support by building and maintaining strong reputations with all their key stakeholders in the first place.

After 9/11 BA probably reinforced its reputation by taking decisive and immediate action but also in the way in which its executive team, key sales and customer service people in particular responded to an unprecedented situation. Indeed it is increasingly in our response to uncertainty that value can be created or added. This is actually what managing strategic change is all about.

Fig. 3.2 Nature of change

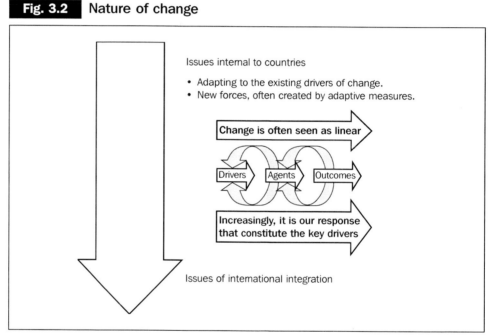

Source: Royal Institute of International Affairs, 2000.

Defining risk

Much current practice in risk management is an attempt to codify organizational processes rather than manage risk itself. This is itself a risk as it can encourage dangerous narrow tick-box processes to ensure compliance. One recent survey of UK managers from the Scottish ICA (2001) actually found that 'managers are risk taking when confronted with losses but become risk averse when considering gains'. How does this happen and why?

Traditionally, risk management has focused on two factors: first, avoiding the hazards associated with risks, and second, complying with legal and regulatory guidelines. As a result, most risk management resources and expertise have focused on financial controls and issues relating to legal and corporate compliance. In viewing risks as hazards, managers typically refer to potential negative events (which may or may not become public knowledge). These events can include financial loss and fraud (affecting shareholders), environmental contamination (affecting regulators and society), product recalls (affecting customers) and even absence through stress, injury or death in a company facility (clearly affecting employees). The common denominator is risk viewed only from a downside perspective.

Another way of approaching issues around risk is to analyse and grade a particular risk by looking at its component parts, which include:

- whether it is a strategic or tactical risk

- how near in the future it might occur

- how likely it is that it will occur

- whether it can be managed in any way

- whether it is an operational risk or a reputational risk (and hence the impact it will have on the organization).

Risk management has several elements which are often overlooked because they are not made explicit.

Identification	What kind of risk? ■ in relation to tangible assets ■ in relation to intangible assets.

Assessment	■ Who assesses the risk, e.g. to what extent is the board (or even credible NGOs) engaged in the process for those that are most critical?
	■ How do we establish its importance in terms of:
	  – probability (the evaluated probability of a particular outcome actually happening, including the anticipated frequency)?
	  – impact (the evaluated affect or result of a particular outcome actually happening)?

Management	■ Who manages the risk?
	■ Who is accountable?
	■ How do we manage the risk?
	  – transfer
	  – tolerate
	  – treat (which includes measuring)
	  – terminate.

What is perceived to be a hazard to one organization may be perceived as an opportunity to another and there are situations in which a negative outcome from one perspective is a positive outcome from another. This is a departure from the conventional view of risk as a hazard to be addressed through crisis management and compliance measures, aided by a growing army of consultants and process-driven solutions. It is actually also truer to the original meaning of the word 'risk' which – and is this too often forgotten – is derived from the early Italian word 'risicare' which means to dare. Taking a risk and being innovative are clearly linked and taking a risk to improve a corporate reputation is not in itself negative.

On one level the predominant approaches to risk are so narrow because it is often in the professional interest of the main protagonists (the insurance industry and communication consultants) to emphasize loss and crisis management respectively. More constructively, this is because of a lack of balance in asking the right questions (whether for the board member or division head) by focusing on two areas above all else:

■ the up-side as well as downside

■ human/behavioural aspects as well as process and system driven approaches.

Significantly, both areas are central to reputational risk and value creation through understanding two associated areas that are key. This is illustrated in Figure 3.3.

Fig. 3.3 Anatomy of risk

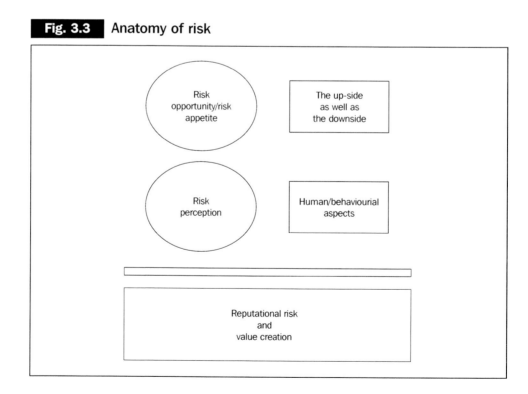

Moreover before managing risk, it is important to identify and then assess risk.

UP-SIDE AS WELL AS DOWNSIDE

In itself crisis management is not enough to provide a proper programme for reputation. It is a last ditch technique, resorted to when all else fails and, all too often, has to be grafted on to an organizational structure which is neither prepared nor equipped to perform properly in the sort of crisis situation implied.

At its inaugural meeting in 2002, the Strategic Planning Society's Risk Group accepted as a baseline assumption that 'risk management can help you seize opportunity, not just avoid danger'. One way to help make decisions has been suggested by Carl Olsson, a senior risk manager at Standard Chartered Bank (2002): 'This can be used to decide whether to take on new risks as well as reassess existing risks and to consider what strategies to use to manage risk.'

Companies need to develop a framework to manage business opportunities and incorporate these to ensure that they do not become unnecessarily risk adverse.

Fig. 3.4 **Probability/impact matrix: risk strategies**

		High	High
PROBABILITY	High	Put in place controls to minimize exposure	Priority for action
	Low	No action required	Put in place a contingency plan
		Low	Higher
		IMPACT	

Source: Olsson, 2002.

This approach, as Olsson himself admits, only helps in a broad sense. The problem is that although reputational risk management is becoming more important, often this is thought of as an internal process to decide what to tell the 'people out there'. Organizations need to build reputation and trust by managing the three Ps (performance, policy and perception) and the three Ts (truth, transparency and trust). The challenge is to manage these by moving to a position of 'listening, learning and engaging' rather than 'deciding, announcing and defending'. The Food Standards Agency, which holds frequent seminars and meetings to explain and engage with the public, is one example of how this process can be managed.

Fig. 3.5 Reputational positioning

A weak reputation – where reputational risk is a negative	A strong reputation – where reputational risk is a positive
■ target of first choice ■ defined by others, especially reputational agents ■ DAD posture (decide, announce, defend).	■ preferred business partner/supplier ■ self-defining, especially via executives' behaviour ■ LLE posture (listen, learn, engage).
Reputation as liability: *un-managed perceptions*	*Reputation as asset:* *managed perception*

How does this relate to performance? Without addressing perceptions of corporate behaviour companies could increase the trust deficit.

Fig. 3.6 Reputation–performance curve

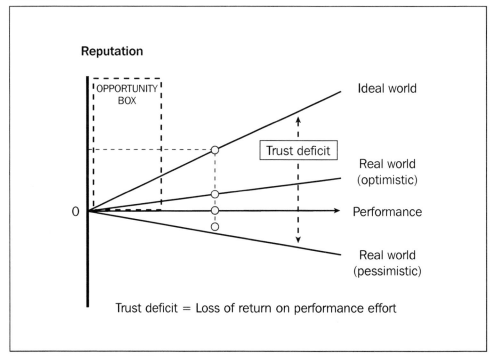

Source: UK Cabinet Office, 2001a.

Case study 3.1

BP uses corporate social responsibility and ethical risks to build its reputation under Lord Browne

Risk

After Shell's reputational disasters over Brent Spar and Nigeria in the late 1990s, BP was very vulnerable given its country exposure and lack of clear action and communication on environmental issues. This was an issue that had the potential, if allowed to develop, to use up much management time and possibly lead to some loss of business, as customers contrasted BP's 'weak' record with Shell's stronger record (especially as the latter attempted to rebuid its corporate brand through its landmark 'People, Planet and Profits' annual report).

Opportunity

BP's Chairman, Lord Browne, in a speech at Stanford in 1999, announced a fresh commitment to the environment. This was further developed in a keynote communication (the Reith Lectures in 2001) and a high profile advertising campaign which also repositioned the corporate brand as 'Beyond Green'.

Solution

The company's board and executive team focused on implementing alignment mechanisms that worked towards ensuring that there was coherence between the company's stated aims and its actions. This commitment to clarity of purpose and alignment started at the board. In 1997, BP's board adopted a set of governance policies that covered its relationship with shareholders, the conduct by the board of its own affairs, and its relationship with the group chief executive.

1 The policies stress the importance of the relationship between the board and the shareholders.

2 They cover board processes to ensure effectiveness, efficacy and integrity of the board. This includes the allocation of specific tasks to different committees, including an Ethics and Environment Assurance Committee, responsible for monitoring all non-financial aspects of the company's activities.

3 They set out how the board delegates authority to the Group CEO. The Goals Policy states desired targets that the board expects the CEO to reach, which are both long term and short term, and financial and non-financial in nature. The board's Executive Limitations Policy sets out restrictions on the manner in which the CEO can achieve these results and covers issues such as ethics, health, safety, the environment, financial distress, internal control, risk preferences, treatment of employees and political considerations. The CEO's performance is assessed against these goals and limitations through a process of dialogue and systematic review. Incentives are aligned to performance in all of these areas.

4 BP also relate ethics, risk and reputation to assurance which is 'knowing that it works as intended and that controls are having the desired effect in the most efficient and effective means possible'. Specifically 'assurance is the justified confidence that the system of internal control is: in place; is fit for purpose; and is working as intended'. Examples of assurance activities include ethical conduct self-certifications; people strategy reviews; and external verification of reported progress on policies.

Specific policies were announced at key moments (the end of political payments, in a speech at Chatham House, as scrutiny of Enron at Congress peaked in early 2002) and a zero tolerance policy on facilitation payments. Subsequent issues, e.g. in Alaska, though damaging BP in the eyes of NGOs and ethical funds, still caused major shareholders like Henderson Global Investors, to maintain their holdings.

Key lesson

Reputational risk is about managing 'relationships' with stakeholders. In order to do this, BP seeks to understand how social, ethical and environmental issues might impact on these relationships. It then assigns responsibility for managing these reputation risks to the line managers who manage the relevant relationships. In other words, reputation is managed directly, and is managed by line managers and not the PR department.

Impact

In the *Financial Times* surveys of the 'World's Most Respected Companies', BP has been named as the firm which commands the most public respect for its environmental record.

Even the *Guardian's* George Monbiot, one of the most ardent critics of multinationals, acknowledged at the end of 2002 that 'by common consent BP is the most environmentally and socially responsible of all big companies'.

For too many people, corporate social responsibility (CSR) is all about risk – what do we have to do to avoid the cost of getting it wrong? However, to an increasingly large minority in business, CSR is predominantly about opportunity. Opportunities to build trust in their brands, to create innovate products, to reduce costs by becoming more efficient, to access funds controlled by socially responsible investors.

Those who have embraced CSR as an opportunity have not waited for the irrefutable evidence that good CSR management = an extra £3.2 million profit per year. They know that to wait for such clear-cut evidence is to wait too long, because CSR can only be a true opportunity for a few. By its very nature, opportunity management rewards the proactive but penalizes the majority.

Once a business has carved out a niche for itself in a sector as the most responsible or most trusted, its competitors will find it doubly difficult to usurp its position. They will appear followers, rather than leaders. They will have missed out on the best, most innovative solutions, tied up by patent or contract by the sector leader. They will have missed out on the best staff, drawn to the leader, tied into its vision.

A key challenge is to understand what the boundaries are. Rank's head of risk management, Paul Hopkin, cautions that although 'opportunity risks are intended to provide a positive outcome, the outcome could be negative'.

Many companies have addressed the basic requirements set out by Turnbull (1999) (which actually makes no direct reference to 'risk appetite') and yet are still dissatisfied with the value created by the risk management processes put in place. One of the keys to unlocking that value is to understand, define and communicate risk appetite.

This is linked to opportunity risk and is the level of risk which the Board and management believe to be appropriate for the culture and capability of that particular organization. The greater the risk appetite, the greater the potential up-sides (opportunities) and downsides (risk incidents). An organization's risk appetite is defined by the extent to which it tolerates risks as described by performance indicators, operational parameters and process controls. This implies a degree of uncertainty as the argument that taking on more risk is acceptable as long as the reward is commensurate with the risk, can only be supported only so far because there comes a point where you begin to bet the business on the future turning out as you expect it to.

Fig. 3.7 **Risk and uncertainty**

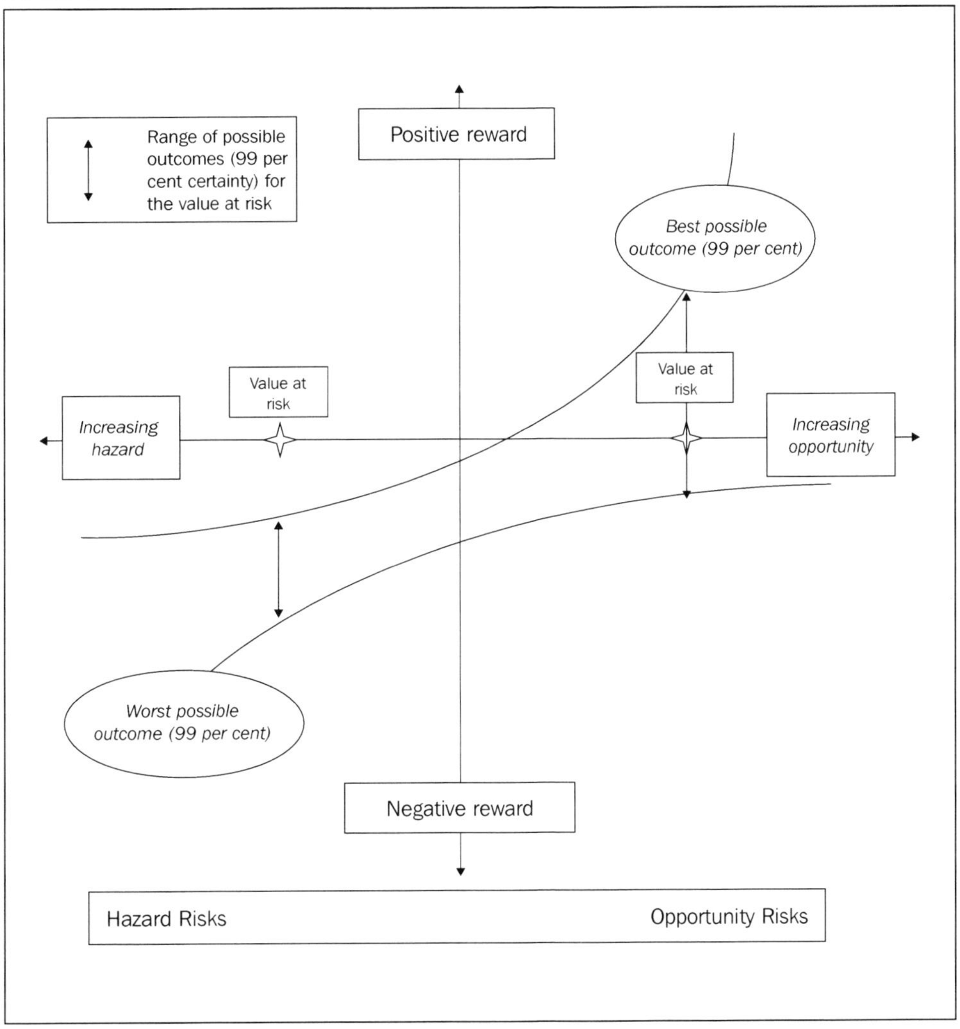

Source: Hopkin, 2002.

One of the keys to successful risk management is the clear identification of both organizational objectives and the appetite for risk that exists and is associated with these objectives. When organizations fail to do this, the result is an internally focused, process-driven organization with little appreciation of new business opportunities or potential threats.

In identifying their appetite for risk taking, companies need to acknowledge and understand the implications of the growing research on risk perception and how biases in decision making can result in inappropriate risks being taken – or risks being ignored altogether.

HUMAN/BEHAVIOURIAL DIMENSIONS OF RISK

- Why did Enron's non-executive directors fail to effectively monitor its risks – despite one Audit Committee member also being the head of the Press Complaints Commission at the time which may have led him to exercise greater scrutiny?
- Why did a psychologist win the Nobel Prize for Economics in 2002?
- Why did Allied Irish Bank suffer a $691 million currency trading loss at its Allfirst subsidiary in 2002?

The crucial factors linking all these cases were the human aspects of risks.

People, the organizations in which they work and the environments in which they exist are dynamic and non-linear in nature. However, when the topic of managing any type of risk is discussed, it frequently revolves around the techniques used to quantify risks or the checklists, procedures and systems that it is hoped will reduce the chance of an undesirable outcome. What are rarely discussed or questioned are the innate decision-making processes that we all use and whether or not they can be compromised.

There is a growing body of evidence that effect and emotions play an important role in people's decision processes for choices when there are uncertain outcomes. The significance of emotion in risk perception was well illustrated when Stanley Prusiner gave evidence to the BSE inquiry in 1998. Prusiner, by virtue of his Nobel Prize for his work on prions, arguably outranks all the other scientists in the debate. In his evidence he declared himself unconvinced by the evidence so far produced that a connection had been established. He was asked if he had changed his diet since learning of BSE. This is what he said:

> *I have worked in this field for 25 years ... did I go out and eat lamb chops, did I go out and eat lamb brain, sheep brain? The answer was 'no', but it was not based on scientific criteria, it was based on just emotion. ... At a scientific level I cannot give you a scientific basis for choosing or not choosing beef, because we do not know the answers.*[2]

But what do we really know about the impact of culture on risk?

Until recently there was a knowledge gap in the circumstances in which managers make inconsistent choices about risk and the attitudes to risk of employees within firms. In a survey by the ICA of Scotland (2001) into attitudes of UK managers to risk and uncertainty, 88 per cent of managers believed 'the culture of the organization played a crucial role in the risks which managers were willing to take' and 'attitudes to actual and perceived company operations involving risk were shaped by the strategies and priorities of the group'. In particular, 'options are edited and framed in accordance with company strategy and culture. Managers did not calculate probabilistic measures of risk such as variance and instead tend to rely on instinct and experience as well as conformity with corporate culture.'

However, having a strong risk culture is not an end in itself. Drawing on his extensive overseas experience in emerging markets with Standard Chartered Bank, Carl Olsson (2002) emphasizes that 'what is important is the behaviours that it drives in pursuit of an organization's goals'.

Fig. 3.8 **Risk culture and the pursuit of objectives**

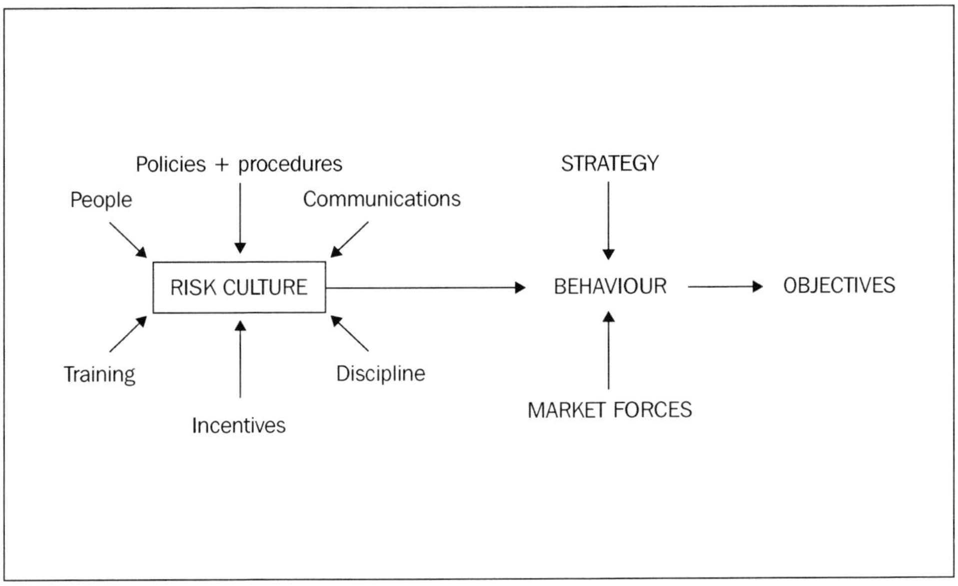

Source: Olsson, 2002.

How does all this connect to reputational risk?

There is a real need to balance the usual emphasis by risk managers on rational factors in decision making with evidence that points to its subjective nature. One area in which reputational risk can be manifested is when organizations cling to existing strategies due to mental fixations (e.g. perhaps BT in terms of its international aspirations before it divested of its Japanese investment in 2001 after 15 years with the arrival of a new chairman and CEO the same year).

Set out in Table 3.1 are factors that affect how we perceive risk. This is often not adequately acknowledged in mainstream risk analyses and underlines the significance of subjectivity in how risks are perceived, *before* they can be managed. A management strategy that acknowledges the individualistic and variable nature of risk perception and enables the open discussion and reconciliation of such differences will increase the effectiveness of decision making.

Table 3.1 Checklist of risk perception factors

Risk perception factors	Description
Understanding risk	In financial economic accounts, risk is generally regarded as a combination of the expected magnitude of loss or gain and the variability of that expected outcome. Human perception of risk works rather differently. There are two other important components of risk that influence our perceptions: ■ Fear factor – how much we dread the potential outcome. ■ Control factor – the extent to which we are in control of events.
Loss and gain	■ One major component of risk perception is how we perceive loss and gain. Our perceptions of our current state of loss or gain influence the extent to which we seek or avoid risk. When people are in a position of gain, they become increasingly risk averse and unwilling to accept gambles because they wish to hold on to their gains. When people are in a position of loss and as losses increase, they become more risk-seeking because they have nothing much to lose. This asymmetry applies to financial loss and gain, but can also apply to less tangible factors such as reputation or the desire to maintain a positive mood. ■ What we perceive as loss and gain is not straightforward. We all have internal reference points that determine whether we perceive an outcome as a loss or gain. ■ Effects of loss, gain, and the reference point can also operate at the group, or team, level. ■ Economic and financial theories often assume that one makes optimal use of available information as a basis for rational decision making. In practice, research (and everyday experience) shows that human behaviour departs significantly from that assumption.
Psychological biases	■ *Confirmation bias*: Having formed a view, most of us have a tendency to pay more attention to information that confirms that view than to information that contradicts it. ■ *Overconfidence*: We usually underestimate the range of possible outcomes from uncertain events. We assume that the more extreme possibilities, both good and bad, are much less likely than they really are so we focus on a spectrum of possibilities that is far too narrow. The consequences of overconfidence can be to take excessive risks or to pass up attractive opportunities. We are more likely to underestimate the risks rather than the opportunities because of optimism. ■ *Illusion of control*: Control beliefs are an important aspect of risk perception. We all hold beliefs concerning the extent to which we are able to exert control over events in which we are involved and over tasks we undertake. Many of these beliefs are perfectly reasonable and arise out of experience. However, there is a great deal of evidence that in some circumstances people systematically behave as if they were able to exert control in circumstances

Table 3.1 *continued*

Risk perception factors	*Description*
	where this is impossible or highly unlikely. This tendency is known as the illusion of control. If I suffer from the illusion of control, this can mean I invest all my efforts in trying to change a situation when it would be more appropriate to focus on adapting to it. Further, when judging risks I am more likely to underestimate the risk I am taking, because I will believe (wrongly) that I can control the situation in such a way as to reduce such risk.
	■ *Excessive optimism* leads us to expect results that are better than what a dispassionate assessment of the odds would justify. Most of us exaggerate our ability to control events and we underestimate our ability to control events and we underestimate the probabilities of bad outcomes that are, in fact, out of our control.
	■ *Faulty hindsight*: We misinterpret past events. We cannot adequately reconstruct what we thought about the probability of an event before that event occurred. Once we know what happened, we honestly believe that we assigned a much higher probability to the event than we actually did at the time. Events that we had considered highly unlikely or had not even imagined, we now claim to have forecast as likely or even inevitable. This tendency to rewrite history to gloss over our surprises and disappointments makes it difficult for us to recognize the errors produced by our environment and over-optimism.
	■ *Overcompensation*: We overcompensate when our success in reducing one type of risk tempts us into behaviour that causes us to take too much of other types of risks, leaving us in a riskier situation than we intended.
	■ *Myopia*: One form of myopia is to look only to the recent past for clues about the future (historical myopia). Another form of myopia is failing to imagine what might happen beyond the near future. It is not that the distant past or future is always relevant to making a decision; often they are not. However, ignoring the distant past or future should be deliberate judgement rather than an unconscious habit.
	■ *Ignoring warning signs*: Overconfidence can lead people into excessively sanitizing the world of hazards and thereby ignoring timely signs of impending danger. The tendency to dismiss potentially injurious events in order to make the world seem a safer place can cause people to fail to recognize the significance of warning signals and thereby paradoxically allow a dangerous situation to get worse. People's beliefs are slow to change and can still persist even when the holders are presented with evidence that demonstrates their view is inappropriate.
Personality and risk perception	■ *Sensation seeking*: This aspect of personality comprises the four elements of thrill- and adventure-seeking, experience-seeking, lack of inhibition, and susceptibility to boredom. Research studies have

Table 3.1 *continued*

Risk perception factors	Description
	linked sensation seeking with a number of risk behaviours such as making risky financial decisions and taking large gambling bets. ■ *Complacency*: This causes us to be unduly uncomfortable with familiar risks, e.g. air travel and the danger of synthetic pesticides and chemicals in the food supply. We may derive false comfort from something that is unfamiliar. ■ *Zealotry*: We become zealots when we seize upon only one possible scenario for the future and steadfastly ignore other possibilities. When we focus excessively on a single scenario, we avoid, reject or distort any information or opinion that conflicts with that scenario. One variant of zealotry may be found on Wall Street when a risk manager focuses on a financial model and forgets about the approximations and simplifying assumptions that it inevitably depends on. This suggests an unwillingness to recognize the losses and with risk and asset managers rationalizing their inertia by assuring themselves that the markets will soon return to 'normal' and the losses will disappear.

Why are risks taken even when the evidence points the other direction?

For the tens of millions of pounds it had invested in market research, BA and its CEO at the time still persevered with a re-branding exercise in the late 1990s which alienated key stakeholders, not least many front-line customer service staff.

Two reasons may lie in understanding:

■ how commitment escalates

■ how people's biases are framed.

1   Commitment escalates when individuals and organizations strongly commit further resources to an action. Escalation situations invariably involve the opportunity to either persist with, or withdraw from, the course of action and subsequent investment may reverse or compound earlier losses. Although the final outcome (i.e. success or failure) is unknown in advance, the decision maker continues to invest in the failing course of action. In other words he or she persists despite information that indicates the outcome is unlikely to be successful. Non-rational escalation occurs – because of perceptual biases and judgemental biases.

Case study 3.2

McDonalds serves up the wrong recipe

The McDonalds libel case, the longest libel trial in legal history was also arguably one of the biggest failures of understanding in business history.

When McDonalds issued a writ for libel against two unemployed environmental activists, they failed to understand that they were only the tip of the iceberg and the outward manifestation of a formidable and implacable force of trade unionists, environmental pressure groups, sympathetic and highly capable lawyers, potential witnesses and former employees of McDonalds. Even more dangerous, it was a counter culture that McDonalds little understood. It could be argued that if McDonalds had ignored the leaflets, the damage to their reputation would have been relatively slight. By reacting to the provocation, however, McDonalds took a marginalized protest and made it relevant. In trying to protect its reputation, McDonalds precipitated a public relations disaster.

For a company which appeared to use the law of libel as a part of their public relations, there was a public perception of the case as a victory for David (David Morris and Helen Steel) against Goliath (Ronald McDonald). Moreover inevitably the focus of the media – as reputational agents – was on the findings made against McDonalds and on comments made by the judge which were critical of McDonalds even when McDonalds may have won that particular issue, because of the meaning attributed to the words.

2   'Framing bias' occurs when trivial changes to the way a problem is presented crucially effects preferences for choosing alternatives. Left unchecked, framing bias is likely to undermine the quality of strategic decision making.

Frames develop and depend on group dynamics – on the relationships of individual to each other and to the group. One consequence of this is *groupthink*, 'the dependence on an earlier interpretation of reality that resists contrary evidence' (Mintzberg, Ahlstand and Lampel, 1999). Groupthink can lead to the development of group behaviours that bolster morale at the expense of critical thinking. This can erode value as it can cause a deterioration in mental efficiency, reality testing and moral judgements as a result of group/peer pressures.

Case study 3.3

Even reputational agents suffer from groupthink

One example of how the media are susceptible to groupthink has been highlighted by Harold Evans, former editor of *The Times* and *Sunday Times* and voted the greatest newpaper editor of all time (by readers of *British Journalism Review* and *Press Gazette*):

GW Bush was involved in the Harken Energy Corporation, and as one of its directors and consultants from 1986 to 1990, in the run-up to the 2000 election. Astonishingly, it was ignored. The New York Times, *the* Washington Post, *the* Wall Street Journal *and all the big TV and radio shows, except Tom Brokaw on NBC, failed even to report the Harken revelations, about which they are now making a fuss. The election reporters got themselves trapped in a narrative that was resistant to fact: Gore was a poseur, and Bush was an amiable Forrest Gump. No fact that did not fit the preconceived pattern saw ink or breathed air.*[3]

Groupthink can be an unconscious phenomenon. Moreover where members of a group are subject to its influence, they will tend to apply direct pressure to any member of the group who raises questions or does not show support for the view favoured by the majority. This can prevent open discussion of any evidence that might point to a weakness in the decision and, as a result, could lead to an inappropriate conclusion. There is also a risk that group members stop engaging in rigorous questioning and analysis and reality testing ceases. Few things in fact are more conducive to risk-taking than the conviction that one cannot fail which can even be perceived as management arrogance.

This can be reflected in a belief that size dictates success – for example in the late 1990s in the case of Marks & Spencer ('we're the biggest retailer in the UK so we must be doing it right') or British Airways (as the 'world's favourite airline' with more international passengers than any other airline when customer complaints, employee morale and shareholder value suggested otherwise).

Groupthink can affect the highest levels of corporate decision making – at the board. The recent Higgs review into the effectiveness of non-executive directors highlights the priority that regulators are now attaching to the effectiveness of decision making at the board level.

Table 3.2 Symptoms of groupthink and how it can link to behaviour on the board

Symptom	Content	Board manifestation/solution
Self-censorship and the illusion of unanimity	■ group members avoid speaking up against the majority for fear of being ridiculed ■ no-one wants to be the first to speak against the dominant position.	■ domineering chairman/CEO ■ disincentives to challenge status quo due to generous share option schemes loosely linked to performance.
Pressure on dissenters	Those who insist on dissenting are branded as a nuisance and their loyalty is questioned.	One response is open and trusting atmosphere for genuine debate.
Illusions of invulnerability	A successful track record or the qualifications of group members lead people to assume that 'we can't lose'.	Earnings history, customer volume, industry awards obscure inherent weaknesses.
Stereotypes	Outsiders such as competitors are cast as less ethical, intelligent, far-sighted or committed to the public good. In contrast, the intelligence, commitment and vision of team members are highlighted.	One way to tackle is through genuine diversity on the board – of background, perspective as well as of gender and race.

Groupthink, while useful in showing how reputational risk can increase as a result of blinkered thinking and behaviour, should not be used to label all group failings. This caveat applies not just to groupthink but to overconfidence bias or the confirmation trap as well. Especially in complex real world cases, multiple factors may be at play. However, groupthink can play a role at the board level. The key message is that if boards should (mainly) speak with one voice, they take dangerous risks when they think with one mind.

Two cases highlight how 'institutional entrapment'[4] can work.

Case study 3.4

Groupthink at Marks & Spencer – and a fresh approach to tackling it

In a wide-ranging interview (Davidson, 2001) with Marks & Spencer's former chairman, Richard Greenbury, the interviewer noted that 'when you ask him if he felt he was too controlling as a boss, compared to other company leaders, if M&S's culture carried the seeds of its own destruction, if he felt he mishandled other executives or the press or the City, he is not really sure, as he knows no other company so well'. He then went on to recall where he sought advice: 'Should old bosses be consulted? Isn't it better to cut the link? "I kept on Derek Rayner as a consultant. I wanted to be able to go and speak to him. I used to have lunch with him at his home, he used to come here, and I'd take his advice."'

One consequence of groupthink may be in the use of language: sometimes lack of awareness of the real audience influences our words. Rather than talking to customers in the language of customers, a company might adopt the language of its suppliers and simply assume that customers relate to this language as easily as the company's own buyers do. Some have argued that Marks & Spencer in the 1990s, became increasingly inward-focused and assumed that technical details of fabrics, for example were more important to customers than style and glamour. So 'machine washable' and 'non-iron' became more acceptable descriptions at the point of sale than what looks good.

Marks & Spencer's current approach with its current board and executive team is a much keener awareness of external perception of risk, at a time when its performance is improving.[5]

Case study 3.5

Long-term capital management (LTCM) – a textbook case

The case of LTCM, the supposedly invincible hedge fund and US investment organization, is perhaps one of the best recent examples of the way in which people regard risks, become overconfident, ignore warning signs and can generate groupthink that are generally never made explicit. David Viniar, Goldman Sachs' CFO has acknowledged that 'it is hard to really discuss risk with anyone on Wall Street without thinking – at least a little bit – about 1998'. Even if other real-life examples have arisen, the lessons for understanding how human factors affected risk at LTCM are still very relevant.

LTCM did not fail because there was a problem with the data, the mathematics or the computers that it employed. In the final analysis, it eventually failed because of the assumptions and the decisions made by people about those issues. We need to understand how decision-making processes and social behaviour may affect people's judgement of financial risks. Everyone needs to be aware of the problems that such processes can create, and the ways in which their effects can potentially be ameliorated. A failure to take account of local conditions may well create difficulties that increase the risk of failure from other, unforeseen sources.

A disconnect in:

- financial risks
- decision making
- individual and corporate behaviour.

Can lead to a connect here:

- risk misperception
- value destruction.

Long Term Capital Management (LTCM) was a small limited investment partnership, i.e. by law it was not allowed to sign up more than 99 investors, people or institutions to the fund it created. In the first instance, the fund was set up to trade in the arbitrage of bonds; however, over time LTCM became increasingly successful in its bond-trading activities, and so a decision was taken to expand its business into a number of other, non-core, higher-risk areas, such as options writing, spread trading and futures. The fund had made returns in excess of 40 per cent in the first two years of its existence, and the partners were sure their success would continue.

Investors – who in the main were banks – had by 1998 loaned the partnership sufficient funds to purchase securities worth $125 billion. These assets were subsequently invested by LTCM in thousands of derivative contracts, which endlessly intertwined it with every bank on Wall Street. Thus if LTCM were to fail then each of the investors that had loaned it money would sustain major losses.

In September 1998 LTCM's notional exposure to derivative contracts was in excess of $1 trillion. The crisis occurred because there had been a number of unexpected world events that had radically changed world market conditions. Due to the very highly leveraged investment strategy that it had been aggressively pursuing, the new market conditions meant that instead of making a profit it now had to fund massive losses. Eventually, its situation became so serious that the crisis threatened to take down all of Wall Street and more. At this point, the Federal Reserve Bank facilitated a meeting where it was agreed that the fund should be taken over by some 14 banks. The reasons for the crisis at LTCM lie in undetected socio-psychological biases of key individuals and in the systemic properties of the global markets in which LTCM operated.

There appear to be people who hold an inordinately strong belief that everything, including risks, can be measured. This mindset also appears to have been held by many of those who worked at LTCM, and in particular by a collection of people known as the Arbitrage Group. This group consisted of hand-picked individuals who were all known for their academic ability in the mathematical modelling of financial risks. For example, two of the group, Robert C. Merton and Myron Scholes, shared the 1997 Nobel Prize for their contributions to Economic Science, while other members of this elite group had been awarded PhD and Master's degrees in either finance or economics. Once the Arbitrage Group had been formed their first action was reportedly to download into their computers all of the past bond prices they could get their hands on. They distilled the bonds' historical relationships, and they modelled how these prices should behave in the future. Every price was a 'statement'; if two statements were in conflict, there might be an opportunity for arbitrage.

However, such a view on the nature of risk would appear to be based on the assumption that all else being equal, the future would look like the past – the idea being that with sufficient data relating to past events the future can be reliably predicted.

What the traders at LTCM did not appear to have appreciated was that the future price of the financial instruments they traded could be radically affected by decisions, which they could not predict, being made in the world of politics, i.e. human agencies are involved in such price movements. Markets are dynamic entities that are constantly changing, and while the past price movement of financial instruments cannot be altered, future price movements can. As a consequence, the accuracy of forecasting future price movements within markets stands on potentially shifting sand.

Because LTCM had $125 billion of securities to invest, it was operating on a global scale. Thus when it failed to predict the downturn in economic activity in Asia, and Russia's default on its sovereign debt, it created a situation where the derivative contracts held by LTCM started to make significant losses – which is hardly surprising, since knowledge of past volatilities does not prepare investors for shocks that lie in wait – nor do they signal in advance just when such shocks might choose to occur.

The partners at LTCM held the belief that there would always be liquidity in the markets in which they traded. However, under the prevailing circumstances in the autumn of 1998, this was not to be, and the LTCM traders could not sell the investments that were losing them money. As a consequence, they were locked into a downward financial spiral from which there was no immediate escape, with their underlying capital being eaten away at a frenetic rate. It was at this point that the Federal Reserve Bank sought to find a way forward. LTCM appears to have mistakenly programmed the market for a cold predictability that it never had: they had forgotten the predatory, acquisitive, and overwhelming protective instincts that govern real life traders.

LTCM initially made significant profits based on its approach to trading. Thus such successes would naturally have led it to believe that it was adopting the appropriate techniques and strategy in its trading decisions, and consequently had no reason to question the rationale underlying them. This could have led LTCM to be overconfident, particularly when, having made a decision at the end of 1997 to return the entire principal and profits made to date to a number of investors, some of the latter demanded to stay in but LTCM turned them down.

Other evidence to suggest that those who worked at LTCM might have been overconfident or have sanitized the world of hazards can be found in the fact that Jim McEntee, a partner in the organization, warned on a number of occasions that they should lower the firm's risk. However, his warnings were ignored and LTCM continued to act as if the world would always be its oyster.

The LTCM failure demonstrates faith in one's own ability and such a capacity to ignore warnings, against a backdrop of success, can lead to complacency and professional myopia, where adverse incidents of tremendous proportions can and do take place.

The Arbitrage Group formed the heart of LTCM's financial instruments mathematical modelling team. This small group of people had similar academic interests and backgrounds, and had been brought together for the same purpose. The Arbitrage Group, about 12 in all, became incredibly close. These are just the circumstances that can lead to the groupthink condition. They shared the same view on the nature of risk, were overconfident, ignored warning signs, took large risks and although they would argue about what the risk models predicted, they exerted direct pressure on those who did not conform to group norms. For example, one mortgage trader found its cliquish aspect overbearing and left. Another defector was treated like a traitor; Meriwether (Founding Partner of LTCM) vengefully ordered the crew not to even golf with him.

The Arbitrage Group appear to have held the belief that the quantitative probabilistic risk-analysis trading equations used by them to predict the future prices of financial instruments were as reliable in their predictive power as those used to describe actions in the physical world. However, the markets in which LTCM operated are open systems, created and influenced by the behaviour of human beings.

Consequently while the techniques of quantitative probabilistic risk analysis are undoubtedly useful, those who employ them should realize that they may be unreliable for the evaluation of some types of risk.

Key lessons

- The Bank for International Settlements verdict on LTCM highlighted deficiencies in banking institutions' risk management with respect to some highly leveraged institutions. The lack of financial information on highly leveraged companies led to a reliance on 'non-systemic and largely qualitative assessments of risks', based on 'reputation and perceived risk management capabilities of the highly leveraged company'.

- Many reputations were damaged in the wake of LTCM on both sides of the Atlantic. One example in which reputation acted as 'collateral risk' was in respect to central banks. 'In a rare coup, LTCM even enticed the foreign exchange office of Italy's central bank to invest $100 million. Such entities simply do *not* invest in hedge funds but LTCM was seen not as a "hedge fund" but as an elite investing organisation "with a solid reputation".'[6]

- Other unforeseen sources of risk can flow from issues of corporate governance and reputation to collectively undermine corporate performance. For all its attention to risk, LTCM's management had a serious flaw. Unlike banks, where independent risk managers watch over traders, LTCM's partners monitored themselves. Though this enabled them to sidestep the rigidities of a big organization, there was no-one to call the partners to account.

- Another reputational risk were the gurus – the Nobel Prize winning economics Harvard professors who also became involved in helping LTCM develop its models. Reared on Merton's and Scholes' teachings of efficient markets, the professors actually believed that prices would go, and go directly where the models said they should. The professors' conceit was to think that models could forecast the limits of behaviour. They overlooked the fact that people, traders included, are not always reasonable – or even responsible.

REPUTATIONAL RISK

What existing definitions miss

Existing definitions of reputational risk from regulators and elsewhere can be summarized as follows:

> The range of risks that arise from the company's relationships, brand name, operational failures in products and services, a failure to comply with relevant laws or damage to the organization's credibility and reputation
>
> which are
>
> threats to long-term trust with customers, employees, shareholders, the regulatory bodies and suppliers
>
> and can include
>
> everything from specific policy misjudgements to scandals. For a service organization, it can mean not delivering on its service commitments including failing to meet adequately customer account needs or expectations, unreliable or inefficient delivery systems, untimely responses to customer enquiries or violations of customer privacy.

However, none of the definitions mention:

- political risk
- ethics or value(s)
- corporate governance or leadership
- behaviour, commitment or relationships
- the social context and how people's feelings and experiences affects corporate reputation.

None make a distinction or reference to internal and external reputation (corporate and organizational identity) or suggest reputational risk matters less or more to different companies (manufacturing/service, old/new economy) or even less make a cultural distinction for a US, UK or Japanese multinational.

The Basle 2 Accord is an attempt by banking regulators to prevent another Barings-like disaster. It includes an 'initiative to include operational risks – such as the breakdown of systems or other unforeseen events – in the basket of risks to be covered'. Operational risk as defined by Basle 2 is: 'The risk of direct or indirect loss resulting from inadequate or failed internal processes, people and systems or from external events.' This includes legal risk, but not strategic and reputational risks. Reputational risk is not however a sub-set of operational risk. This is a key point and one shared in a recent Cabinet Office review of risk types (UK Cabinet Office, 2001b).

US banking regulators equate reputational risk with its impacts which has application to companies involved in alliances, joint ventures and subsidiaries:

Spillover effects can result in aggregate risk exceeding the sum of the individual risks of business units within the firm concerns in what might be called reputational or contagion risk, the idea that problems in one part of a diversified firm may affect confidence in other parts of the firm. The situation is one in which such problems cause acute, near-term funding or liquidity problems across the firm, due to questions about whether the losses in the troubled business unit are evidence of as-yet-unrevealed losses in other business lines.

Enron and Anderson's subsequent collapse provides one of the most potent examples in recent corporate history of such 'spillover effects'. Eerily, as the Federal Reserve Bank months before Enron noted:

businesses with massive technology investments [such as Enron] can engender what some analysts call 'strategic risk'. Failure in such ventures may be highly visible and thus likely to have spillover effects on other businesses through the cost of capital, the cost of funding, and revenue effects through the loss of customer approval. Thus, other business lines associated with the troubled entity may see their franchise value erode as a result of difficulties in an affiliated unit. Such strategic risk may be particularly important for institutions for which customer trust is a key competitive advantage. Adverse publicity, legal judgements against the firm, evidence of fraud or internal theft, or high-profile failed business ventures may erode customer confidence in an institution. In the extreme, such concerns may reach the point where the affected firm is no longer viable as an ongoing concern, even though it may technically be solvent.

Cumming and Hirtle, 2001

Reputational risk is:

The comparison that key stakeholders make between how a company or its employees are expected to behave and how they actually behave.

Key point: Reputational risk can therefore be positive or negative.

Reputation needs to be seen as a source of risk in its own right and/or as a consequence of other risks occurring. However, what is striking is how definitions, coming mainly from the insurance industry or communications consultants, take negative approaches synonymous with 'loss/insurance' and 'crisis'. Why?

A key reason may be a failure to focus on the definition of reputation and risk which sees reputation as being about the quality of relationships with stakeholders and risk as having an inherent up-side. Moreover there is scarce recognition of the significance of emotional factors in framing expectations in key stakeholder relationships (i.e. among customers, employees and investors) set out below, which are not linked.

Table 3.3 Emotions among key stakeholders

Stakeholder	Discipline/function	Theme	Link to reputational risk
Customers	Marketing and Communications Customer service and operations. Commercial business development	Human qualities in branding/'emotional branding'.	Stakeholder relationships and expectations.
Employees	Organizational behaviour and Human Resources.	Emotions in organizations.	
Investors	Finance and Investor Relations.	Behavioural finance.	

A synthesis is needed. A focus on corporate governance may provide an emerging common ground.

The Turnbull Report (1999) remains the most considered view on reputational risk within the policy arena and its main authors have since acknowledged that 'many companies now find reputation risk a central cause of concern' (Carey and Turnbull, 2001). The Higgs Report (2003) 'focuses on the conditions and behaviours necessary for non-executive directors to be fully effective' including the need to take account of 'the long-, as well as the, short-term consequences of their actions, the need to foster business relationships ... and business reputation'.

This suggests an enabling framework (*see* Figure 3.9).

Fig. 3.9 Governance and leadership

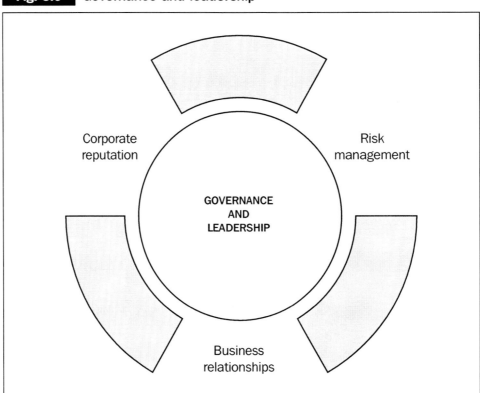

EXECUTIVE SUMMARY

1 Post 9/11, politicians, military and business are now sinisterly terrorist equal targets. People will need to accept more and wider uncertainty not as an occasional feature of the competitive landscape but as being increasingly the norm. Companies need to move from a 'make and sell' mindset to one of 'sense and respond'. In this, context becomes more important than strategy and monitoring for external signals is key.

2 Much current practice in risk management is an attempt to codify organizational processes rather than manage risk itself. This is itself a risk as it can encourage dangerous narrow tick-box processes to ensure compliance.

3 What is perceived to be a hazard to one organization may be perceived as an opportunity to another. The word 'risk' is derived from the early Italian word 'risicare' which means to dare. Risk management can help you seize opportunity, not just avoid danger. Taking a risk and being innovative are clearly linked and taking a risk to improve a corporate reputation is not in itself negative. It is the behaviours that people exhibit that determine whether this adds or destroys value. A key challenge is to understand what the boundaries of risk-taking are.

4   Predominant approaches to risk are narrow because they fail to focus enough on the up-side as well as downside and acknowledge the influence of human/behavioural factors.

5   Risk appetite is the level of risk which the board and management believe to be appropriate for the culture and capability of that particular organization. The greater the risk appetite, the greater the potential up-sides (opportunities) and downsides (risk incidents).

6   There is a growing body of evidence that emotions play an important role in people's decision processes for choices when there are uncertain outcomes.

7   There are a number of factors that affect how we perceive risk. These include loss and gain and psychological biases. A management strategy that acknowledges the individualistic and variable nature of risk perception and enables the open discussion and reconciliation of such differences will increase the effectiveness of decision making.

8   Groupthink can affect the highest levels of corporate decision making – at the board. The recent Higgs review into the effectiveness of non-executive directors highlights the priority that regulators are now attaching to the effectiveness of decision making at the board level.

9   Existing definitions of reputational risk fail to mention ethics or value(s), behaviour, relationships and how people's feelings and experiences affect corporate reputation. Having a strong risk culture is not an end in itself. What is important is the behaviours that it drives in pursuit of an organization's goals.

10 Reputational risk is the comparison that key stakeholders make between how a company or its employees are expected to behave and how they actually behave. The key point is that it can be positive or negative.

Key message

Risk is subjective. Behaviour matters more than checklists for compliance and are not necessarily linked.

What you must ask of your team/staff/consultants

1   Do we consider what kind of risk-takers we want in our senior management population – or even on the board?

2   How do we assess country risk?

3   Is our approach to risk relevant for the top three challenges facing this organization in the next 12 months?

4 What kind of language do we use when we discuss risk on the board?

5 How different is this if we had a culturally diverse board with people from Japan and India and a woman, or an ethnic minority from our own country, as the senior NED in the room?

What you must do today

1 *Read* the Long Term Capital Management case study. Extract three lessons that are relevant for you and your organization.

2 *Count* how many times you take calculated risks on your journey home.

3 *Ask* what risks you would take with your own reputation.

4 Then *ask* what risks you would take with your company's reputation.

Related websites

UK Cabinet Office
www.risk-support.gov.uk

Notes

1 Chris Patten, the EU's Commissioner for External Relations speaking on Radio 4 'With Us or Without Us' interview, of his experience visiting Washington after 9/11. *http://www.bbc.co.uk/radio4/news/withus/patten/pdf.*

2 Nobel Laureate Stanley Prusiner, BSE Inquiry, 6 June 1998.

3 *Sunday Times*, 14 July 2002.

4 The author is indebted to Joanne Cutler, research adviser to the External Members of the Monetary Policy Committee of the Bank of England 1996–2002 for this term (June 2002).

5 Mike Morley-Fletcher, Head of Risk Assessment, Marks & Spencer (presentation to a Strategic Planning Society meeting on 27 June 2002 chaired by the author).

6 James Blitz, *Financial Times*, 2 October 1998. Arif Zaman is grateful to John Bray, Professor at the LSE and author of the seminal bestseller *False Dawn* (1998) for pointing this out in conversation at the ICA, 5 September 2002.

References

Carey, Anthony and Turnbull, Nigel (2001) 'The Boardroom Imperative on Internal Control' in *Mastering Risk Volume 1: Concepts*. London: Financial Times Prentice Hall.

Cumming, Christine M. and Hirtle, Beverly J. (2001) *The Challenges of Risk Management in Diversified Financial Companies*. Federal Reserve Bank of New York, April. *http://www.newyorkfed.org/rmaghome/econ_pol/2001/201cumm.pdf*.

Davidson, Andrew (2001) 'Interview with Sir Richard Greenbury', *Management Today*. November.

Foster, Richard and Kaplan, Sarah (2001) *Creative Destruction: Turning Built-to-Last into Built-to-Perform*. London: Financial Times Prentice Hall.

Haeckel, Stephen H. (1999) *Adoptive Enterprise: Creating and Leading Sense-and-Respond Organizations*. Boston: Harvard Business School Press.

Hopkin, Paul (2002) *Holistic Risk Management in Practice*. London: Witherby & Company.

Institute of Chartered Accountants of Scotland (2001) *Attitudes of UK Managers to Risk and Uncertainty*. Edinburgh: Institute of Chartered Accountants of Scotland.

Mintzberg, Henry, Ahlstrand, Bruce and Lampel, Joseph (1999) *Strategy Safari: The Complete Guide Through the Wilds of Strategic Management*. London: Financial Times Prentice Hall.

Olsson, Carl (2002) *Risk Management in Emerging Markets*. London: Pearson Education.

Royal Institute of International Affairs (2000) Chatham House Forum, *The Engines of Change*.

Turnbull Report (1999) *Internal Control: Guidance for Directors on the Combined Code*. London: ICAEW.

UK Cabinet Office (2001a) 'Managing risk and uncertainty – the challenge for the next decade'. Seminar. 14 December. *http://www.number10.gov.uk/output/Page3767.asp*.

UK Cabinet Office (2001b) Risk and Uncertainty Project Scoping Note. September. *http://www.number-10.gov.uk/SU/RISK/risk/home.html*

Reputational risk and customers

WHAT YOU MUST KNOW BEFORE YOU START

1 Why the customer is central to understanding and managing reputational risk.

2 The service company difference.

3 Why customer satisfaction alone does not safeguard reputation.

4 Critical drivers of customer expectations – and how they are changing.

5 The connection between brand values and corporate values – and why it matters when building reputation.

6 How channel conflict can sour corporate reputation.

7 What you must know before you start.

8 How the internet often increases reputational risk.

WHY THE CUSTOMER IS CENTRAL TO UNDERSTANDING AND MANAGING REPUTATIONAL RISK

The customer is ultimately the most important stakeholder for every competitive business and commercial operation. This is perhaps a statement of the obvious but in all the focus on shareholders, regulators and even the community since the late 1990s in particular, this needs to be re-emphasized. Shareholders clearly matter but, as we have seen, shareholder value and financial performance is driven from customer satisfaction and experience. Employees may be the most important asset according to the chairman's statement but this is mainly because they are key to delivering value for customers. Companies may increase their shareholder value but if investment analysts have disastrous customer service experiences on a BA flight or in a Marks & Spencer store it is naïve to believe that this does not affect the reputation of BA or Marks & Spencer in their eyes. Equally, BT may have a well-developed community relations programme but if OFTEL takes BT to task over the way it treats its customers, this will harm its reputation more.

THE SERVICE COMPANY DIFFERENCE – AND WHAT IT MEANS FOR ALL COMPANIES

Not all service companies are the same. They differ widely, with varied organizational characteristics that create very different management problems. But which core competences have the strongest influence on improving the performance of different types of service business?

109

Tangibles	Appearance of facilities, equipment, personnel, materials.
Reliability	Ability to perform the service dependably and accurately.
Responsiveness	Willingness to help customers and provide prompt service.
Assurance	Ability to convey knowledge, trust, confidence.
Empathy	Caring, concern, individualized attention.

Which is more important to customers: delivering the right product or service, or eliminating problems in that product or service? It depends on what the customer is buying. Although customer satisfaction depends on both meeting customers' needs and doing so in a trouble-free way, the relative importance of customization and reliability changes dramatically depending on whether the company is delivering goods or services.

For service businesses especially, reliability (eliminating 'things going wrong') is more important than customization (fitting customer needs perfectly). That may surprise some who have been trained that a service company's ability to customize its service to individuals is a primary driver of value. It is also a strong indicator that service businesses should not abandon initiatives to improve internal processes as they strive to meet customer needs. The biggest risk to Microsoft is on the reputation side – 'if the products don't produce' as it has put it. They attempt to manage this risk through various helplines which actively capture feedback and through software updates which happen automatically.

What this means for all companies is that one of the keys to understanding customer expectations is recognizing the role that emotions play in customer relationships.

- Emotions tell us what matters to customers. If service transactions had no value to customers, customers would not have emotions about them. Customers remember events, many times unconsciously, that influence the reality of their current experience. Service providers are often forced to deal with strong customer emotions that have nothing to do with the transaction underway. However, any displayed emotions are related to something that currently matters to the customer and service providers need to interact completely with the total customer experience – because that is what is happening at the moment.

- Customer emotions are influenced by memories which include expectations already formed, the first few seconds and the last few seconds of a service encounter and the personal pride (shame) they feel from their choice of purchases or suppliers.

■ Emotions tell us how customers relate to service providers. Because of the brevity of many emotions, social interactions can change directions emotionally. When there is an audience, customer emotions intensify for most people.

■ Emotions tell us how customers are likely to behave. If customers are angry, they feel threatened at some level and are primed to attack. If customers feel fear, they may be impelled to escape or leave or not come back.

Decisions are often not based solely, or even largely, on economic or functional criteria of value. Products fill more than functional needs; they are also purchased to fill social needs.

WHY CUSTOMER SATISFACTION ALONE DOES NOT SAFEGUARD REPUTATION

If companies focus excessively on satisfaction, they run the risk of not understanding why customers feel drawn to return or the emotional meaning of the service experience to them. Moreover if customer service staff rely on customers to report when they have experienced negative emotional reactions, service providers run the risk of missing subtle emotional communications that may not be expressed verbally.

Common misconceptions

■ *Customer satisfaction influences business performance* This only tells part of the story. Market-perceived relative quality is correlated with profitability. The term 'market' encompasses more than just customers; it includes all potential sources of revenue – customers, competitors' customers and non-users. 'Perceived' means quality as defined and judged by the customer, not by marketing planners or consultants. 'Relative' means quality as compared to the competition, a key differential in the firm's ability to attract and keep customers. 'Quality' in this context means exceeding customer expectations.

■ *Customer satisfaction means doing whatever it takes to keep customers happy regardless of the cost* The ability to establish, maintain and build customer relationships depends on the perceived value of the offering. Moreover customer budgets that are overshot in the first quarter do not provide the means to deliver customer value in the final quarter.

■ *Customer satisfaction leads to customer loyalty* Customer loyalty is best understood as a pattern of behaviour. It is the likelihood of staying with the

111

main (i.e. most often used) service provider rather than switching to a realistic alternative.

■ The primary drivers of loyalty in commoditized sectors are often expressed in comments like 'I tend to use the same shop/bank/airline/computer manufacturer without really thinking about it' or 'I can't be bothered spending time choosing between what different companies offer.' This does not build reputation. Drivers like 'I tend to stick with products/services I know and trust' minimizes the reputational risk and builds reputation. Secondary drivers may relate to convenience and choice where customers find it difficult to know the differences between what companies offer.

There are two forces at play in customer loyalty across BTC and BTB markets:

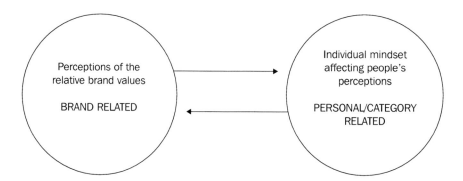

Most marketing campaigns fail to acknowledge the growing importance of how an 'inert' mindset can often be the real cause of apparent loyalty – not brand benefits. This can increase reputational risk. One way to overcome this is to build strong perceptions of relative brand value.

Case study 4.1

British Airways focuses on customer value to drive global relationships forward after 9/11

■ BA's largest on-airport investment is in its cargo business (BA carries more international cargo than Fedex). The commercial strategy recognized that a rationale was needed for customer segmentation of key global business accounts (the freight forwarders – the airline's traditional intermediaries). Moreover a value was needed beyond traditional customer satisfaction measures.

■ The product and customer service strategy was tailored to high value customers; the contact strategy from communication to booking involved more contact from senior levels for high value customers; there was a clear pricing strategy for each distinct segment; and for operational excellence, operational priorities were set by the value of customers.

- Business partnership programmes involved devising appropriate schemes by segment/customer; marketing strategy focused on investing money on high value segments and in cost-effective targeted campaigns. In the business development strategy, low-value customers had to use cheaper channels.

- To implement all this a commercial organization structure was established to maximize value from customer relationships.

A cross-functional project team made up of operational research staff and the global key account management team segmented the top customers. Then:

1 A brainstorm of what was meant by 'value' resulted in a focus on the actual business *and* behaviours.

2 Agreed factors for a model recognized monetary factors upfront (e.g. market share, relative average yield) – but *also* non-monetary factors (e.g. support for sending freight on the airline's leased freighters, the fit of the product offering, price sensitivity and the strength and openness of the end-customer's relationship).

3 A survey of customers was devised and populated in internal workshops.

4 Results were aggregated to achieve a global perspective.

5 Weightings were agreed for all factors.

There is no simple relationship between increasing the performance and quality of services and increased level of user satisfaction. The level of satisfaction or dissatisfaction that results from an encounter between a service user and provider depends both on the user's expectations of the service they will receive and their perceptions of the service they have received.

Different factors make different contributions in determining people's perceptions of the service they have received. The absence of some factors – for example, reliability – can have a strong impact on dissatisfaction levels. However, the presence of reliability may sometimes be taken for granted and hence increased performance may not lead to higher satisfaction levels. Moreover, people may be willing to tolerate small movements in some of these factors without any impact upon their satisfaction with a service. These points are explored further:

Types of factors

- *Dissatisfying factors* If such factors are perceived to be inadequate, then dissatisfaction will result, but any increase in performance above adequacy has little effect on perceptions. For example, the presence of a dirty fork is likely to make customers dissatisfied, but a very clean fork is unlikely to add to satisfaction.

- *Satisfying factors* are those which when improved beyond adequacy have a positive effect on perceptions. When these factors are absent though, there is little effect on satisfaction. For example, if a waiter does not remember you from your last visit to the restaurant you are unlikely to be dissatisfied, but if he does and also remembers your favourite wine, you are likely to be delighted.

■ *Critical factors* are those where changes in performance affect both satisfaction and dissatisfaction ratings. In the example of a restaurant, slow service can cause dissatisfaction, while speedy service can increase satisfaction.

■ *Neutral factors* Satisfaction is not responsive to changes in performance.

Is satisfaction related to objective measures of inputs or outputs?

Satisfaction is linked to some inputs of service quality and some objective measures of service output. As satisfaction measurement covers a wide range of factors, including subjective impressions such as friendliness, it is not surprising that the relationship is not perfect.

Case study 4.2

Service and reputational risk: train reliability after the Hatfield crash

In 2000, before the delays in the months following the Hatfield crash the relationship between performance and satisfaction was strong. In 2001, during the aftermath of Hatfield, performance significantly worsened. Satisfaction ratings did not move in tandem with performance – and the relationship between satisfaction and performance broke down slightly. This suggests satisfaction consists of many different components and some have a greater influence at certain points. For example some companies were better at providing accurate information and 'recovery' – the actions taken to correct a mistake after it is made and so lessened the immediate reputational risk.

Steve Marshall, CEO of Railtrack Group from November 2000, three weeks after the Hatfield rail crash, until March 2002 has pointed to wider lessons learnt in reputational risk:

■ Your reputation will always mirror the absolute reality of who you are. This has enormous implications. Anyone who thinks that they can change their reputation without changing the company is mistaken. Spin, in other words, can never change a reputation and can help damage it.

■ The most deadly sign of a reputation in trouble is when staff admitted to covering up their papers while on a train because they did not want people to see that they worked for Railtrack.

■ Railtrack did not have a grip on its contractors and from that stems catastrophic business risk. It destroyed the brand's integrity.

Suggested strategies:

1 Focus more on scanning the horizon than dealing with crises.

2 Keep breast of changing attitudes. The reactions of different stakeholders change. Public tolerance of a rail crash is now much lower than it was 20 or 30 years ago. The frequency of crashes has not increased. It is the tolerance that has reduced. Risk managers have to assess not just the reputation risk but how it changes over time.

CRITICAL DRIVERS OF CUSTOMER EXPECTATIONS AND BRAND EQUITY

Customers do not evaluate a product or service on its own. They do so relative to their expectations. When customer expectations are too high and the delivered product does not meet those expectations the customer will not repeat purchase. Thus a critical factor in retention is the difference between the customer's expectations and the delivered quality of the product or service.

User identification (Figure 4.1) and experience is a key driver of brand equity. This implies a much stronger focus on employee motivation as, especially in a service industry, front-line customer service staff create the atmosphere and are the principal conduit for engaging the customer in the experience.

THE CONNECTION BETWEEN BRAND VALUES AND CORPORATE VALUES – AND WHY IT MATTERS WHEN BUILDING REPUTATION

Traditionally the focus of trust between buyers and sellers was on a promise or unique selling point and whether it was delivered or not. However, the flows of information are no longer controlled by brand managers – the power of pressure groups (especially NGOs) and media as reputational agents has been noted earlier. Added to this there is rising consumer sophistication. The generation reaching retirement age is the first to have reached their adult lives in a full blown brand marketing, media-intensive environment.

Empowered consumers are demanding ever higher standards in terms of quality and value for money. Consumers are more 'cash-rich, time-poor' than they have ever been. Some strategies for dealing with this that enhance reputation need to meet or exceed customer expectations, often not at great cost.

Fig. 4.1 Drivers of brand equity

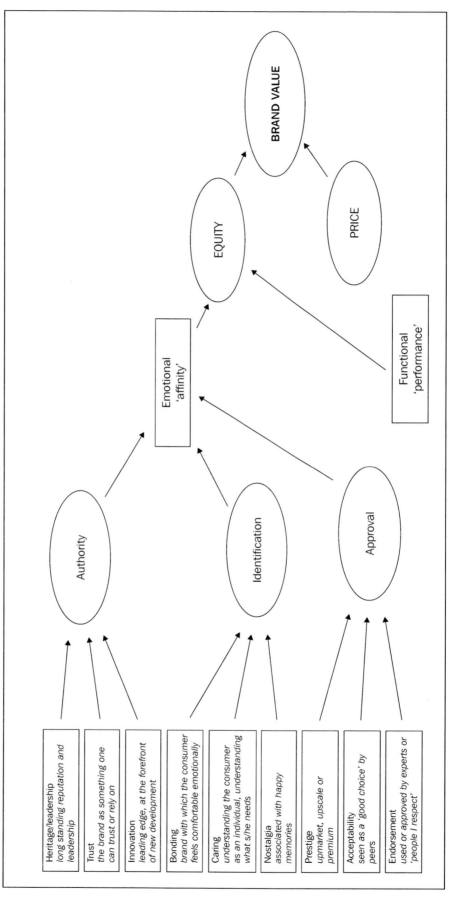

Source: Major FTSE company in the service sector.

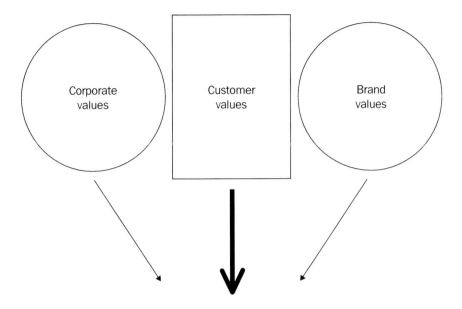

What do we do	How do we do it
Understand the value of time.	Minimize time-wasting on cumbersome processes.
Manage relationships through flexibility and problem-sharing.	Encourage a team approach by front-line customer service staff.
Identify opportunities to leave a positive customer experience.	Exceed expectations by adding surprise little touches in service delivery.
Do not lose sight of the value of personal contact.	Call centres are a prime culprit for this in the number of auto prompts required before it is possible to speak to a live person.
Fairness – a more flexible attitude to look for alternative solutions to problems.	Not telling customers there is only one way; focus on outcome not process.

Case study 4.3

Camay soap in India

A disconnect in corporate and brand values can sometimes be manifested in brand arrogance. When Procter & Gamble launched the Camay soap in India it was done so with scant regard for the Indian consumer's aspirations. The assumption was that Camay was a well-entrenched brand all over the world and that India was just one more territory in which the company had to make the brand available. The advertising did not even mention the benefits of the brand. Camay had prejudged the Indian consumer who then failed to support the brand. To date, there are no traces of the brand in India.

Consumers are also becoming more aware and active on a wide range of environmental, social and ethical issues. Concerns about the ethical working practices of businesses are having a significant effect on purchasing decisions around the world (Weber Shandwick Worldwide, 2001) and the company's ethical approach must be in step with those of its valued customers. This is no substitute for a company being clear what it stands for and reputational risks can grow when gaps develop unchecked between how a company behaves in the minds of its customers and how it is *expected* to behave.

- While reliable and good value products are still most important to consumers all over the world, people are also increasingly concerned with other factors.

- Most consumers in Australia (71 per cent), the US (67 per cent), Germany (62 per cent), Singapore (56 per cent) and the UK (55 per cent) 'would consider buying a different brand of product if they were concerned about how the company making their current brand treated its employees, harmed the environment or used child labour'.

- 'Leading edge' consumers are more likely than other consumers to say they have considered changing brands because of 'bad corporate behaviour'. This suggests that companies should pay particular attention to the views of this more affluent, better educated group of consumers on issues of corporate behaviour, as this group is likely to lead the way on changes in consumer purchasing behaviour.

Generation Y consumers have shown the most social activism since the baby boomers in the 1960s. They are likely to base much of their consumption on the values they associate with the companies providing goods and services. This means that companies will have to make a far greater effort to ensure that the values communicated to consumers are consistent with its internal values. If it is not, they will be exposed.

HOW CHANNEL CONFLICT CAN SOUR CORPORATE REPUTATION

How can companies take advantage of a new and growing sales channel while managing relationships with existing channels? There a number of conflict-management levers (variables under marketing's control) that can be used to increase or reduce the risk of conflict with incumbent channels.

In the interest of mitigating channel conflict, each of the levers can be employed in a variety of ways. The range of current approaches suggests no shortage of options for companies aiming to minimize conflict when launching an on-line sales channel.

Fig. 4.2 Risks and opportunities from conflicts in marketing and distribution channels

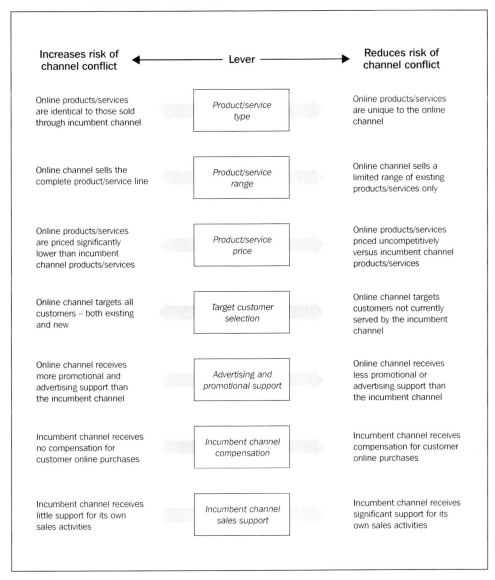

Source: Marketing Leadership Council, 2000.

Table 4.1 Levers that can reduce the risk of channel conflict

Product/service type	Online products/services made distinct from traditional channel products/services via:
	■ Customization or digitization of existing products for the web
	■ Creation of new, Internet-only products/services
	■ Creation of new, Internet-only brands.

Product/service range	Online sales restricted to a subset of the products/services sold in other channels: ■ Peripheral products/services only ■ Low-margin products/services only ■ Products without servicing requirements only.
Product/service price	Online prices rendered uncompetitive (vs. other channels' prices) via: ■ Prices above manufacturer-suggested retail prices ■ Subscription fees for online access ■ Shipping and handling fees.
Target customer selection	Online channel sells to unique customer segment(s) by targeting: ■ Market niches only ■ Untapped geographies only ■ Small account sizes only.
Advertising and promotional support	Online channel provided limited promotional support in the form of: ■ Limited advertising ■ Restricted use of popular retail promotions (e.g. sales, coupons).
Incumbent channel compensation	Traditional channel partners provided 'extra' compensation in the form of: ■ Commissions for online sales ■ Shared online profits.
Incumbent channel sales support	Traditional channel partners provided sales support in the form of: ■ Agent/dealer website development ■ Online-generated leads ■ Online ordering capabilities.

Source: Marketing Leadership Council, 2000.

HOW DOES CUSTOMER RELATIONSHIP MISMANAGEMENT IMPACT REPUTATION?

Customer relationship management (CRM) has been a recent mantra as electronic solutions from vendors to customer relationships have proliferated. Many of the problems have increased reputational risk by playing directly into what customers expected and what they experienced. In many cases these problems have stemmed from cultural and organizational issues or simply inadequate planning rather than fundamental problems with the technology.

1   *Inadequate testing* An online service that is launched too quickly risks severe embarrassment if the system fails. One of the most high-profile examples of

this was when Encyclopaedia Britannica went online and people became increasingly frustrated when unable to access something which perhaps to them represented the ultimate knowledge bank.

2   *Poor back-office integration* Companies often fail to realize the depth of back-office integration that is needed. One example of how this can be manifested is when a customer asks an insurance company for a quote on the Internet and call centres use the same quote (unless there is a conscious decision to maintain differential pricing).

3   *Front-end applications fail to communicate* For continuity, applications need to be able to speak to each other. Without that, for example, new services coming online will not be tightly integrated with those the customer already has. Banks have found they need to ensure that screen statements mirror in near or real time the movement of money from accounts.

4   *Lack of departmental integration* Of consumers, 70 per cent receive duplicate emailings, generated from the same source, on a regular basis. To prevent this and the ensuing frustration of the customer that damages reputation, CRM systems must enable different departments to coordinate their communication. An e-mail marketing service from a recording company that alerts rap music customers with links to classical music web links (events and merchandise) is likely to cause customer antagonism and undermine any corporate claims to be at the forefront of technological innovation (unless of course customer interests coincide).

5   *Lack of channel integration* As online sales and marketing channels have developed, so has the challenge of integrating them with existing means of customer contact. Since privatization, utility companies, for example, have not only had to gear up customer services to support their traditional businesses, but have moved into new ways of doing business in an attempt to capitalize on their existing relationships with customers. Moving customers online lock, stock and barrel may position the company as being e-savvy with shareholders who may well encourage moves to reduce selling costs but do not necessarily deliver value in the customer's eyes. It may also erode value or ROI (in the original systems investment) by slowing any migration from customers using paper-based communication to electronic channels. To build confidence and credibility (i.e. trust) in the online system, keeping it linked with paper and telephone billing operations is vital (for example customers may feel better if they receive paper bills even if they are paying electronically). This could enable information provided to customers to be consistent and ensure that companies log communications as easily with customers when they communicate via e-mail as when they write or call.

6   *Lack of real value for the customer* Many companies focus on solving internal hiccups but then do not feed that back to the customer. For example,

a company may well succeed in linking the data bases and applications that deal with customers over the phone, web and face-to-face, saving operating costs in the process, but does this produce benefits that customers appreciate and value? What this may mean in practice is that if customers call with a query, whoever deals with them will have details of all their previous correspondence to hand to ensure *the customer's* time is used effectively.

7 *Sloppy data handling* Quality data processing is crucial for CRM, for example in the area of customer segmentation which has grown in importance as personalization has grown. One solution may be to combine a reporting and analysis tool in use like business objects with a segmentation and sampling tool that accelerates query performance. The net result is more agile data handling, speedier complex customer modelling and a much more manageable timeframe for online marketing campaigns.

8 *Failure to see CRM as ongoing* Constant changes in technology (for example the take-up of broadband) and more sophisticated consumer demands require systems to adapt regularly or the service to the customer will fall below an acceptable level. New strategic relationships and changes in the competitive environment mean that CRM should not be seen as an isolated investment with limited review processes.

9 *Failure to educate your staff* To make a customer relationship management system work, the workforce need to be committed believers in the system. Training will reduce any board level view that CRM is a quick fix solution by pointing out that it is a mapped-out endeavour that is intended to last many years and needs to be implemented in stages. It can encourage and nurture the right skills for staff who may be experiencing changes to internal working practices. Showing staff how they fit into the bigger picture and how their actions can make a difference to the organization will help to get them on side.

10 *Long customer response times* One of the most effective ways of ensuring that systems work from the customer's perspective is by speeding up the response times to customer requests. Failure to do so can frustrate the customer and give them the impression that their business is not valued. When companies are overcome with customer responses which they had not anticipated, one approach may be to identify common queries and then – and this is often where many companies fall down – make it easier for customers to access the answers to them. This is more than just directing customers to a 'FAQ' list but perhaps letting the customer ask the question in their own language and style – and then using hidden but sophisticated and deep search processes to deliver the answer back in a way that is quick but relevant.

While the phrase 'customer focus' tends to involve two key activities – building a superior understanding of customer priorities and aligning the organization to deliver against them – companies vary in their goals for customer-focused initiatives:

■ *Building deeper customer relationships* Building on ongoing collaboration with customers to identify new opportunities for value creation, companies are trying to forge longer-term, more profitable relationships with their customers.

■ *Offering a more compelling customer experience* By embedding customer focus across the organization – particularly in staff and processes at key customer touchpoints – companies seek to provide a truly differentiated experience for the customer.

■ *Creating better or more innovative products or services* Companies hope that by consistently developing a complete understanding of customers' needs and preferences, they can help build a portfolio of products and services superior to those of their competitors.

However, the execution of a customer-focused strategy has proven very difficult for most companies. The path from implementing one-off customer initiatives to embedding customer focus in all organizational processes presents a number of potential pitfalls which have arisen because of mismatch of customer expectation and experience (*see* Figure 4.3).

HOW THE INTERNET OFTEN INCREASES REPUTATIONAL RISK

Building and maintaining trust is a fundamental part of any e-business strategy. Among e-business partners, trust is the product of each organization's history, reputation, track record and patterns of behaviour. Companies that fail to assure third parties of the integrity, security and reliability of their business processes run a very real risk of failure. This is a point worth emphasizing as companies interact with consumers at unprecedented levels and across channels, such as e-mail, text chat, Voice over Internet Protocol (VoIP), and multi-functional call centres, just to name a few.

Despite the popular depiction of the Internet as a channel for commerce, the public views it mostly as a source of information and these uses continue to explain its popularity much more than its utility as a way to shop, bank or invest. Moreover people who use the Internet are becoming more conservative, visiting a small number of websites to get their information.

Fig. 4.3 How reputational risk increases when customer focus is lost

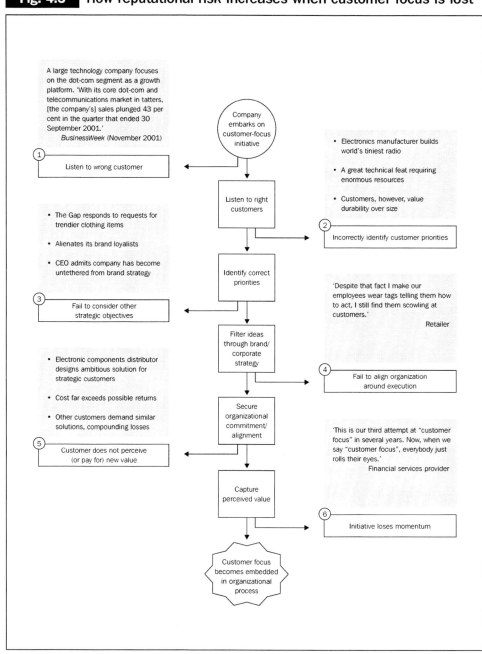

Source: Marketing Leadership Council, 2002.

What are the implications for companies?

Corporate websites need to be seen as a library, a place where information can be found. It means that almost eight out of ten visitors to your website are sceptical about the trustworthiness of the content they will find. You need to be extra vigilant to ensure that your content is accurate. In the eyes of the great majority of people who use the Internet, you are a publisher. However, a publisher whose information is not trusted does not have a long-term business model.

One study found that 75 per cent of respondents believe that content on the web is 'poor quality'. On English-language websites, content is between 75 per cent and 91 per cent accurate. Recent FBI operations in the US have alleged that more than 90 companies and individuals had illegally taken almost $120 million from over 55,000 consumers on the web. The American Federal Trade Commission receives more complaints about deceptive technology advertising than for any other industry. AltaVista estimate that as many as 20 per cent of web links that are more than a year old may be out of date.

We live in the digital age in which everything possible is being reduced to its most basic digital elements. In this environment, however, it has become increasingly clear that trust is not too easily digitized. With the heightened awareness over consumer data privacy issues, the issue of trust has emerged as a key concern. In B2B e-commerce, trust is often a core principle in the mission statement for market-places and exchanges. The challenge is that creating trust early on has little to do with being 'e' or electronic, and everything to do with 'p' for people, as significant human capital is required to stimulate and support online activity.

While much can be discussed regarding implications for the softer issues around trust in B2B e-commerce and electronic markets, the bottom line is that delivering on the promise of a clear value proposition is fundamental to generating trust. Consequently, to ensure that none of the critical early stage transactions escalate the reputational risks, companies should rely significantly on human touch to reduce the risk of poor fulfilment. Increased human involvement will be required early on to guarantee a satisfying customer experience.

Other key elements to establishing trust include preserving neutrality and respecting needs to data privacy. When trying to aggregate both sides of a transaction, neutrality is vital and this often requires strict rules for governance of a market's activities with clear implications for not following established rules. Without such neutral governance, transactions will be tough to come by because liquidity does not come without integrity.

Related is the notion of data privacy, which should be another obvious requirement, but given the experiences in B2C, and the far greater sensitivity in B2B, it warrants emphasizing that electronic markets must fully respect rights regarding the use of participant data.

While there will likely be numerous enabling technologies to help build trust in electronic markets, companies must simply deliver on promises, preserve neutrality, and respect customer data to maintain reputation and trust.

Table 4.2 Building blocks for trust in electronic relationships

What	Elements	How
Seals of approval	Symbols can reassure visitors that sites have established effective security measures.	Recognized seals of approval which enhance reputation by testifying to the safety of a vendor's site, its technology and the network behind it.
Brand	A company's implicit promise to deliver specific attributes, based on a company's reputation and visitors' previous experience with its products.	Includes online and offline brand recognition, portal or other marketing affiliations, community building and the sense of a site's breadth of product offerings.
Navigation	The ease of finding what a visitor is looking for.	Helped by understandable terms, the consistent placement of a navigational system, clear instructions to help customers find their way round seamlessly.
Fulfilment	How clearly a site indicates the way orders are to be processed, its return policy and how well it explains the way customers can seek recourse to problems.	The assurance that a customer's personal information will be kept secure and private is a key attribute of fulfilment.
Presentation	Ways in which the look of a site communicates meaningful information.	On the home page, a site's purpose is clear to the first-time visitor.
Technology	Visitors evaluate technology largely in terms of speed and function.	Reliability of site's operational performance and how quickly each page loads.

PRIVACY: THE KEY ISSUE

A fundamental cornerstone of trust in the virtual environment is the protection of Internet users' privacy. Failures in security are failures in meeting the implicit and explicit commitment in the customer relationship.

The Internet deconstructs existing value sets by focusing on:

- 'people and products' not 'place and production'
- arms length transactions
- implicit consent on transactions.

Key to privacy is an individual's right to:

■ control the information collected about them

■ control what that information is used for

■ control who has access to the information

■ access their personal information.

Although a significant number of individuals accessing the web are concerned that their personal information will be misused or abused, the actual level of concern differs in different parts of the world. As a result, consumers' online behaviour and the regulatory approaches to protecting their concerns diverge among jurisdictions. For example, the legal and regulatory approaches adopted by the various country-by-country implementations of the 1995 European Directive on Data Protection contrast sharply with the broadly self-regulatory approach adopted in the USA.

It would be wrong to see trust and privacy in purely defensive terms. Users will tend to migrate to providers that excel in protecting their personal privacy especially given consumers' readiness to provide personal information varied with the degree of trust they felt in the organization they were interacting with. There is growing evidence that consumers are increasingly attracted to do business through those companies they perceive to be strong, open and trustworthy on e-privacy.

FOCUSING ON THE USER EXPERIENCE

Interactivity on the Internet is often vastly over-hyped. Words like 'interactivity' and 'community' have been hugely abused and devalued as web usage has grown. A Jupiter Media Metrix survey of 250 retailer websites in 2002 found interactivity sorely lacking.

■ 30 per cent of websites surveyed responded within 6 hours

■ 18 per cent took 6 to 24 hours

■ 18 per cent took 1 to 3 days

■ 34 per cent took longer than 3 days or failed to respond at all.

Even if initial forecasts of e-commerce uptake at the height of the Internet bubble in 2000 were unrealistic, web use is growing. Moreover as more consumers make purchases over the Internet, online customer service has been a challenge for most companies. While people are embracing the Internet for customer service needs, many are dissatisfied with the customer service experience and are seeking online support that is better integrated with traditional forms of communication. One survey conducted by Modalis indicates that:

- people are demanding multiple forms of contact, such as e-mail, online chat and scheduling a callback on the web

- customers would rather use the Internet to receive information about a company or product. More than one-third of respondents who have used a shopping cart online have abandoned it because of a lack of information about the product online.

Companies can address their user experience issues at a low cost without necessarily having to invest in new technologies. The best website is the one that gets them the right content fastest. People want pages that download quickly. Jupiter has found that:

- 59 per cent of people want more product information

- 40 per cent will visit a site more often if its pages load faster

- 36 per cent want personalization features

- only 20 per cent are interested in multimedia or rich media features on a website

- only 12 per cent are interested in mobile commerce facilities.

Broken links are a serious problem on the web. There are a number of reasons for this:

- a large number of websites are being closed down

- websites are not being properly maintained

- website information architecture is constantly being changed.

Even so, links are an essential infrastructure that allow web content to be navigable. Link management is thus an important part of the activity of running a website. A broken link is a sign of an unprofessional website. Study after study shows that people are becoming more conservative in their use of the web. On a daily or weekly basis, they go to fewer and fewer websites. A broken link is a guaranteed way to feed that user scepticism of site value.

Case study 4.4

Staples.com

Staples.com has made a success of selling office supplies on the web. It has done this by finding out what its customers want and giving it to them. Its number one priority has always been to make its website usable.

Staples has five guiding principles – listen, watch, prioritize, execute and stay focused. The growth in use of Staples.com has come from focusing on what people want and providing it to them, i.e. much quality product information (that maintains trust for savvy e-shoppers) and that downloads quickly and can be read easily. This implies avoiding the need to pander to technologists (with a bias to push new technologies), marketers (with a bias to drive image-rich messages) or graphic designers (with a bias to showcase their art school training).

Understanding web users in various cultures is becoming a greater concern for web designers. Targeting the design of a website, as with any product or service, to the needs and wants of its market segment is a requisite for successful acceptance though not all big name sites do equally well in terms of adapting to local markets' perceptions of what is good usability.

Usability assessments of websites should consider user perceptions of site navigation and help documentation since these two factors are the main drivers of overall site appeal. Intuitive navigation is the primary component of overall site appeal. The combination of intuitive navigation and robust help/documentation account for 70 per cent of the variance in website appeal.

Addressing the experience of users is key to understanding online reputational risk. Warning signs that user experiences are failing need to be detected early with the establishment and development of a user experience team.

Reputational red flags that online user experiences are failing

- Customers are complaining about the experience – via all other possible channels.

- The site fails the 'First Use' case: log files indicate that users are arriving – and leaving – without doing anything.

- Log files indicate that users are entering search terms that should be readily apparent in the site navigation.

- The user activities and behaviours that drive the business case – performing certain tasks or transactions or customizing the experience – never get completed. Worse yet, they never get initiated.

- Log files indicate that customers are 'jumping channel' – such as picking up the phone to call customer service – before completing transactions.

- Your brand proposition statement does not hold for the online channel.

- The metrics that determine business success for the online channel – such as number of completed transactions or rate of adoption of features – are moving in the wrong direction as measured over time.

Action to take – things to know about building a user experience team

Make sure each team member clearly understands the underlying business case for the user experience and the measures of success.	For team members whose formal background does not include business or marketing, make sure the business goals and drivers are explained in a language they can understand. 'Maximize channel return'

	means nothing to team members who are not fluent in the concept of ROI.
Executives and managers should set the standard for 'customer-centric' behaviour.	Customer-centric means the customer comes first, all the time. Executives may even make fun of customers during usability testing, behind the one-way mirror but in front of marketing and development teams. Behaviours like this set a precedent for team members to believe the customer experience is a joke.
Hire only team members who are driven to develop the best customer experience – for the customer.	One best practice among firms that have developed successful online experiences: hire only people who are excited about developing the best user experience for the customer. Employees should not be taken on for the jazziest designs for their portfolios or because they have just shown off their technical prowess.
Make ongoing conversation about user experience a part of the company culture.	Hold a monthly lunchtime discussion about user experience, discussing the top usability issues that are challenging the development team or showing up in testing. In an inclusive – not accusatory – manner, discuss how to best deal with these issues effectively.
Be fluent in the analysis of customer experience data.	Understand how the blend of qualitative (observational) and quantitative (analytic) techniques now tie performance of the user experience to the satisfaction of business goals. Use the most appropriate and cost-effective tools – ranging from using off-the-shelf website log-file analysis tools, low-cost usability testing or hiring a specialist firm to perform the analysis and provide a report.
Understand the impact of integration – or lack thereof – on the user experience.	The best customer experiences fail if their value is hindered by a lack of integration. Know how the delivery platform(s) and the

	underlying pipes impact the user experience. For example, if dependencies on an underlying personalization engine constrains the layout of the front-end user interface, know how users will react and how these constraints will affect the business.
Encourage team members to continually learn about new techniques, practices and technologies to enhance their skills in developing better customer experiences.	While some techniques never change – like the time-honoured usability technique of observing users performing tasks – new practices, techniques and thinking are constantly adding to what we know about the discipline and practice of user experience. Encourage team members to be active learners to continually enhance their skills in developing, designing and measuring the success of user experiences.

Source: Adapted from Karen Donoghue, 2002.

EXECUTIVE SUMMARY

1   The customer is ultimately the most important stakeholder for every competitive business and commercial operation.

2   Service companies are not all the same. They differ widely, with varied organizational characteristics that create very different management problems. One of the keys to understanding customer expectations is recognizing the role that emotions play in customer relationships.

3   Decisions are often not based solely or even largely on economic or functional criteria of value. Products fill more than functional needs; they are also purchased to fill social needs.

4   Customer satisfaction alone does not safeguard reputation. If companies focus excessively on satisfaction, they run the risk of not understanding why customers feel drawn to return or the emotional meaning of the service experience to them.

5   The level of satisfaction or dissatisfaction that results from an encounter between a service user and provider depends both on the user's expectations of the service they will receive and their perceptions of the service they have received.

6   Different factors make different contributions in determining people's perceptions of the service they have received. The absence of some factors – for

example, reliability – can have a strong impact on dissatisfaction levels. However, the presence of reliability may sometimes be taken for granted and hence increased performance may not lead to higher satisfaction levels.

7 Customers do not evaluate a product or service on its own. They do so relative to their expectations. When customer expectations are too high and the delivered product does not meet those expectations the customer will not repeat purchase. Thus a critical factor in retention is the difference between the customer's expectations and the delivered quality of the product or service.

8 User experience is a key driver of brand equity. This implies a much stronger focus on employee motivation as, especially in a service industry, front-line customer service staff create the atmosphere and are the principal conduit for engaging the customer in the experience.

9 Brand values should connect with corporate values. Traditionally the focus of trust between buyers and sellers was on a promise or 'unique selling point' and whether it was delivered or not. However, the flows of information are no longer controlled by brand managers and are increasingly influenced by reputational agents and rising consumer sophistication. This matters in the following ways:

■ Consumers are also becoming more aware and active on a wide range of environmental, social and ethical issues. Concerns about the ethical working practices of businesses are having a significant effect on purchasing decisions around the world and the company's ethical approach must be in step with those of its valued customers.

■ Generation Y consumers have shown the most social activism since the baby boomers in the 1960s. They are likely to base much of their consumption on the values they associate with the companies providing goods and services. This means that companies will have to make a far greater effort to ensure that the values communicated to consumers are consistent with its internal values. If it is not, they will be exposed.

10 Channel conflict can sour corporate reputation. There are a number of conflict-management levers (variables under marketing's control) that can be used to increase or reduce the risk of conflict with incumbent channels. To reduce channel conflict, each of the levers can be employed in a variety of ways.

11 Customer relationship mismanagement can impact reputation by playing directly into what customers expected and what they experienced. In many cases these problems have stemmed from cultural and organizational issues or simply inadequate planning rather than fundamental problems with the technology.

12 The execution of a customer-focused strategy has proven very difficult for most companies. The path from implementing one-off customer initiatives to

embedding customer focus in all organizational processes presents a number of potential pitfalls which have arisen because of mismatch of customer expectation and experience.

13 Building and maintaining trust is a fundamental part of any e-business strategy. Among e-business partners, trust is the product of each organization's history, reputation, track record and patterns of behaviour. Companies that fail to assure third parties of the integrity, security and reliability of their business processes run a very real risk of failure.

14 To ensure that none of the critical early stage transactions escalate the reputational risks, companies should rely significantly on human touch to reduce the risk of poor fulfilment. Increased human involvement will be required early on to guarantee a satisfying customer experience.

15 Although a significant number of individuals accessing the web are concerned that their personal information will be misused or abused, the actual level of concern differs in different parts of the world.

16 Failures in security are failures in meeting the implicit and explicit commitment in the customer relationship. However, it would be wrong to see trust and privacy in purely defensive terms. Users will tend to migrate to providers that excel in protecting their personal privacy especially given consumers' readiness to provide personal information varies with the degree of trust they feel in the organization they interact with. There is growing evidence that consumers are increasingly attracted to do business through those companies they perceive to be strong, open and trustworthy on e-privacy.

17 Interactivity on the Internet is often vastly over-hyped. Good usability is a more important driver of a positive experience with a site than superior technical performance.

18 Companies can address their user experience issues at a low cost without necessarily having to invest in new technologies. Usability assessments of websites should consider user perceptions of site navigation and help documentation since these two factors are the main drivers of overall site appeal. Intuitive navigation is the primary component of overall site appeal.

Key message

The customer is the most important stakeholder and narrowing the gap between customer expectation and experience is key to mitigating reputational risk and creating value in customer relationships.

What you must ask of your team/staff/consultants

1 When we are just about to report our first ever quarterly loss or staff morale is at its lowest, who is the most important stakeholder?

2 Do we measure our understanding of what matters to the customer in terms of how satisfied they are – or the top three ways in which we build and maintain trust in their eyes?

3 Who are our most valuable customers – and what do they want from their relationship with us?

4 Is our website built around user experience – or ours?

5 How many people failed to transact through our website yesterday? Were the reasons fundamentally due to the technology or other (softer) factors?

What you must do today

1 At the end of the day, reflect on the most effective customer interaction you had and why.

2 Identify what your brand values are – and then your corporate values.

3 Try and transact (externally) through your own corporate website – and then through a competitor you fear most and a company from another sector you admire most for their customer service?

4 Ask a front-line service employee who your most valuable corporate customer is.

Related websites

Marketing Leadership Council
www.marketingleadershipcouncil.com

Built for use
www.builtforuse.com

British Airways
www.britishairways.com

Amazon.com
www.amazon.com

Sony
www.sony.com

References

Donoghue, Karen (2002) *http://www.humanlogic.com/builtforuse/index.html*.

Marketing Leadership Council (2000) *Managing Channel Conflict: Practices for Firms Launching Direct On-line Sales*. Washington: Corporate Executive Board.

Marketing Leadership Council (2002) *Driving Customer-Focused Decision-Making: the Theory/Practice Divide*. Washington: Corporate Executive Board.

Weber Shandwick Worldwide (2001) *Understanding the Consumer Mindset in Brand Selection: a Global Review*. *http://www.webershandwick.com/*.

5

Reputational risk
and employees

WHAT YOU MUST KNOW BEFORE YOU START

1   How employee expectations and commitment are changing.

2   Understanding employee communications and the relationships they support.

3   How commitment relates to performance and productivity.

4   What factors affect employees' perception of corporate image and reputation?

5   How internal and external reputation connects.

6   How to mange talent and develop leaders.

7   Employee branding – where it's worked, why it falls down.

HOW EMPLOYEE EXPECTATIONS AND COMMITMENT ARE CHANGING

There is a clear challenge for managers to grapple with understanding how employee expectations and commitment are changing:

- indifference of staff is the cause of 68 per cent of customer defections
- 80 per cent of employees lack commitment to their work
- only 5 per cent of organizations have the trust of their workers
- an undercurrent of tension is coming to the surface, made apparent by escalating workloads, increases in workplace conflict, bullying and job insecurity and the growing use of office politics
- managers considering a move to a different organization want an opportunity to broaden their skills (53 per cent), more challenging work (44 per cent), greater appreciation (43 per cent), more money (41 per cent) and a better match between their own values and those of their organization (37 per cent)
- 88 per cent of managers want their organizations to act socially and environmentally responsibly, for example, through respecting diversity.

Internal rivalry, hidden agendas, lack of trust and strained working relationships were rife in the workplace in 2002. Specifically:

- lack of trust in organizations is acting as a barrier to high performance, resulting in inappropriate management styles, harassment, conflict, espoused but not practised values and resistance to change
- 9/11 appears to have triggered among managers a growing awareness of their own mortality, with many looking for 'meaning' in their lives and the chance to do something worthwhile, at home and in the workplace

- the majority of employees feel less loyal to their employer than in the past and they are no longer prepared to put work ahead of everything else

- work–life balance is becoming such an important issue for managers that many are prepared to downshift in order to gain more time for their out-of-work interests

- of respondents, 67 per cent claim their organization embraces diversity, though this often means they merely have an equal opportunities policy.

What people expect from their employers is changing. Even before the bursting of the Internet bubble, job security was increasingly becoming an oxymoron. 9/11 and the combination of terrorism and war risk with economic weakness has put employment prospects beyond what both employers and employees can plan for. In this context perhaps the greatest responsibility that companies have to their employees is not to keep them employed but to make them employable. This also connects with the trend for length of service to reduce at a time when people see their career as less being in a fixed role but more as a set of experiences, perhaps simultaneously, through 'portfolio working'.

Most employers enter into written contracts with their employees. However, employers and employees also have a psychological contract with each other. This is based on the expectation that both employer and employee have of the other in terms of their working relationship. The psychological contract is the mutual expectation which both parties have of each other. It is not the formal contract of employment, enforceable in law. It is more about the implicit and informal set of expectations and understandings which the two sides have of the employment relationship, the 'deal' which employees believe they are entitled to expect from their employer. It underpins the way each of us relate and work with colleagues, customers and suppliers. Moreover it is central to understanding the employment relationship and employee attitudes and behaviour.

Reputational risk in relation to employees is the gap between the promises and commitments made and delivered by the organization

When the psychological contract is violated, unmet expectations create a sense of inequality which stifles morale, erodes customer satisfaction and, ultimately, destroys shareholder value. Key to managing reputational risk is understanding how the psychological contract is established and subsequently renegotiated in a changing business climate.

Key components of the psychological contract are:

- it is concerned with expectations and obligations
- it is implied and unwritten

- it is mutual and two way
- we have strong feelings about the way our psychological contracts are fulfilled which determine our behaviour and actions.

How it works:

Fig. 5.1 How the psychological contract works

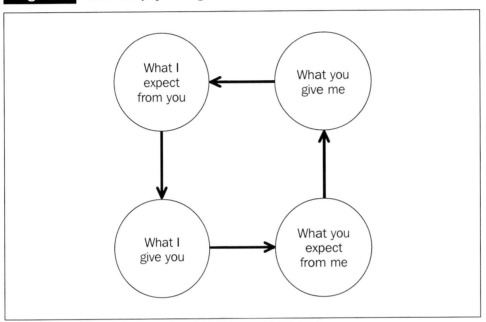

How this translates in practice can be seen in the context of talent management.

What I want from the company.	<ul><li>Know what is expected.</li><li>Have equipment I need.</li><li>Able to use talents.</li><li>Having a supervisor who cares.</li><li>Encouragement to develop.</li><li>My opinions listened to.</li></ul>
What the company gives.	<ul><li>Current employment.</li><li>Job content rewards.</li><li>Leadership and trusting culture.</li><li>Pay and benefits.</li><li>Consistent and fair human resource management practices.</li></ul>
What I decide to give the company.	<ul><li>Fully engage with the organization.</li><li>Apply talents to work.</li><li>Develop colleague relationships.</li></ul>

What the company wants.	■ High performance to meet corporate goals. ■ Commitment to deliver stakeholder value. ■ Talent retention.

What drives psychological contracts are pre-employment experiences, recruiting practices and early on-the-job social contact. Prior to employment, workers can possess beliefs regarding work, their occupations, and organizations generally, that set in motion certain responses to joining with an employer. Recruitment experiences create understandings regarding the promises workers and employers make to each other, and social contacts, once recruits join, then continue the processing of new information regarding the employment relationship and promises related to it.

Shared information is critical to what people perceive as what has been agreed to or not – and it is this which determines mutual understanding regarding promises and obligations. Moreover as the psychological contract works as a process, not a one-time event, the quality of the relationship over time is crucial. A common frame of reference between two parties promotes perceived and actual agreement.

There are two components of the psychological contract – transactional and relational as seen in Figure 5.2. These emphasize different types of relationships between the employee and employer.

Until the 1990s there was a relatively stable alignment between business goals and employee expectations as expressed in the psychological contract. This was built on a deep acceptance of paternalism: that decisions would be made by the employer and accepted by the employee and that the employer would look after the employee. Now there are few companies which display this stable alignment.

Contemporary business realities of economic uncertainty impact psychological contracts in the following employer positions being taken:

■ We will employ you as long as you create business value – when you do not, you will be fired.

■ We will provide opportunities to learn and take on more challenging work – but make no promises.

■ You are expected to update your skills and mindset so you can continue to add value.

■ You need to adapt and do different things to maximize your contribution and value.

■ To maximize your value you are expected to come up with ideas on how to maximize performance.

Organizations are struggling to fulfil components of the psychological contract that their employees value most (e.g. open and honest communication). These discrepancies (between perceived importance and perceived fulfilment) significantly impact employee satisfaction and intention to leave the organization. These discrepancies also affect employee performance.

The psychological contract is broken – and reputational risk increased – once either the employer or employee fails to live up to the expectations of the other. Employers should therefore ensure that they do not promise what they cannot deliver in terms of creating realistic expectations in the minds of employees. Growing evidence suggests that, properly managed, the psychological contract delivers hard, bottom-line results. Effective people management practices are the basis for a positive psychological contract, which leads in turn to improved business performance. The communications process is at the heart of the psychological contract. This is because it is directly responsible for influencing employees' perceptions of the content of the deal: both what they are required to do and what they are entitled to expect. Implicit in this is understanding the transaction and relational elements of the relationship between employees and employers (*see* Figure 5.2).

Fig. 5.2 The employee–employer relationship

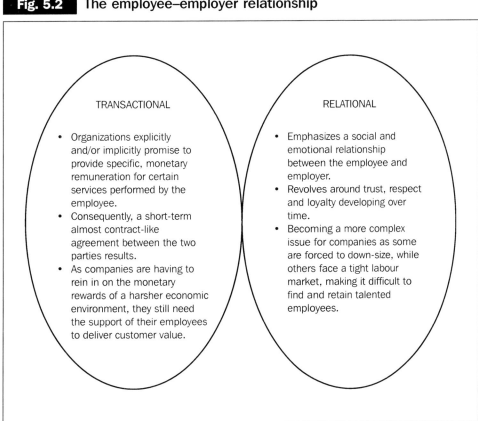

TRANSACTIONAL

- Organizations explicitly and/or implicitly promise to provide specific, monetary remuneration for certain services performed by the employee.
- Consequently, a short-term almost contract-like agreement between the two parties results.
- As companies are having to rein in on the monetary rewards of a harsher economic environment, they still need the support of their employees to deliver customer value.

RELATIONAL

- Emphasizes a social and emotional relationship between the employee and employer.
- Revolves around trust, respect and loyalty developing over time.
- Becoming a more complex issue for companies as some are forced to down-size, while others face a tight labour market, making it difficult to find and retain talented employees.

There is a central role that line managers have to play in delivering business performance. The personnel function has to design and monitor implementation of a range of people management practices. Senior management has to be clear about the job to be done and the messages they want to convey. However, the way that line management communicates with frontline employees is fundamental to how those messages are understood and to what kind of service is delivered to the customer.

The psychological contract is linked to the concept of social intelligence or emotional intelligence. Traditional measures of intelligence are based on rational thinking. However, throughout the business world, those that are most successful are not necessarily the most intelligent in terms of IQ. Successful people often have highly sophisticated social and emotional skills, which mean that they are not only aware of other people's emotional needs, but are able to manage their own emotions very effectively.

Employees place a high level of importance on all areas of the psychological contract and are increasingly aware of the non-monetary rewards that companies are willing to provide. This is not to say that employees do not pay attention to money; however, it does imply that employees take other aspects of the psychological contract very seriously. This implies that recruiters need to go beyond a discussion of compensation and benefits and highlight aspects of their organization that job candidates will find intrinsically satisfying. Employers could also seek alternative and creative ways to understand and communicate not only an employee's role with the organization but also the culture and expectations of the firm.

Case study 5.1

Connecting with employee expectations

Cisco Systems has been successful at recruiting individuals whom the organization calls 'passive' job seekers (i.e. individuals who may not be actively looking for new employment). On the company's web page, a potential new hire can be connected with a current Cisco employee who works in a similar position/role in the organization. The current employee, not the trained recruiter, gives an inside view regarding the cultural expectations and work life at Cisco. Allowing current employees to discuss and convey Cisco's expectations is not only a valuable selling tool to attract competent and talented employees, it also gives current employees a voice in the continued growth and development of the organization. As a result of many of these recruiting innovations, turnover is low (at 6.7 per cent p.a. against an industry standard of 18 per cent p.a.).

Organizations do not work like machines. Solitary references to 'drivers' and 'delivery' suggest that senior management can deliver results simply by issuing appropriate instructions. However, this model of management is increasingly seen to be moribund, if not actually dead. Employees who increasingly have discretion about how to deliver services effectively are more likely to need help and support than a repeat of instructions already given. Line managers can contribute to managing the psychological contract by:

- interpreting instructions from above in the light of local circumstances and refining or explaining the message, where necessary; to accommodate local realities

- actively managing employee expectations, recognizing that these are influenced by many sources, and not just by the proclamations of senior managers

- not disappointing employees' expectations, or if this is unavoidable, explaining why

- when recruiting and appraising staff, being honest about what they can expect

- seeing that rhetoric and reality are in line, and that, so far as possible, the organization is effectively implementing the policies it has endorsed

- supporting the use of attitude surveys to monitor employee responses, and being prepared to act on the findings.

EMPLOYEE COMMUNICATIONS AND THE RELATIONSHIPS THEY SUPPORT

How business leaders communicate to their employees significantly affects the bottom line. Not only is this common sense, it is increasingly supported by research evidence. Organizational culture and climate is largely influenced by the CEO and is strongly linked to increased profits, reduced employee turnover and the increased self-esteem of employees.

Employee communications and the relationships they support are increasingly being asked to deliver demonstrable business benefit. A pleasant glow in the boardroom is no longer enough as organizations grapple with economic slowdown, pressure on margins, and the failure of the new economy to deliver shareholder value. Communicating organizational climate and culture to employees is, therefore, crucial. A performance culture stresses goal-attainment and the value of effort and quality while a people culture emphasizes employee involvement, trust and commitment. Both are important and they largely emanate from the top – from the CEO and the top management team. Key findings from recent research (Henley Management College, 2003):

- While CEOs appear to be more involved, methods used are not always the most effective.

- The negative impact of IT on the quality of communications does not seem to have diminished its attraction as one of the main platforms for communication.

- Although most organizations survey employee opinion, the majority may not be asking the right questions.
- Face-to-face communication is the most effective, but instead, extra effort is going into the use of IT.
- Investment in employee communications is not being maintained.
- CEO commitment to employee communications is patchy.
- The emphasis remains on providing information, rather than on employee involvement.
- IT alone will not solve the communications conundrum; e-communications should be used to support other more two-way methods of communicating and not replace them.
- Organizations seem to be missing the point in their employee surveys by asking the wrong questions.

Such evidence should stimulate organizations to put new impetus into evaluating and improving their relationships with employees. The aim should be to measure the extent to which their staff trust, and are committed to, the organization and what they intend to do about this. These consequent actions can either help or hinder the attainment of company objectives. It should be possible to track back to find what the firm has done to make them feel this way, so that the company can take decisive action to strengthen its relationship with employees. This, in turn, will improve the organizational climate and culture and will then enhance company performance.

Communications has the biggest causal impact on staff trust in the organization. This must be two-way communication, however, with a greater emphasis on listening and involving, rather than informing. But which kinds of communication are most effective? There are three broad kinds of communication between management and workforce.

1 Downward communication, for example, through company meetings or mission statements: this is generally seen as least effective of all.

2 Communication occurring mainly around the recruitment process and including job descriptions, staff handbooks and initial training: although widely used, these forms of communication are not necessarily particularly effective.

3 Job-related and personal communication: these methods are very effective. They include setting individual objectives and targets, performance appraisal, informal day-to-day interaction, training and development and briefings by line management. They are much more clearly linked to behaviour and therefore reputation, both individual and corporate.

Communications needs to be seen as a two-way process.

Fig. 5.3 How we assess our colleagues

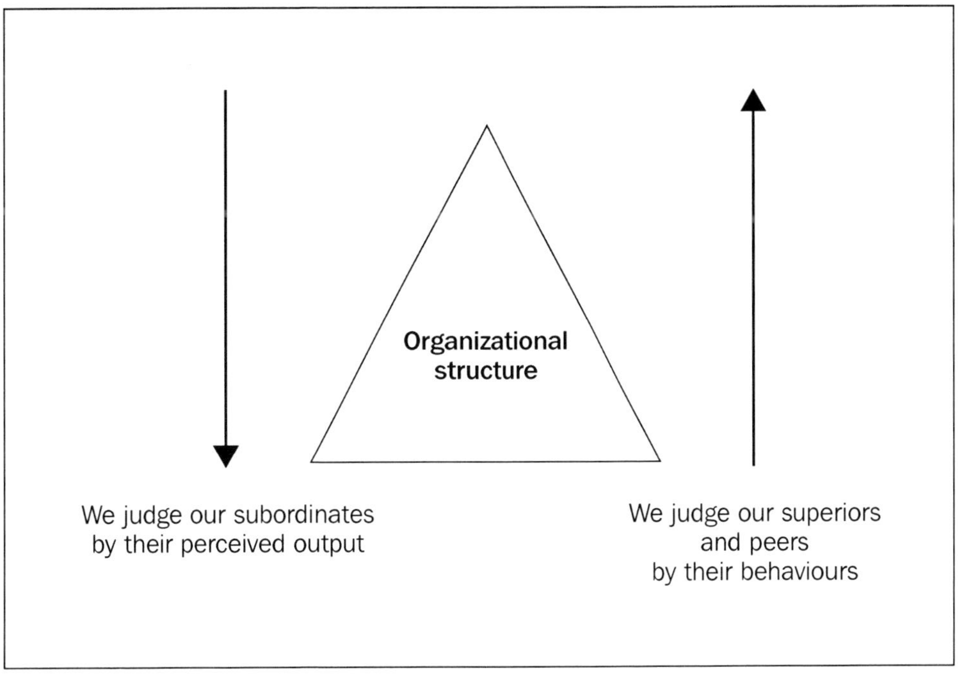

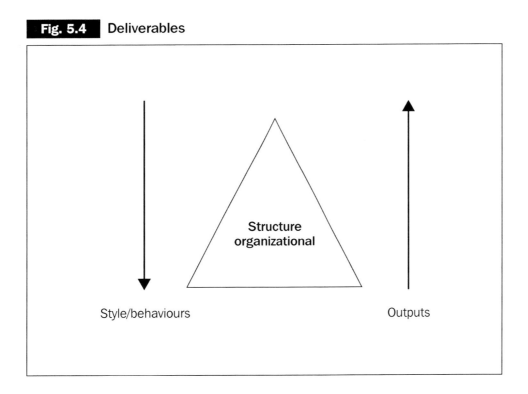

Organizational
structure

We judge our subordinates
by their perceived output

We judge our superiors
and peers
by their behaviours

In this process, there is direct correlation between how managers behave and how effective the required outputs are.

Fig. 5.4 Deliverables

Structure
organizational

Style/behaviours

Outputs

Companies need to be aware of the messages they are giving at different stages in the management process and think about how far they are consistent with one another, and how they will be understood by employees. Managers at all levels can have an influence on employees' perceptions of the psychological contract. It is, however, the relationship between individual employees and their line manager that is likely to have most influence in framing and managing employees' expectations.

If cues and messages to employees – via people policies and processes, communication and management behaviour – lack integration and cohesion, people will create a sense of meaning which is far removed from the aspirations of the organization. If these frames and meanings are removed from the business goals, the performance of the business will suffer.

Why do mixed messages to employees occur?

- Organizations create multiple or conflicting business goals which may not be coherent.
    - there are messages around the importance of delivering long-term customer service, yet the predominant goal is to maximize short-term profits at the expense of what is best for the (valued) customer and the longer-term relationship with that customer
    - the need to innovate and be creative is a key business goal while at the same time people are punished for taking risks and encouraged to be 'right first time'

    Key point: multiple strategies need not be in conflict but if they are not resolved at a corporate level the dilemmas they create are played out at an individual level.

- Outdated processes and systems – these need to be updated over time and seen to be so.
    - the reward system may still reflect a time when hierarchical power structures dominated, when managing your boss was more important than working collectively as a team, for instance in a nationalized utility company now in the private sector
    - the promotion system may still reinforce and reward individual excellence and accomplishment even as the current goals are for excellent team performance and collegiality.

- Not being consistent in what is meant. Meaning is created in organizations from many sources – what senior managers say, how colleagues and peers behave, their values and norms of behaviour; the expressions of the company policy on reward and appraisal and how these work in reality (e.g. in the proportion of ethnic minority managers at senior levels across the organization); and the understanding of the history, heritage and reputation of the organization and how this is represented to customers. As business goals change, so the meaning of the organization changes.

COMMITMENT, PERFORMANCE AND VALUE

Individuals' identification with work is complex. Why people work and what they expect from work varies from person to person. However, there is evidence that there is a growing divide between those who identify with their work and those who do not.

Some people love work and identify strongly with it – so much so that there is no boundary between work and home. With an increased perception that the world is riskier and more uncertain than ever, some individuals are searching for a place of belonging. Some have located that place in work. Work for them provides appreciation, recognition, some control, some self-expression and often a real sense of community. For these 'willing workers' work is good. For 'wage slaves', work holds no appeal. They work because they have to and often their jobs lack some or all the criteria of a 'good' job. They derive little of their identity from work and even less satisfaction from their jobs, which lack appreciation, recognition, control and self-expression.

In fact some factors are important for instilling commitment and retention in all age groups (e.g. career advancement, development opportunities, and pay for organizational performance), others matter more to specific ages. Pay for individual performance and work–life balance are more salient to Generation X, while the most senior workers attach more importance to job security.

Personal development opportunities may be more important in the creation of trust and commitment for younger employees. Perception of unfairness in career opportunities can be more important for commitment and trust in groups of older employees. The implication is that, among older employees, it pays to use fair career management procedures since their commitment towards organizations can be increased by careful attachment to procedural concerns and enforcing non-discriminatory policies.

People's expectations of work are changing, particularly in countries with close to full employment. Increasingly, people are turning towards their jobs as a means of achieving personal validation, rather than the traditional institutions of family or faith. Accordingly, more people are looking to their places of work as a means of providing the social support, networks and values that were previously maintained by other institutions. In terms of selecting a prospective employer, the ultimate deciding factor for most people is still financial remuneration. However, other factors are becoming more important. A recent survey of UK professionals by the Industrial Society,[1] for example, found that a high proportion of respondents actively seek jobs in companies that reflect their own personal values (*see* Figure 5.5).

Commitment relates directly to value. This is seen in the action-profit linkage (APL) model. Unlike the service-profit model, this encourages companies to eliminate some of the uncertainty in defining linkages between company actions and profits. It allows managers to see how any action within any corporate function affects overall profitability. Managers can identify and measure key drivers of business success and profit, develop causal links among them and stimulate the impact of actions to bring them about. The attention shifts from individual performance metrics to an awareness of how those metrics function as a system and how they can increase profit and shareholder value. Central to this is commitment and behaviour.

Fig. 5.5   Role of company values when choosing a job

	% agree	% neutral	% disagree
I would not work for an organization whose values I did not believe in.	82	12	6
I chose my current organization because I believe in what it does and what it stands for.	59	28	11
I do not care if the company I work for behaves responsibly or not.	0	1	99
What I do, and the organization I work for, gives people an idea of what I am like.	66	20	14

Case study 5.2

How Canadian Imperial Bank of Commerce (CIBC) used an APL model to understand how actions affect customer loyalty and profits

Situation

In 1996, CIBC faced increased competition and deregulation, resulting in a customer defection rate at 10 per cent and an additional 15 per cent of its customers estimated close to defection. Seeking to re-establish the bank's market position and learn how management's own behaviour affects customer retention, executives developed a model that links management behaviour to employee commitment, customer loyalty and profits.

Action

Working backward, CIBC linked shareholder value (profit) to customer actions (customer-loyalty behaviour) and employee commitment.

Establishing the links Recognizing the bank's precarious situation, CIBC senior managers relied on intuition and business experience to hypothesize and define the links driving the company's current performance. The bank used surveys to gather considerable information required for analysing the established links. CIBC also invested in a customer-information warehouse, collecting more than 1,000 data attributes per customer and 25 months of rolling data. CIBC's model asserts that employee commitment affects customer behaviour, which directly impacts profits. In addition, executives concluded that leadership from management influenced employee commitment.

Defining metrics and collecting data CIBC analysed the data and defined customer loyalty variables. Variables included the intentions of customers to continue to use purchased banking services, to recommend the bank to other customers, to purchase more of the bank's services and to use the bank's services exclusively. CIBC then linked those loyalty variables to their individual drivers: customers' attitudes toward the bank's core services, non-core services, banking fees, image and barriers to switching to other banks. The company found that factors such as customers' evaluation of the local brand and the bank's problem-solving efficiency impacted customer's core-services loyalty.

CIBC then linked customer-loyalty behaviour with employee commitment by polling its workers. Variables of employee commitment behaviour, which demonstrates employees' satisfaction with and loyalty to the company, included responding efficiently to requests, meeting commitments, recommending the company as a place to work and establishing employee tenure. CIBC then identified employee commitment drivers such as company culture, degree of customer orientation, reward and recognition, workload, learning and development and leadership.

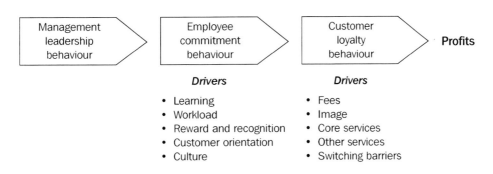

Result

By analysing the links in the model, CIBC management learned that a 5 per cent increase in employee commitment yielded a 2 per cent increase in customer loyalty, which increases profitability by $72 million. Managers at CIBC achieved this payoff by carefully identifying, articulating and measuring the causal relationships between actions and profit.

Source: Marketing Leadership Council, 2002.

Employee commitment is increasingly needed in the security-conscious environment that confronts business after 9/11. In the past, organizations focused on specific risks like loss-prevention, but now the risk is much more general. To counter these general risks, many organizations are moving away from a security model based on compliance, towards a commitment-based approach that involves all employees within an organization. Traditional security programmes focus on loss-prevention and personal safety. Most programmes are not designed to face the new reality of thwarting an attack. Protecting inventory from shrinkage is not the same problem as maintaining product integrity or enhancing social responsibility. Most security solutions are biased toward the use of technology. They rely on cameras, locks, alarms, fences, badges and sensors. In an environment where the risk is non-specific and can come from anywhere, technological solutions should not be the only answer.

Commitment-based security is where all employees view security as an integral part of their job. Not only are the employees ever-vigilant, but their ideas are eagerly solicited and acted upon by leadership. With all employees involved in security and actively aware of the risks facing their organization, the chances of catastrophic losses are reduced. Creating a safe and secure workplace requires a shift away from seeing technology, surveillance and employee compliance as the sole answer to security problems.

The best security programmes focus on three critical elements: initial detection, delay of the risk and a response capability. Physical security measures obviously play a major role in all three of these elements. These measures have their limitations and the most glaring of these is expense. However, the greatest asset to any organization's security programme – and the one most often ignored – is the one that cannot be bought or sold: the commitment of the employees who work there. Employee commitment can be the single biggest factor in detecting, delaying and responding to a security breach.

INTERNAL AND EXTERNAL REPUTATION AND THE RISK OF CORPORATE AMNESIA

There is a close reputation between internal and external reputation. This reflects the relationship between organizational and corporate identity that has been referred to earlier. In Figure 5.6 the central box labelled 'employees' images and reputation of the company' represents an intangible asset for the company which needs to be nurtured if performance is to be maximized. This is the 'employer brand' equity in the minds of its employees.

Employees' perceptions of the organization builds up over a sustained period. Even so, business history's value as business as a tool for management development is often overlooked. It can be an extremely useful resource in a world where the labour market is becoming more flexible and many companies are turning over their entire workforce in a regular cycle. Moreover corporate history can help us to learn from past successes and failures and avoid re-inventing the wheel.

Fig. 5.6 Factors affecting employees' perception of corporate image and reputation

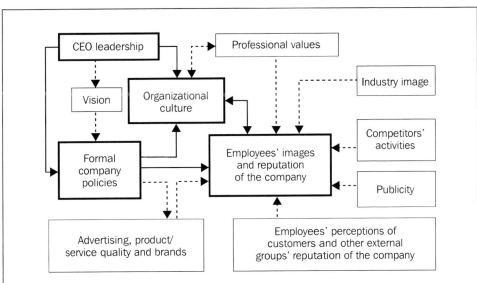

Source: Dowling, 1996.

Organizational memory

- Perhaps the most important constituent of any institution's durability.
- For the individual company, whose staff can today be displaced every five years, corporate 'memory' is increasingly other employers' experiences, which is not necessarily always relevant.
- Organizations have already paid for their memory at least once. If it is not to pass beyond reach, it needs to be managed professionally – just like any other corporate asset.
- It disappears through inherent short and selective memory recall, natural wastage when employees leave to join other organizations, the retirement of key individuals and/or redundancy, even through job rotation.

Corporate amnesia

- When organizational memory disappears, the organization's ability to learn and develop naturally is interrupted, often with expensive consequences.
- Is it greater in larger organizations?

As companies restructure and shed employees in a depressed economic climate, they need to recognize the organic – and evolutionary nature – of corporate knowledge. Above all this is inherited and represents a set of cumulative experiences. However they are filtered, all management decisions are made through a set of cultural constructs. To fully understand it – and work within it – an organization needs to be aware of the contributory experiences that shaped its development – and these may go back many, many years. In the case of a Reuters, Marks & Spencer, Barclays Bank or British Airways this may be several generations – testified by how these companies safeguard and celebrate air crew uniforms or old bank symbols in their corporate archives.

All boards of directors and senior executives have a key role in protecting and developing their 'corporate memory' on both the hard intellectual property generation side and the soft vision, culture and values and behaviours side. If they neglect this, then often they risk 'corporate amnesia'. Organizations need to codify and diffuse their learning so that they are forced to use, or abuse, their scarce resources to keep re-learning that in which they have already invested.

TALENT MANAGEMENT AND LEADERSHIP DEVELOPMENT

It is important for companies to have a nuanced understanding of the job offer and development preferences of high-value and high-potential employees amidst the insecurities of the current economic climate and given the predicted leadership shortfalls ahead. Surveys continue to indicate that companies are failing at the talent management practices most valued by their employees, including providing development opportunities such as on-the-job training, mentoring and feedback. This is against growing evidence that effective talent management practices – in particular, better alignment of leadership development strategies with leader preferences – may have a direct impact on financial performance.

Internal reputational risks increase when a focus on talent leads to a mindset which devises policies on individuals at the expense of teams and organizational systems. The 'war for talent' is to some extent a distraction from companies' real task of devising cultures and management styles that fully maximize human and intellectual capital, not just the skills and knowledge of an elite cadre.

Moreover 'war for talent' imagery overlooks the fact that often the case-effective teams outperform even more talented collections of individuals, that individual talent and motivation is partly under the control of what companies do and that what matters to organizational success is the set of management practices that create a trusting culture. However, it is not just that the war for talent is the wrong lens through which to see organizational success. Fighting the war for talent itself can cause problems. Companies that adopt a talent war mindset often end up venerating outsiders and downplaying the talent already inside the company, set up competitive, zero sum dynamics that makes internal learning and knowledge transfer difficult, activate the self-fulfilling prophecy in the wrong direction and create an attitude of arrogance instead of an attitude of wisdom. For all of these reasons, even fighting the war for talent may be hazardous to an organization's health and detrimental to doing the things that will make – and keep – it successful.

Organizations significantly mis-allocate precious leadership development resources – and it is leaders who perceive their organizations to be least effective in delivering the programmes they view as most valuable to their continued growth. The context for leadership development is changing and a failure to recognize and respond to this increases internal reputational risks. Leadership development – demanding practical experience – will be increasingly tailored to the individual. It may evolve into coaching relationships with a number of advisers skilled in different areas – business, emotional, intellectual, spiritual and physical. New ways of accelerating leadership development are required. They will probably include challenging assignments, formal development plans at all levels, participation on senior executive teams and in shared leadership teams and coaching and mentoring relationships.

Too many current and future leaders are poorly prepared for their roles. Some common failings include:

- To grow emotionally: the leaders who have high intelligence quotients (IQs) and low emotional quotients (EQs) are often clever and charismatic but destructive.

- To make creative connections: leaders who see the connections between A and B and B and C rarely see how A and C connect. They miss the more subtle patterns and ones that extend beyond the quarterly reporting period.

- To empathize: they often look at numbers or surface behaviour and lack an understanding of others' true needs and aspirations.

- To manage ego: deadly self-inflation, or hubris, frequently leads to derailment or nemesis.

- To overcome personal alienation and boredom: these leaders simply stop feeling the exhilaration of learning.

How can companies respond in ways that strengthen not weaken reputation and trust? They need to move beyond a product, service and distribution focus and elevate relationship building by:

- developing skills and values that lead to increased empathy and knowledge among all who would be part of relationship building

- measuring and rewarding appropriate relationship-building activities.

They also need to acknowledge that feedback and relationship programmes are the most effective leadership development strategy.

Fig. 5.7 Distribution of importance scores for development programmes

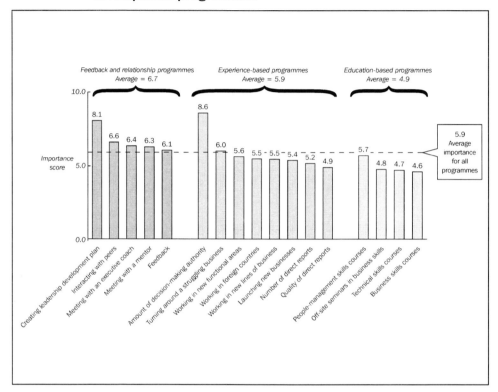

NB: Measures relate to the relative importance leaders place on each programme for the development of their leadership skills

Source: Corporate Leadership Council, 2001.

Feedback and relationship programmes operate on several levels which relate to how effective they are.

The key point is to think out of the box in seeing how these may operate in practice. Costs constraints may not permit 'many sessions with a mentor assigned to you by your company through a formal mentoring programme' but developing mentoring programmes with key customers, suppliers, government departments and community groups may meet organizational objectives and build corporate reputation.

This does mean there is no place for experiential learning in minimizing reputational risk. Many challenges to corporate orthodoxy and groupthink and barriers to innovative thinking can come from unexpected quarters – and links between how perspectives are developed at home and in the workplace may be blurring.

Table 5.1 Employee development programmes: from laggard to leader

Development programme	Level 1: laggard	Level 2: below par	Level 3: above par	Level 4: leader
Creating a leadership development plan	No leadership development plan.	A leadership development plan that is appropriate for your position but not customized to you.	A leadership development plan that is somewhat customized to you.	Many sessions with an executive coach from outside your company.
Feedback	Feedback on your skills as a leader from case-based interviews on hypothetical business problems.	Feedback on your skills as a leader from written tests that assess personality characteristics.	Feedback on your skills as a leader from performance reviews (e.g. 360-degree reviews).	Many sessions with a mentor assigned to you by your company through a formal mentoring programme.
Meeting with an executive coach	No sessions with an executive coach (from outside your company) to talk about leadership issues.	One or two sessions with an executive coach from outside your company.	Several sessions with an executive coach from outside your company.	
Meeting with a mentor in a mentoring programme	No sessions with a mentor assigned to you by your company through a formal mentoring programme.	One or two sessions with a mentor assigned to you by your company through a formal mentoring programme.	Several sessions with a mentor assigned to you by your company through a formal mentoring programme.	A great deal of interaction with peers to discuss leadership issues.
Interacting with peers to discuss leadership issues	No interaction with peers to discuss leadership issues.	Little interaction with peers to discuss leadership issues.	Some interaction with peers to discuss leadership issues.	A leadership development plan that is extensively customized to (by?) you.

Source: Adapted from Corporate Leadership Council, 2001.

Table 5.2 Leisure and business

Leisure pursuits which have shaped business thinking	% of participants responding	Comment
A social conversation on holiday.	72	The growth of independent holidays to emerging market destinations by a younger generation of business executives (e.g. Vietnam, Cuba and China) may increasingly provide perspectives that play directly into an appreciation of business risk, not typically provided by economic reports or security consultants.

Leisure pursuits which have shaped business thinking	% of participants responding	Comment
Personal insight from participating in a sport or outdoor activity.	39	Some corporate cultures, e.g. high-performance may be linked to an active sports club programme where office politics may be transferred to the soccer field.
Insight from professional activity outside work (school governor, charitable trustee, local councillor, etc.)	35	This now links directly to corporate governance with the Higgs Review (2003) suggesting that one way to increase diversity among non-executive directors is to tap talent in the non-profits sector.
The perspective of a historical figure in a non-fiction book.	15	The autobiography of the cult CEO (e.g. Jack Welch) may make for richer reading in the wake of their association with corporate excess and subsequent reputational fallout post-Enron.
The perspective of a fictional character in a novel.	12	Novels and films may increasingly come to reflect real-world context in a post 9/11 world.

Source: Syrett, Michael and Lammiman, Jean (2002). Survey from Roffey Park Management Institute (1998) with comments added by author.

EMPLOYEE BRANDING

The employer brand establishes the identity of the firm as an employer. It encompasses the firm's values, systems, policies and *behaviours* toward the objectives of attracting, motivating and retaining the firm's current and potential employees.

These are the key trends:

Employer branding is still going through a growth spurt.	Corporate brands are still much more common, but companies are focusing branding efforts more and more on employees.
Funding for employer branding efforts has increased.	Further growth is expected especially as employee commitment cannot be taken for granted at a time of economic and geopolitical uncertainty.

Corporate and employer brands are closely related.	Companies treat the relationship between corporate and employer brands in different ways. Some have built employer brands on established corporate brands, while others claim a strong employer brand without a corporate brand. In some cases, development of an employer brand provide the impetus for corporate branding.
Employer branding may be especially important for companies that face difficulties in establishing strong brand images.	This is because their products or services are sold to other companies and lose much of their product brand identity before reaching end users.

There is a need – especially in big, diversified companies – to convey unified, coherent brand messages in ways that are appropriate to different sites and cultures. Common risks are not starting branding efforts early enough, not making it intensive enough or senior management failing to give employee branding a high enough priority, in actions as well as words.

Table 5.3 Reputational risk and employee branding

Employee branding initiative	Risk
The brand the company creates says, 'this is a great place to work'.	But how does this broad claim differentiate the company not only from its competitors but from any other company offering the same brand message?
The brand is just the company's mission statement rehashed.	But how many mission statements really differentiate companies and how many express what is at the company's core? How many employees actually believe mission statements – and how many become empty statements, subject to employee derision?
Management (or consultants) create a brand for the company and 'parachute' it to the employees.	In such a situation it is questionable if employees buy into the brand – or even if they understand it.
The company creates a brand because the competition has created a brand.	The result is unlikely to capture the true essence of the firm. The brand will not be true or complete if it is drafted out of fear or only as a reaction or response.

Employee branding initiative	Risk
The company creates its employer brand but it remains a separate effort – with a different message – from the marketing brand.	Effective brand efforts need to be unified and mutually reinforcing.
The company creates marketing and employer brands with the same message.	… but the connections between the two are shady at best and inexplicable to the employees.

Employee branding can build reputation and create value if it is …

Employee branding initiative	Opportunity
… Holistic.	It applies throughout the company and throughout the internal and external markets.
… Known and understood throughout the company.	All employees know the brand's message and (more importantly) how it applies to them.
… Known and respected in the employment market-place.	Candidates will be familiar with the brand and will be applying to the company on the strength of the brand.

In the face of unexpected declines in hiring needs for entry-level talent, a number of US employers have recently been forced to rescind or defer a significant volume of campus job offers. Some of these companies have employed a variety of creative strategies (e.g. pre-employment severance packages, long-term start date deferrals) aimed at quelling the pain associated with such actions. From a strategic perspective, these tactics (and their accompanying publicity) represent an investment in employment brand – across the long term, such investments might mitigate potentially devastating levels of employment brand-erosion on key campuses. Perhaps most notably, these brand-building investments have been deemed valuable enough to survive waves of cost-cutting initiatives at many of these same organizations.

EXECUTIVE SUMMARY

1   Job security is becoming an oxymoron. 9/11 and the combination of terrorism and war risk with economic weakness has put employment prospects beyond what both employers and employees can plan for.

2 Perhaps the greatest responsibility that companies have to their employees is not to keep them employed but to make them employable.

3 The psychological contract is the mutual expectations which both parties have of each other. It is not the formal contract of employment, enforceable in law and is about the 'deal' which employees believe they are entitled to expect from their employer.

4 Reputational risk in relation to employees is the gap between the promises and commitments made and delivered by the organization. The psychological contract is broken – and reputational risk increased – once either the employer or employee fails to live up to the expectations of the other. Employers should therefore ensure that they do not promise what they cannot deliver in terms of creating realistic expectations in the minds of employees.

5 The communications process is at the heart of the psychological contract. This is because it is directly responsible for influencing employees' perceptions of the content of the deal: both what they are required to do and what they are entitled to expect.

6 Employee opinion surveys often suffer from many weaknesses, e.g. not asking the right questions and befitting from varying degrees of CEO commitment.

7 Internal reputational risks increase when a focus on talent leads to a mindset which devises policies on individuals at the expense of teams and organizational systems. The 'war for talent' is to some extent a distraction from companies' real task of devising cultures and management styles that fully maximize human and intellectual capital, not just the skills and knowledge of an élite cadre.

8 Too many current and future leaders are poorly prepared for their roles. Some common failings include making creative connections, being empathetic and managing ego.

9 Experiential learning has a role to play in minimizing reputational risk with many challenges to corporate orthodoxy and groupthink and barriers to innovative thinking coming from unexpected quarters.

10 The employer brand establishes the identity of the firm as an employer. It encompasses the firm's values, systems, policies and behaviours toward the objectives of attracting, motivating and retaining the firm's current and potential employees.

Key message

Understanding employee expectations – what drives them, how they are changing and how to manage them while maintaining morale in a harsh business climate – is a top management priority.

What you must ask of your team/staff/consultants

1   Are we really convinced we know what our employees – particularly those with talent we want to retain – expect of us, in hard and soft terms?

2   Has work–life balance improved or worsened since 9/11? If worse, does this worry us?

3   Is our management development built around keeping our employees employed with us or employable?

4   How do we celebrate our history and heritage – and capture key lessons learnt?

5   Is our employee opinion survey global and how do we track and communicate back any concerns raised regarding top management performance?

6   How do we communicate strategic messages – and how do we know this works?

7   Do we have or need an employer brand?

What you must do today

1   Go home at 5.00 p.m.

2   Review your CV in the light of today's FT headlines.

3   Reflect on how your expectations are being met by your employer.

4   Schedule a chat with your mentor, if you have one, to discuss any or all of the above.

5   Identify the most talented person you work with – and ask them what would make them leave the company.

Related websites

Corporate Leadership Council
www.corporateleadershipcouncil.com

The Work Foundation (formerly the Industrial Society)
www.theworkfoundation.com

DTI Partnership at Work Fund
www.dti.gov.uk/partnershipfund/index.html

UK Black MBA Association
www.blackmbauk.org/pages/home.htm

Note

1   Now called The Work Foundation.

References

Corporate Leadership Council (2001) *Voice of the Leader: a Quantitave Analysis of Leadership Bench Strength and Development Strategies*. Washington: Corporate Executive Board.

Dowling, Grahame (1996) *Corporate Reputations: Strategies for Developing the Corporate Brand*. London: Kogan Page.

Henley Management College (2003) See *http://www.henleymc.ac.uk/henleymc 02.nsf/files/CORREmployeeRelationshipsCommunicationsReport2002.pdf/$FIL E/CORREmployeeRelationshipsCommunicationsReport2002.pdf*.

Higgs Review (2003) *Review of the Role and Effectiveness on Non-executive Directors*. London: DTI. *http://www.dti.gov.uk/cld/non_exec_review/pdfs/ higgsreport.pdf*.

Marketing Leadership Council (2002) *Linking Employee Satisfaction with Customer Satisfaction*. Washington: Corporate Executive Board.

Syrett, Michael and Lammiman, Jean (2002). Survey from Roffey Park Management Institute (1998).

6

Reputational risk and shareholders

WHAT YOU MUST KNOW BEFORE YOU START

1 Why and how markets are less efficient than they may appear.

2 How do investor relationships work?

3 What is market sentiment – and how does it affect market expectations?

4 Where does corporate governance stand after Enron?

5 What is the special role of non-executive directors (NEDs) in managing reputational risk?

6 What are the pressure points for shareholder activism?

7 What is responsible shareholding and long-term fiduciary duty?

8 Why does mainstream interest in socially responsible investment matter?

ARE MARKETS REALLY THAT EFFICIENT?

With the financial world turning upside-down, it was fitting that the Nobel Prize for Economics in 2002 went to two academics for pointing out that large chunks of traditional neo-classical economics are wrong. Psychology matters, people are irrational, markets do not always work. According to the 'efficient market' theory, prices more or less reflect the value of the company – though often they do not. The Internet, media telecom bubbles make it hard to explain in a rational way valuations that made absolutely no sense. The way corporate reputation in the financial markets is made and unmade has more to do with understanding behavioural finance (partly a collection of market anomalies) than has been often realized.

The 2002 Nobel Prize for Economics went jointly to:

■ Vernon Smith (an economist) – he is interested in how markets work. He took abstract economic theory and put it to the test in experimental laboratories, where he used students as guinea pigs to demonstrate how financial bubbles could be created or how electricity markets can be deregulated. He found that under test conditions, simple markets do work as forecast by economic theory. In more complicated markets however such as auctions, where uncertainty is important, he found that people did not behave according to theory.

   Smith discovered that the price likely to be achieved by sellers in Dutch flower auctions – those where the price starts high and gradually falls until someone shouts 'stop' – is lower than that in a sealed bid auction. Theory says these two types of auction are equivalent – but in experiments it seems that people are influenced both by the price and the suspense of waiting, which they enjoy. So they systematically underestimate the risk of holding out for a lower price, and indeed the price does fall further. Such experiments are now regularly used in auction design, as well as energy markets and the pricing of runway slots at airports.

- Daniel Kahneman (a psychologist) – is interested in how your brain works and how you make decisions. He showed how quirks in human behaviour, such as a tendency to avoid risk or to be over-confident, leads people to behave in ways economists would consider irrational or that do not always bring positive outcomes. He found that people do not behave as economic theory suggests.

As a psychologist, Kahneman showed that people have developed sophisticated and quick techniques to comprehend the world and to make decisions. Because humans learn by their mistakes, these will normally be rational, but in some areas people tend to leave strict rationality behind. In numerous studies, he showed that we are bad at understanding randomness, we put too much emphasis on the status quo and we place greater emphasis on making losses rather than profits. One of the implications is that investors carry on buying stocks during a bubble when rational valuations tell them not to.

The key message is that each Nobel laureate violates an important economic principle. Together these failings imply that most of us believe fund managers who beat the markets for two years or even twenty years are good rather than lucky; that people hang on to shares after they have fallen even though they would not buy them given what they now know; and that we tend to save too little because the immediate loss of consumption weighs more heavily on our minds than the future benefits.

The argument that asset prices are set by rational investors is part of the grand oral tradition in economics and is often attributed to Milton Friedman, one of the greatest economists of the last century. There are five areas in which behaviour in the real world seems most at odds with the theories in textbooks and the ways in which many people reared on them think financial markets work (*see* Table 6.1).

Table 6.1 How psychological biases influence asset prices

Volume	- Standard models of asset markets predict that participants will trade very little. The reason is that in a world where everyone knows that traders are rational (I know that you are rational, you know that I am rational, and I know that you know that I am rational), if I am offering to buy some shares of IBM and you are offering to sell them, I have to wonder what information you have that I do not.
	- Pinning down exactly how little volume should be expected in this world is difficult, because in the real world people have liquidity and rebalancing needs, but it seems safe to say that 700 million shares a day on the NYSE is much more trading than standard market models would expect.
	- The standard approach would not expect mutual fund managers to turn over their portfolios once a year.

Volatility	■ In a rational world, prices change only when news arrives. Economists have realized that aggregate stock prices appear to move much more than can be justified by changes in intrinsic value (as measured by, say, the present value of future dividends). ■ Stock and bond prices are more volatile than advocates of rational efficient market theory would predict.
Dividends	■ In an efficient market with no taxes, dividend policy is irrelevant. Under the US tax system, however, dividends are taxed at a higher rate than capital gains and companies can make their taxpaying shareholders better off by repurchasing shares rather than paying dividends. ■ This logic leaves us with two major puzzles, one about company behaviour and the other about asset prices. Why do most large companies pay cash dividends? And why do stock prices rise when dividends are initiated or increased? Neither question has any satisfactory rational answer.
The equity premium puzzle	■ Historically, the equity premium in the US and elsewhere has been huge. For example, a dollar invested in US T-bills on 1 January 1926, would now be worth about $14; a dollar invested in large-cap US stocks on the same date would now be worth more than $2,000. ■ Although one would expect returns on equities to be higher, because they are riskier than T-bills, the return differential of 7 per cent p.a. is much too great to be explained by risk alone.
Predictability	■ In an efficient market, future returns cannot be predicted on the basis of existing information. Thirty years ago, financial economists thought this most basic assumption of the efficient market hypothesis was true. Now, everyone agrees that stock prices are at least partly predictable on the basis of past returns, such measures of value as price-to-earnings or price-to-book ratios, company announcements of earnings, dividend changes, and share repurchases and seasoned equity offerings. ■ Although considerable controversy remains about whether the observed predictability is best explained by mispricing or risk, no one has been able to specify an observable, as opposed to theoretical, risk measure that can explain the existing data pattern.

Source: Adapted from Thaler, 1999.

To understand how this operates in practice, consider the manipulation of corporate earnings. Investors process financial information relative to performance thresholds, such as whether profits meet analysts' expectations. Recognizing this, companies manipulate earnings so as 'not to disappoint', possibly at great future cost. Empirical studies bear out such manipulation: there is a dramatic disproportion of earnings meeting or slightly beating thresholds, with very few just below.

This affects individual investors. People have a strong tendency to expect the past to repeat itself – and to do so right away – and thus buy the assets they wished they (owned) last year. People are averse to recognizing their losses, a point that helps to explain stock market behaviour. Suppose, for instance, an investor buys stock at £5 per share and it jumps to £7. If the stock seems overvalued at £7 per share, the investor would be inclined to sell it for a profit. However, researchers found that if the investor instead bought the stock at £9 per share and it fell to £7 per share, investors are less inclined to sell it, even if it still seems overvalued at that price.

Managers' financial reporting behaviour provides further evidence.

- Managers make many decisions motivated, at least partly, by a desire to make it harder for investors to uncover information that the managers do not want to affect their firms' stock prices.

- Managers choose and lobby for accounting methods that improve highly visible statistics, such as earnings-per-share and debt-equity ratios, and conceal expenses and liabilities in less visible footnote disclosures.

- Managers classify arguably ongoing expenses as non-recurring or extraordinary items, while reporting arguably unusual gains as part of operating income.

- Managers develop 'rainy day' reserves to maintain the capacity for positive accruals to boost earnings in the future.

- Managers announce pro forma earnings numbers that emphasize improvements relative to their own strategically chosen benchmarks, while making it more difficult for investors to observe other measures of performance.

Recognizing the irrationality of markets has benefits. Three forms of irrationality seem particularly useful as a basis for understanding overreactions:

- *Over-reliance on unreliable data.* Many experiments find that people tend to react too strongly to statistics that have little information content, because their reactions are determined by how salient the information is and how strongly it is emphasized, rather than by its statistical validity. Markets might overreact to persistent earnings trends because the older earnings numbers have very little power to predict future earnings, but are very salient to investors. Similarly, markets might overreact to repeated publication of interesting but relatively uninformative evidence, such as income from debt-equity swaps, pro forma earnings announcements, or analysts' projections.

  A special case of this error arises when investors fail to completely account for the incentives of reporters to distort their information. Recent investigations into the influence of misleading and self-interested analyst reports suggest that such a lack of scepticism may have played a part in the overpricing of Internet stocks. Investment banks' equity research continues to suffer from credibility problems. In the US two-thirds of recommendations on Thomson Financial/First Call are still a 'buy' or 'strong buy' – although that has dropped from 73 per cent in 2000.

- *Aggressive trading by less-informed investors.* Markets might overreact because investors who collect little information fail to recognize their informational disadvantage in the market. This error, found in countless experiments, causes relatively uninformed traders to trade too aggressively and influence prices too much. This behaviour, in turn, causes market prices to overreact to statistics that are collected by relatively uninformed investors who collect little other information.

- *Inappropriate information collection.* Economic models assume that traders can predict others' decisions accurately but experimental tests of similar settings find that they often have trouble doing so. If traders underestimate how many others collect highly publicized statistics, then they will trade too aggressively on those statistics, causing market overreactions.

INVESTOR RELATIONSHIPS

The biggest blow to BAA's solid business reputation came on the day Mike Hodgkinson became CEO in October 1999, when he was forced to issue a profit warning because the group had miscalculated the effect of the abolition of duty-free sales in Europe.

People want to invest in companies they trust, understand and believe in. Financial analysts are no different, only their opinions can profoundly affect the price of a company's stock and can persuade investors to purchase – or sell – your company's shares.

Externally, the financial community is split into two main areas that the investor relations department targets: the sell-side and the buy-side:

- The buy-side represents individual and institutional investors and all relevant functions such as analysis and portfolio managing. These are the 'buyers' of the firm's shares. They have grown in importance as fund managers have become increasingly wary of the sell-side and prefer to rely on internally generated research. The extent to which they can gain access depends on the credibility of the firm, the size of their actual or potential shareholding and the experience and expertise of their analysts in the sector. They can have a strong feel for the preoccupations and trading strategies of the funds. Buy-side analysts look for quantitative and qualitative information and check with sell-side analysts, especially about whether 'news' is significant or just 'noise'. They seek information about quality of management – often tracking managerial statements for five years – as a means of establishing trust.

- On the sell-side are the investment banks and various forms of brokers that sell the firm's shares to the buy-side. These analysts matter because they use the information disclosed by the company and other sources of 'newsflow' to form a rating on the stock, which in turn will influence investment decisions. Besides supplying these analysts with reliable, accessible and complete financial information, it is important to go further than providing only that which is required by regulations since companies' stock should gain from less asymmetries of information.

The dotted arrows in Figure 6.1 show the relationships between companies, both sides of the investment decision and the media. These take the form of all sorts of reporting, meetings and company visits and form an important part of the firm's investor relations efforts. Companies as a whole and investor relations departments in particular also deal with regulating bodies such as the SEC or similar organizations, consultants and accountants in their investor relations efforts. These all provide information and guidance in the disclosure process and related investor relations issues.

Fig. 6.1 **Investor relations constituents and their relationships**

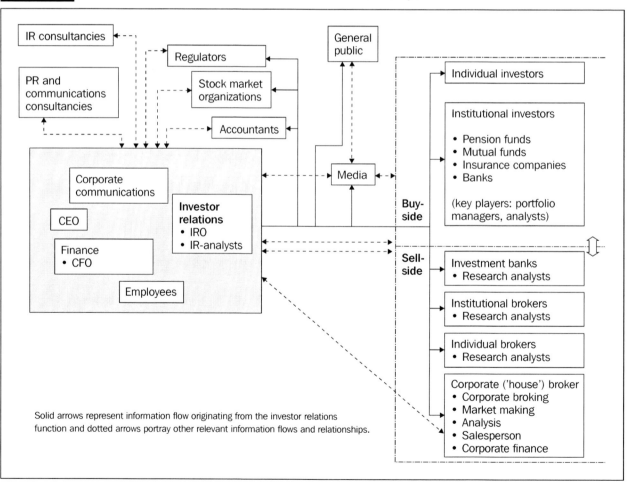

Source: Larsen, 2002.

In their marketing to corporates, investment banks have successfully encouraged the notion that sell-side analysts are critical to the institutional buy or sell decision. The reality is often different. However, if institutions listen to sell-side analysts but are little influenced by their stock recommendations, this does not mean that they do not find them useful. At a time when analyst objectivity is under severe scrutiny, companies need to be more proactive in understanding what matters to investors to build effective relationships.

Table 6.2 What investors really want (from sell-side analysts)

Overall rank	Attributes
1	Country/industry knowledge
2	Trustworthiness
3	Accessibility/responsiveness
4	Independence from corporate finance
5	Useful/timely calls
6	Written reports
7	Management access
8	Stock selection
9	Special services (sector-based conferences organized by broking firms where buy-siders can listen to presentations from companies and analysts)
10	Earnings estimates
11	Communication skills
12	Quality of sales force
13	Marketing pricing/execution
14	Primary market services

Source: All-Europe Research Team Survey, 2002 (institutional investor website).

Trust is a significantly key factor – among a community often criticized for its acknowledgement of soft factors. This also affects the buy-side: in two hours with one of the largest pension fund managers in the US weeks before the collapse of Enron (to which they had significant exposure), the most emotional part of the meeting was when the pension fund manager expressed absolute exasperation when describing how telephone calls were not returned.

On one level this may seem minor – but as a possible indicator of evasive behaviour it becomes far more serious. Company executives may brush off a failure to return calls promptly as part of the pressures of a working day but they increase reputational risk if the person making the call owns a large slice of the company. This is trust-building behaviour at a basic level but it is amazing how often the impact of simple actions is often overlooked by companies – especially when combined with the scarcities of time, attention and trust (described in Chapter 1) which affect analysts as much as anyone else.

In financial markets credibility is a function of three things: corporate performance, consistent truth and a clear willingness to deal forthrightly with the public and those who analyse securities on the behalf of the public. The public dimension is increasingly important and clearly links corporate reputation in the minds of the public and shareholders. Business leaders and their financial performance have become news – whether a Michael Dell at Dell, a Philip Green at BHS or a Richard Branson at Virgin (even if in the case of the latter the company is unquoted and half owned by Singapore Airlines). People buying cars, computers, domestic appliances and many other products are increasingly interested in the companies behind their purchases.

Shareholder value has shifted from past performance to future performance and future expectations increasingly rely on a company's intangible assets such as reputation and relationships. Sell-side and buy-side investors alike make their own decisions about non-financial performance and then act upon these evaluations. Fund managers use the following factors to assess quality of management:

- How well do the managers know their business?
- Do they know their markets?
- Have they got a clear sense of direction and strategy?
- Are they working for themselves or their shareholders?
- How credible are they?
- Do they do what they say they are going to do?

Other sources of information are also used by fund managers to evaluate companies and their management teams and are particularly valuable when trying to assess:

- whether deteriorating performance is due to exogenous, market-based factors or endogenous management failures
- whether managers are taking full advantage of the opportunities available to the company and have the necessary competence to do so.

The instigation of strategic or management changes by institutional shareholders may typically be triggered by:

- the announcement of poor financial results for the current period or results which are below market forecasts, particularly if caused by business activities or risks not previously disclosed or discussed with fund managers

- a bearish trading statement or a profits warning about future performance, particularly if these indicate that a prior deterioration in the company's performance has not been arrested over the timescale previously forecast by management

- plans being announced which contradict previous statements made or assurances given by the company to fund managers.

It is more likely to be the *discrepancy* between expectations, assurances and actual events, rather than the shorter-term availability of new information *per se*, that is likely to trigger intervention by fund managers. This underlines the significance of the adage that 'the market does not like surprises'. Too many annual reports provide a catalogue of carefully selected activities and achievements without any convincing glue – the why as well as the what.

There are growing indications that companies are having increasing difficulties in communicating effectively with their shareholders. There is substantial evidence that profit warnings, trading statements and other information 'surprises' are increasing share price volatility. In the case of profit warnings, there appears to be a tendency for changes in share price to exceed the announced change in expected earnings, in some cases by a factor of two or more.

The recent evidence is not encouraging. Global companies are less inclined to discuss 'bad news' or their business prospects in 2003 than they were in 2001, according to one recent survey of 50 of the world's largest 1,000 companies (*Financial Times*, 2003). Of the 50 firms, 6 have no investor relations information on their home page. Only 18 per cent of the companies included forward-looking statements in their annual reports, down from 79 per cent two years ago. Only 30 per cent had any discussion of 'bad news' in their annual reports, down from 50 per cent two years ago. Among the worst performers were Tesco and Walt Disney. More findings:

- 44 per cent of chairmen mentioned strategies in letters to shareholders

- 36 per cent of annual reports included objectives, compared with 76 per cent in 2000

- 44 per cent of companies described possible risks or uncertainties they face compared to 70 per cent in 2000.

Time spent by CEOs on nurturing good relations with investors and the City can pay dividends. Creating positive relationships with those who influence share prices and investor attitudes is an insurance policy. Giving accurate and plentiful data is a good start, but the tenor of exchanges between companies and those who monitor them can colour the way that information is assessed. Time spent on nurturing positive relations with investors and the media can even go some way towards compensating for poor performance: if business leaders are well liked, they stand more chance of being given the benefit of the doubt when things go wrong.

Case study 6.1

How weak relationships increase reputational risk and destroy value

1 Jeffrey Skilling was, briefly, president of Enron. Enron's fate had been determined by dubious dealings before Skilling assumed the presidential mantle, but he probably hastened the end when, in a conference call with analysts, he took exception to a probing question and dubbed the enquirer an 'asshole'. Analysts do not respond well to public put-downs; neither do journalists. If they encounter hostility, they are likely to return it.

2 Sir Richard Greenbury could not disguise the contempt that he felt for those, generally very much younger and less experienced than he, who challenged what he was doing at Marks & Spencer. Although M&S paid people to deal with press enquiries, the tone of relationships is set at the top. After years of Greenbury's stewardship, M&S had few friends among the analysts and even fewer in the press. When the company's trading turned down, the pent-up antagonism that Greenbury's attitude had fostered flowed into print. When M&S was trouncing the competition, the reviews had to reflect that success – but Greenbury had ensured that when he faced problems, those he had treated so disdainfully did not look so charitably on his predicament.

Key points:

■ Individual relationships matter especially and, with the CEO and CFO as the typical public face of the company to investors, the way these people behave is critical whether in briefings, body language or private actions (e.g. selling shares in the company which can be interpreted as signalling a lack of confidence in the company's strategic direction).

■ These relationships can continue when CEOs become non-executive chairmen.

There are three questions companies need to answer (and review every quarter in fast-moving markets) when considering the effectiveness of their investor relationships:

1 What do you do to create value (the opportunity dimension of risk)?

2 What can happen to destroy value (the hazard dimension of risk)?

3 What degree of confidence do you – and your largest institutional investor, your most valuable customer and your most talented employee – have in the estimated distribution of outcomes (the uncertainty dimension of risk)?

MARKET SENTIMENT AND EXPECTATIONS

Reputational risk in financial markets is driven in large part by market sentiment. There is however seldom any analysis of what market sentiment is, even less how it operates. Essentially market sentiment is a way of describing the central mood that drives individual share prices, sectors and the equity market as a whole. It is an emotional reaction to a piece of corporate or other stock-market related news. It can affect individual companies and sectors (for example airlines after 9/11) and can continue for weeks or even months. Sentiment is a residual – the element in a share price that cannot be explained by reference to the fundamentals.

The best way to view market sentiment is either a pair of sun glasses or a life jacket. A pair of sunglasses in that it enables the market to view any announcement as always bad news or always good news. Thus the same two companies, one with a positive backing, a good feeling to it, a positive response, a positive branding image within the City can come out with the same news item as a company with a weak corporate branding. Handling it well against handling it badly can see a share price increase 10 per cent instead of falling 30 per cent. What this means is the market either views one item of news as the glass being half full or as being half empty. An example would be current market conditions where due to economic and geopolitical uncertainty, the market views everything as a glass half empty because it has bad news about the economy and the whole of the market. This can increase reputational risk for a particular company or sector.

This is made worse where there is the slightest doubt about a company's credibility, honesty, the opacity of its accounts – where even minor items hidden away should not have been, that can trigger more negative feeling towards a company or sector. This may relate to subsidiaries, franchises, finance leases – anything that will affect the company's reputation when people look at that side. If confidence is shaken, rumours will go round the City rapidly and people will not afford to take the risk buying after a profits warning even if the stock is cheap. The value of the company will then sink further and further and eventually may even disappear or be taken over. Thus market sentiment is important to manage to give each company a cushion against the fact that there will be unexpected bad news somewhere along the line.

A positive sentiment can often be viewed if sector or company is perceived as well-run – when analysts do not have doubts about it or have questions about the honesty of the management. The attitude in the City is 'so what if they've had a profits warning, I'll buy after the profits warning' and so it is the life jacket that enables the company to come up again and survive. This can increase reputational opportunity.

Case study 6.2

Lloyds TSB

Lloyds TSB was held up as a paradigm of a perfectly run bank for several years. In the last 3–4 years it has been a laggard by a very large margin against all the other banks in the UK. This is not directly because of how the bank is run (which is run well) but because there were no up-side surprises and people became bored. It is still the best and the most efficient bank in the UK but now it languishes on a bit of a discount to the rest of the banking sector because there is no excitement. Indeed this may also be due to what was referred to as 'the Pitman premium' after its highly respected chairman who retired in 2000 – he may have generated that excitement because the earnings numbers have not really changed.

If everyone in the market knows the consensus estimate – the one the companies have helped develop and fully expect to beat, if only marginally – they also know that the quarterly earnings report will offer little or no valuable information unless it is negative. The focus then turns to estimating how much the company's estimate will exceed the consensus estimate. This process is accelerated by the Internet which has led to a proliferation of gossip and news easily available to everybody. Financial gurus of various sorts publish online the letters of privileged information that they used to address to their corporate clients. Even in a bear market and with greater regulatory scrutiny after an abuse of trust by several highly-paid analysts, the 'whisper numbers' matter.

'Whisper numbers' are the 'real' earnings forecasts that the sell-side analysts are providing favoured institutional clients, or so the market believes. One definition from an Internet-based information service at the height of the bubble defined them as 'unofficial and unpublished earnings per share forecasts that circulate among professional traders on Wall Street, securities analysts and big investors specifically meant for the favoured and very wealthy clients of the top brokerage firms'. Specialized firms such as *www.earningswhispers.com* post on the Internet rumours and leaks that in the past did not diffuse beyond initiated circles.

Case study 6.3

www.earningswhispers.com

The first source for a whisper number is a contact associated with a company. If this is not available, it seeks information from a vendor or a corporate customer. They query brokers and investors who might already have some whisper numbers. Finally they search Internet message boards.

All of this information goes into calculating a whisper number which is then compared to analysts' estimates, particularly those that have been accurate in the past and to the company's past performance in beating expectations.

US reporting focus on quarterly earnings and forecasting of cash flow (now being proposed by the EU) has moved not only from giving results but in giving pre-warnings, pre-results and 'warnings seasons' before the results come quarterly. All of that is shifting it more and more away from the actual numbers as they come out towards actual perception. Before market sentiment turned away from the technology sector, some of the tech US companies came out with extremely bad numbers but because they managed to keep the whisper number down far enough before announcing their bad numbers, and their bad numbers are better than the really bad whisper numbers, their stock price went up. The result is that they were perceived to have successfully navigated their way through that period.

Availability of information however does not guarantee accuracy and whisper numbers themselves fall far short of being purely unbiased. Nonetheless academic research supports the view that whisper numbers are more important to market prices than consensus estimates. Nearly 70 per cent of companies that met the consensus estimate but failed to live up to whispered expectations saw their share prices drop over a five-day period and more than 56 per cent saw it drop over a 24-hour period.

This has also been described as 'moral anchoring' – where the market is tied down by people's comparisons of the intuitive force of stories and reasons to hold their investments against their perceived need to consume the wealth that those investments represent. Thus when a company misses its forecast by a few pence and the corporate reputation is weak, the market talk may confirm an assumption that it may have lost its edge. Analysts could then recalculate not only the height of a company's future projected earnings but its duration as well.

The key message is that although they are less influential than they were at the height of the Internet bubble, whisper numbers still exist and companies need to acknowledge that a weak reputation in the market (e.g. in regularly revising profits forecasts) fuels their use. This matters because whisper numbers reinforce a short-term orientation and increase the amount of time and energy being spent just prior to the earnings announcements.

All this has made successful communication and management of people's expectations probably the number one or number two priority for a CEO. The head of equities strategy for a big 4 UK bank has described how this works:

From the point of view of the share price in the short term and given the fact that chief executives tend to be pretty short these days, s/he may well be better managing expectations than managing the company. That suggests that it's a vital thing to do and if you look at the people who lose their jobs as chief executives it's almost invariably as a result of mismanagement of investment and financial expectations. That may well be, and almost invariably is, combined with a big push factor from underneath. Somebody who is mismanaging expectations is probably (a) got a company that is probably disappointing and therefore there's bad news to bring forward, and (b) is trying to gloss over it and so is probably unpopular within his own business. But investors don't see that and they don't get into the depth of the business. They just see the chief executive or the finance director and so managing those expectations badly tends to end up with people losing their job.

A good example is Rentokoil which was one of the top 5 in the whole of the UK market for 15 years with 20 per cent earnings growth year-in and year-out. Every sensible analyst knew it couldn't be sustained but Clive Thompson decided to maintain that it could be sustained for ever. When he came in with less than 20 per cent (I think he only came in with 17 per cent in the first year), that was viewed as a big shock. His reputation was shot to pieces. Then it came out over time that to get the 20 per cent in the previous years, there had been the best possible gloss on the results. They had not been running the business on a long-term perspective but just squeezing everything to get the 20 per cent per year. In fact they ended up not quite but almost destroying what is a very good company and still is a good company – but the reputational damage has seen their share prices halved and has seen investors view them as a very poor investment.

Zaman, 2003.

In a business climate where visibility at best (and trust at worst) on financial performance numbers is low and as the proportion of value determined by future growth increases, expectations become a more critical determinant of how markets react to new information. Understanding expectations largely explains why share prices change in ways that do not seem consistent with the news being announced (good earnings news leads to share price drops, bad earnings news results in share price increases) and market volatility in general. Recent research at Wharton (Rogers and Stocken, 2002) has found that when it is more difficult for market participants to detect forecast bias, financially distressed companies are more optimistic than healthy companies (and companies in concentrated industries are more pessimistic than those in less concentrated industries).

When asked what his secret to BA's success in its transformation from public utility to publicly quoted company was, Lord King, BA's previous chairman, once confided that it was all down to a ruthless focus on cash flow. We need to probe this to understand how it connects to expectations. The value of a company is the present value of the expected cash flows on the company and implicit in these expected cash flows and the discount rates used to discount the cash flows are investors' views about the company, the behaviour and credibility if its management and the potential for excess returns.

■ *Risk is measured relative to expectations* The risk in a company does not come from whether it performs well or badly but from how it does relative to expectations.

■ *Good companies do not always make good investments* It is not how well or badly a company is managed that determines stock returns but how well or badly managed it is, relative to expectations.

Managers can respond by:

1 *Focusing on information about the value drivers* The requirements of the Operating and Financial under forthcoming changes to UK company law are a good place to start (discussed later in this chapter).

2   *Finding out what is expected of them* If managers are going to be judged against expectations, it is critical that they gauge what those expectations are. While this translates for many companies into keeping track of what analysts are estimating earnings per share to be in the next quarter, there is more to it than this. Understanding why investors value the company the way they do and what they think its differential (rather than pure competitive) advantages are, is much more important in the long term. Central to this understanding is a strong relationship with investors where communication is trusted, open, clear and consistent.

3   *Learning to manage expectations* When companies first go public, managers and insiders, abetted by their PR consultants, sell the idea that their company has great potential and should be valued highly. While this is perfectly understandable, managers have to change roles after they go public and learn to manage expectations. Specifically they have to be brave or humble enough and, in a male-dominated environment (Marjorie Scardino remains the only female FTSE 100 CEO at Pearson plc), possibly even less macho, in talking down expectations. This may be when they feel that their company is being set up (sometimes by financial journalists or quasi-consultant-led research) to do things that it cannot accomplish. Again, though, some companies damage their credibility when they talk down expectations incessantly, even when they know the expectations are reasonable.

Steve Balmer, Microsoft's CEO, has developed a reputation for talking down expectations and then beating them on a consistent basis. Rod Eddington at BA is an example of a CEO who is much better at managing (internal and external) expectations than his hapless predecessor, Bob Ayling. Moreover Eddington's experience at News International, where he remains a senior NED and his multilingual fluency (e.g. in Japanese, Korean and Mandarin), doubtless helps his credibility with investors and reinforces the point that even CEOs can grow their reputation from a bit of professional development.

4   *Not delaying the inevitable* No matter how well a company manages expectations, there are times when managers realize they cannot improve expectations any more, because of changes in the sector or the overall economy. While the temptation is strong to delay revealing this to financial markets, often by shifting earnings from future periods into the current one or using accounting ploys (which still persist post-Enron as the regulatory investigation into Ahold suggests), it is far better to have the courage to deal with the consequences immediately. This may mean reporting lower earnings than expected and a lower share price (to maintain trust) but companies that delay their day of reckoning tend to be punished much more.

Case study 6.4

Market sentiment and GSK

In May 2003, the GlaxoSmithKline board suffered a historic defeat of over pay and rewards. However, a number of elements were already contributing towards negative sentiment towards GSK even before the pay award was presented to investors:

■ honeymoon period over

Jean-Paul Garnier became CEO of the merged GlaxoSmithKline in 2001. Garnier had a hard task in being the first CEO of the merged group and after two such highly respected executives had left the scene, namely Richard Sykes and Jan Leschly. By November 2002, GSK's shares had underperformed the sector by 30 per cent since mid-2001. Garnier's management style was coming in for open criticism with a boardroom reputation as a table-thumper who may engage in debate but rarely concedes a point.

■ reassurance needed that the new decentralized research was working

There had been a radical reorganization of GSK's research which was still in its early stages, which was an attempt to revive R&D after setbacks that saw promising drugs failing late-stage clinical trials or flopping once they reached the market.

■ lack of visibility on the product pipeline

GSK's early stage drugs were still emerging. Its long-awaited R&D meeting with investors, when companies showcase the drugs in their research laboratories with high potential, the first such 'R&D Day' since the February 2001 merger, was still awaited. In the meantime competitors such as Pfizer and Astrazeneca had been setting the pace. There were more blockbuster drugs in circulation and more aggressive low-cost generic competitors.

■ brain drain and morale issues

Since the GSK merger there had been a worrying drain of top executives. In an industry where product innovation is directly linked to talent retention, analysts were especially concerned about the departure of senior members of the research and development team and possible morale problems among GSK scientists.

CEO pay award and weak investor relationships

To this cocktail of context, GSK's Chairman, Christopher Hogg, had had to acquiesce to shareholder pressure to abandon a plan to double Garnier's already generous annual pay package to a potential $18 million (£11.4 million) in November 2002.

■ Analysts saw it as unlikely to accelerate the departure of senior staff, as it further distanced Garnier's remuneration from those GSK needed to retain. Investors were also surprised at the timing of the demand. Having seen their investment decline by a third since the merger – slightly more than the FTSE 100 – they were not inclined to be generous.

■ Many investors dismissed the argument that Garnier's pay should be aligned with peers at the top US groups such as Pfizer and Merck, where share packages are twice as generous. Even if post-Enron, such deals were seen by some to be discredited, Pfizer's growth in shareholder value, for example, already put GSK on the defensive. Sidney Taurel, CEO of Eli Lilly, took only $1 in salary and cancelled executive bonuses after sales of its lead drug Prozac plunged.

■ The arguments were put across by Sir Christopher Hogg, GSK's chairman in his first meetings with shareholders since he took the chair six months previously. Hogg is also chairman of Reuters, a post he has held for almost two decades (well beyond most of his peers) and also under pressure there from investors for weak shareholder value.

■ Hoggs' argument was that if GSK, the world's second biggest drugs group, wants to retain its top executives, their pay must match its peers. Several large institutional investors made it clear that no-one was that indispensable, even the CEO.

■ One issue was how much time Garnier spent in the US, where about half of GSK's business was done against how little he spent in the UK, where 70 per cent of GSK's shareholders were. However, the real issue was a weak relationship between the CEO and institutional investors. Garnier lived in the US where he had been for more than 20 years, taking joint French-US nationality. In November as an earlier crisis over his remuneration package mounted, he was perceived as laying low in Philadelphia, leaving his chairman and corporate relations team to take the flak, perpetuating a reputation for sidestepping difficult issues.

Result

Sir Christopher Hogg stepped back from chairing GSK's nominations and corporate social responsibility committees. Sir Peter Job (ironically Reuters' former CEO under Hogg in the 1990s) was appointed to the remuneration committee, beefing up the British contingent and following criticism of American influence on determining executive pay.

Lessons

1 GSK angered shareholders not only through the sheer quantum of rewards proposed for Garnier but also by appearing to present the package as a *fait accompli*.

2 Some reassurance was needed that the new decentralized research was working. This in fact came in early 2003 but some early evidence could have been used to build credibility at a time when shareholder value was weak.

3 The R&D meeting with investors needed to be signposted again to build confidence with anxious investors in difficult market conditions, e.g. was it expected in Q1 2003?

4 How serious was a brain drain and morale issues? Had management recognized this as an issue and even if it was not, were they still prepared to talk about it, given any inevitable post-integration issues?

5 How was the pay award agreed? Was the timing not seen as a reputational risk – and did anybody flag it as such at the board level? As one institutional investor said, as a result of apparent weak internal processes, the issue quickly grew to became one of governance and not just top executive pay. Ironically, GSK had put it quite well itself in its submission to the Higgs Review only a few weeks earlier by pointing out that 'Audit Committee … effectiveness is ultimately influenced by the quality and calibre of the individuals involved'.

6 Were initial soundings taken from any major institutional investors, e.g. in the hurdles to receiving the options being seen as too low? If not, was this because relationships with key investors were too weak?

7 Hogg needed to re-develop his own credibility with the City given contemporary performance issues under his watch at Reuters. Moreover his argument that the pay deal was vital if GSK was to retain its top executives was a weak one given recent performance at GSK and developments at Eli Lilly. In a depressed financial market and one in which investors were being expected by regulators to be more assertive with underperforming companies post-Myners and with Higgs drafting his report at that very moment on NEDs, it was easier for investors to state that no one was that indispensable – even the CEO.

8 Garnier needed to have more personal exposure with GSK's key institutional investors in the UK as well as the US to build trust. The objective must be to develop a stronger relationship with GSK's key stakeholders and reputational agents, its investors, analysts and media, in breadth and depth.

CORPORATE GOVERNANCE AFTER ENRON

Evidence for a strong reputation for sound and solid corporate governance is compelling. A February 2002 Survey by KPMG of the largest international takeovers consummated at the height of the bull market show that a third are now being unwound. Businesses acquired at great cost are being disposed of for fractions of their acquisition costs. Since that report was compiled the evidence has become even stronger. The firms where the greatest, indeed almost total loss of shareholder value has occurred were serial acquirers of other companies – for instance Enron, Tyco, WorldCom – whose high stock market ratings required continuous acquisitions. This ultimately unsustainable process was supported by compliant boards and often shady accounting practices which are now leading to numerous prosecutions.

There is a growing body of international studies providing strong evidence that superior governance can both significantly increase corporate value and substantially reduce the risk of corporate failure. A McKinsey survey of many major institutional investors in April/May 2002 was conducted in 31 major countries in five continents with the Global Corporate Governance Forum. It covered 200 major investors who with their parent organizations had $9 trillion under management. It showed that 70 per cent – 80 per cent of investors would pay a premium for a well-governed company defined *inter alia* as follows:

- a majority of outside directors, truly independent, i.e. no ties with management
- formal director valuation in place
- a very responsive attitude to investor information requests on governance issues.

Governance remains a great concern for institutional investors worldwide, one on a par with financial indicators when evaluating investment decisions. An overwhelming majority will pay a significant premium for good governance, 14 per cent in America and western Europe, 12 per cent in the UK and rather more elsewhere where governance standards are less well developed. These premiums are down on a similar survey of two years ago (18 per cent then for the UK and the US) but in view of the flood of American corporate scandals in the few months following the survey, the American premium would be higher today. The much higher recent falls in the share prices of companies with complicated financial structures is further evidence of the worth of good governance.

But how does this affect emerging markets? In April 2001, the Emerging Markets team at Credit Lyonnais Securities (Asia) or CLSA published a report that studied 495 companies in 25 emerging markets. CLSA ranked the companies in seven key corporate governance areas: discipline, independence, transparency, accountability, fairness, responsibility and social awareness.[1] CLSA found that (at least for 2000), there was a strong correlation between corporate governance on the one hand and financial performance and share price increases in emerging markets companies on the other.

Now, thanks to Enron, the phrase 'corporate governance' has now entered the vernacular. As SEC Chairman at the time Harvey L. Pitt told Congress, Enron's rapid demise 'changed how citizens look at the *safety* of the markets, the *truth* of corporate disclosures, the *dependability* of financial statements, the *validity* of analyst recommendations and the *reliability* of rating agency evaluations'.

But what exactly do we mean by 'corporate governance'? A set of rules for governing directors' duties and describing the processes that underpin them – or something more? The question has to be asked in the context of the behaviour of four major institutional investors who all had, or considered having exposure, to Enron months before its collapse at the end of 2001.

- A fund manager with one of the UK's top company pension funds and a FTSE 100 company which avoided Enron because she did not believe the earnings numbers and forecasts of growth that the company executives claimed – and was given no information by Enron to reassure her.

- A leading UK ethical investment fund group which had Enron exposure and found the UK company representatives friendly and accessible.

- One of the largest pension funds in the US which held significant exposure to Enron and also helped set up the kind of off-the-books partnerships that ultimately sent Enron down.

■ A leading UK institutional investor which avoided Enron due to its political risks and community confrontations in India.

The common denominator in all of these was trust and confidence, and in the case of Enron, misplaced. Asia is a region often associated with the importance of relationships in business success. In a speech to the Japan Business Federation in 2003, Sir Stephen Gomersall, the British Ambassador to Japan, set out some of the key features of corporate governance which could apply to boards everywhere:

> *Corporate Governance is not just about balancing the rights of those with an interest in a company's activities – be they customers, shareholders, employees or the wider public. It also concerns the information flows and decision making within a firm so that it is able to make the right strategic choices; to set the right controls; and to provide the necessary objectivity to ensure responsible and ethical business behaviour ... An effective board is as much about encouraging and establishing appropriate behaviours and relationships within and outside the board as it is about formal structures.*

Niall Fitzgerald, chairman of Unilever, has also captured several of the key elements of effective corporate governance:

> *Transparency and accountability lie at the heart of good corporate governance. Only if you have transparency can you engender trust – and it is trust, trust of the management, its policies, of the employees and what they do, that is the essential bedrock of economic success.*
>
> Fitzgerald, 2003.

At its core corporate governance is about nothing less than creating value from the quality of decision making. This simple definition puts a focus on:

1 Value: creation and maintenance.

2 Accountability: decisions for whom?

3 Consensus: something that is agreed by more than one person, if the board is to avoid being a rubber stamping group for major strategic decisions and to have a balanced understanding of risk.

4 Action: corporate governance is about deciding as well as debating and moving forward as well as reflecting on the past and present.

5 Quality: acknowledges the increasing importance of softer factors, especially in global boards which practice rather than preach diversity (not so much of gender and race but more of perspective – which may mean one and the same thing in many companies). Included in 'quality' is business integrity (the

author is grateful to Guy Jubb, Director of Corporate Governance at Standard Life Investments, for this distinction).

It also implies communication as decisions reached need to be recorded, even if confidentiality precludes their wider dissemination. Good corporate governance is evidence of the practice of quality governance together with the care and skill in making business judgement calls. It emphasizes the importance of public reporting to shareholders on long-term issues as well as those which will have an impact on current year profitability. Such disclosure increases the vulnerability of management to criticism but in corporate governance terms this may be no bad thing: companies are a great deal more than the sum of their executive directors or even the whole board. Governance is about:

- the accountability of companies to their shareholders

- the transparency of the relationship between shareholders, particularly institutional investors, and companies

- the quality of corporate governance processes which are progressive and positive.

In an address to Chatham House in February 2003, Mervyn King, chairman of the King Committee of Corporate Governance in South Africa, suggested six questions (*see* Figure 6.2) to ask in order to practise 'qualitative corporate governance'.

The UK Company Law Review White Paper (2002) indicated that companies should provide more qualitative and forward looking reporting, in addition to information that is quantitative (e.g. the balance sheet), historical (e.g. the financial results in the past year) or about internal company matters (e.g. the size of the workforce). Moreover information about future plans, opportunities, risks and strategies are seen as just as important to users of financial reports as a historical review of performance.

How does all this link with reputational risk? Best practice is emerging fast and from interesting quarters. Listed public companies in Australia will now have to report annually on their corporate governance procedures in relation to certain principles and will have to identify and explain any divergence from them. Specifically corporate governance guidelines pending (effective by July 2004) state that the board's risk oversight and management policy should include a focus on 'reputation risk – the potential in loss or gain from changes in *community* expectations of corporate behaviour'.

This is not quite leading edge thinking – as it restricts the term to community. As we have seen throughout this book, reputational risk is a much more powerful creator of corporate value if seen in relation to an organization's key stakeholders – customers, employees and shareholders (without which a commercial organization will have no resources or capabilities to deliver anything of value to the community). What is useful though about the Australian Stock Exchange's

Listing Rules is that for the first time a major or probably any stock exchange/ regulatory authority uses the language which has been used in this book i.e. *expectations of corporate behaviour*. Is this the language that your board uses when discussing issues matters relating to reputational risk?

Fig. 6.2	**Qualitative corporate qovernance**	
1	Is there any conflict of interest?	■ Personal or immediate family. ■ No interest needed. ■ Disclose and vote or excuse from voting. ■ Conflict leads to deceit by omission and/or commission.
2	Do I have all the facts to enable me to make a decision?	■ Objectively speaking. ■ Acknowledge past prejudices and present needs. ■ Focus on facts not assumptions.
3	Is this a rational decision based on all the facts?	■ Balance risk and reward. ■ Time might show the wrong decision. ■ This may be subject to a legal microscope years later. ■ Remember the probability in legal cases as a guide: 50 per cent are winners, 50 per cent are losers.
4	Is the decision in the best interests of the company?	■ Long term rather than short term.
5	Is the communication transparent?	■ Substance over form. ■ Negatives and positives. ■ Non-financial aspects. ■ Prompt – no surprises.
6	Is the company acting in a socially responsible manner?	■ Good corporate citizen. ■ Non-discriminatory. ■ Non-exploitative. ■ Safety, security, health and environment. ■ Business ethics.

Source: King, Mervyn 2003 (adapted).

ROLE OF THE NON-EXECUTIVE DIRECTOR (NED) FROM 2003

The role of the non-executive director is under more scrutiny than ever before. Codes of practice from the Cadbury and Hampel Committees, along with increasing pressure from institutional investors and judicial requirements and most recently the Higgs Review, have brought about a focus on the changing role of the non-executive director and the expectations attached to that role.

Non-executives are required to have a view of the company's affairs which is independent from that of the executive directors. They are expected to get sufficiently close to the business to understand its risks in some detail while maintaining both a strategic and monitoring position. They now have three problems in particular:

1   There is a danger that as a result of recent events, NEDs will be expected to become all things to everyone. For example, while they have a monitoring and watchdog role, they are not auditors and neither do they have the resources ostensibly available to auditors to investigate independently or to verify all the information which management provides them.

2   They have time constraints which are often arguably not adequately compensated for. On the whole, most NEDs are expected to spend around 24 days a year working for their companies. This means that it would take them around ten years in the business to work the same number of days as a full-time employee works in each year of employment.

3   The recent decision of the board of Equitable Life to sue its former directors has highlighted the financial risk which NEDs take on in addition to the reputational risk of which they should be aware (though Higgs made several suggestions on Director liability to address this).

Relying on management to provide enough information to enable the non-executive to carry out their role is not sufficient and directors must know the right questions to ask to ensure they have the information necessary to carry out their duties efficiently. In this the role of the chairman is key. This includes 'the promotion of constructive relationships, management of the discussion processes, encouraging challenging and effective contributions in board meetings and ensuring appropriate information flows. The building of trust between all members of the board will also be part of this process and will enhance board performance.'[2]

The Higgs Report (2003) acknowledges that:

corporate governance provides an architecture of accountability – the structures and processes to ensure companies are managed in the interests of their owners. But architecture in itself does not deliver good outcomes. The Review therefore also focuses on the conditions and behaviours necessary for non-executive directors to be fully effective.

A strong sense in which NEDs need to retain a focus on corporate reputation pervades the report. Higgs sets out the personal attributes required of the effective non-executive director as founded on:

- integrity and high ethical standards
- sound judgement

- the ability and willingness to challenge and probe
- strong interpersonal skills.

Table 6.3 Role of the non-executive director

Strategy	Non-executive directors should constructively challenge and contribute to the development of strategy.
Performance	Non-executive directors should scrutinize the performance of management in meeting agreed goals and objectives and monitor the reporting of performance.
Risk*	Non-executive directors should satisfy themselves that financial information is accurate and that financial controls and systems of risk management are robust and defensible.
People	Non-executive directors are responsible for determining appropriate levels of remuneration of executive directors and have a prime role in appointing, and where necessary removing, senior management and in succession planning.

* In response to a question from the author in a plenary session of the 2003 annual conference of the International Corporate Governance Network, Derek Higgs stated that this included non-financial risks such as reputation too.

Source: Higgs Report, 2003.

Table 6.4 Personal attributes of NEDs

Integrity and high ethical standards.	First and foremost, integrity, probity and high ethical standards are a prerequisite for all directors.
Sound judgement.	Essential for each of the elements of the non-executive director's role.
All non-executive directors must be able and willing to enquire and probe.	■ NEDs should have sufficient strength of character to seek and obtain full and satisfactory answers within the collegiate environment of the board. The objectivity and fresh perspective acquired through their relative distance from day-to-day matters, combined with experience acquired elsewhere, is the basis for questioning and challenging the accepted thinking of the executive. ■ Questioning does not only serve to raise specific concerns, it can also prompt stronger executive performance. Skilful questioning can be penetrating and demanding. The response can both reassure the non-executive director and stimulate reflections and actions that contribute to more effective executive performance. Executive directors especially value informed and constructive debate with non-executive directors.
Strong interpersonal skills.	Much of a NED's effectiveness depends on exercising influence rather than giving orders and requires the establishment of high levels of trust.

Source: Higgs Report, 2003.

In addition there are several specific references to reputation:

1 'Directors' duties are to act for the success of the company for the benefit of its shareholders as a whole. In determining how best to promote the success of the company, directors must, where relevant, take account of "material factors". These include long- as well as short-term consequences of their actions, the need to foster business relationships, including with employees, suppliers and customers, impact on communities and the environment, business reputation and fairness between different shareholders.'

   Key implication: this is consistent with the changes in the White Paper on the company law review. It is also a central argument in this book which sets out a relationship-driven view of corporate reputation in relation to an organization's key stakeholders.

2 'The composition of a board sends important signals about the values of the company. A commitment to equal opportunities which can be of motivational as well as reputational importance is inevitably undermined if the board itself does not follow the same guiding principles.'

   Key implication: diversity among NEDs for women and especially for ethnic minorities is now a reputational risk for companies. This is because they need visible practices as well as paper policies to demonstrate corporate commitment to equal opportunities as a tangible expression of their values. Moreover given the weak position of many companies in this area, action on diversity provides a reputational opportunity and can increase motivation among current and potential executives and NEDs.

   One major institutional investor usefully cited the Lex column which puts it only too clearly:

> *It is hardly disputed that non-executive directors should, as the Higgs report formulates it, 'bring wider experience and a fresh perspective to the boardroom'. If they are to fulfil this requirement, recruiting only the usual suspects – pale, male, stale and already on a FTSE 100 company's board – does not do the job. Companies need to recognize that greater diversity on their boards – including that of age and experience, as well as gender and ethnicity – leads to better decision making.*

The incestuous nature of corporate governance partly reinforces boards current composition. Not only do directors often meet on different boards; they may also be members of the same country clubs, industry associations and charitable foundations. Such extracurricular connections can make directors insular and when boards come unstuck from established corporate governance norms, insularity and groupthink is often an important factor. A recent list of the 500 largest companies in the world by market capitalization reveals the best-connected companies and directors:

- The list of the top 20 best-connected companies contains only 5 US groups (in descending order, Verizon and SBC Communications from the telecommunications sector, Pfizer, the pharmaceuticals group, and SunTrust, Allstate and JP Morgan Chase in finance).

- All the other companies in the ranking are German or French, with the best-connected being Allianz, the German insurer, Axa, its French rival, BNP Paribas of France, and Eon, Germany's largest utility. The best-connected directors in the world are also German and French.

3   'At a time when the perceived risks associated with being a non-executive director are growing … encouraging greater provision of [directors' and officers'] insurance, while it might reduce the personal exposure of directors, would not remove [their] reputational risk and paradoxically it would mean that there would be more to gain financially in taking action against directors.'

Key implication: NEDs have to live with a reputational risk that is individual as well as corporate. This could go with them and could apply in their membership of other boards (perhaps one reason why Higgs recommends a maximum that 'a full time executive director should not take on more than one non-executive directorship, nor become chairman, of a major company' and that 'no individual should chair the board of more than one major company').

Wider issues of accountancy and audit reform were considered concurrently with Higgs in 'Audit committees – Combined Code guidance' by the Smith Committee (Financial Reporting Council, 2003). This stipulated that 'the audit committee should review related information presented with the financial statements, including the operating and financial review, and corporate governance statements relating to audit and risk management'. As the Ahold scandal intensified in 2003, the EU has also unveiled far-reaching plans on corporate governance and statutory audits including a call for independent directors to supervise pay and audits.

Role of the Audit Committee

- to monitor the integrity of the financial statements of the company, reviewing significant financial reporting judgements

- to review the company's internal financial control system and, unless expressly addressed by a separate risk committee or by the board itself, risk management system

- to monitor and review the effectiveness of the company's internal audit function

---

- to make recommendations to the board in relation to the appointment of the external auditor and to approve the remuneration and terms of engagement of the external auditor

- to monitor and review the external auditor's independence, objectivity and effectiveness, taking into consideration relevant UK professional and regulatory requirements

- to develop and implement policy on the engagement of the external auditor to supply non-audit services, taking into account relevant ethical guidance regarding the provision of non-audit services by the external audit firm.

Audit Committee's role in internal financial controls and risk management

- it should monitor the integrity of the company's internal financial controls

- in the absence of other arrangements, e.g. a risk committee, the audit committee should assess the scope and effectiveness of the systems established by management to identify, assess, manage and monitor financial and non-financial risks

- management is responsible for the identification, assessment, management and monitoring of risk, for developing, operating and monitoring the system of internal control and for providing assurance to the board that it has done so. Except where the board or a risk committee is expressly responsible for reviewing the effectiveness of the internal control and risk management systems, the audit committee should receive reports from management on the effectiveness of the systems they have established and the results of any testing carried out by internal and external auditors

- except to the extent that this is expressly dealt with by the board or risk committee, the audit committee should review and approve the statements included in the annual report in relation to internal financial control and the management of risk.

Source: Smith Committee, 2003.

The key message from Smith is that the audit committee needs to act as the fulcrum which brings together reporting on reputational and other risks for discussion and decision by the full board.

A critical area which ties together the work of the NEDs set out by Higgs and the Audit Committee set by Smith is the Operating and Financial Review (OFR). The White Paper on the company law review (DTI, July 2002) recommended that all OFRs should 'consider matters which affect or may affect the company's reputation' and 'include three elements:

1 The company's business and business objectives, strategy and principal drivers of performance.

2 A fair review of the development of the company's and/or group's business over the year and position at the end of it, including material post-year-end events, operating performance and material changes.

3 The dynamics of the business, i.e. known events, trends, uncertainties and other factors which may substantially affect future performance, including investment programmes'.

Beyond these core elements disclosure should also extend to other areas including 'policies on employment, social and environmental issues'.

In addressing how to manage reputational risk for value creation, companies (supported by their auditors) need first and foremost to find a common language. This book sets out to respond to precisely this challenge by setting out what reputational risk might mean in the context of relationships with customers, employees, shareholders and society. Once understood this could provide a real template for companies in disclosing how they perform through the OFR.

SHAREHOLDER ACTIVISM – AND LIFE AFTER GSK'S 2003 AGM

Institutional investors have grown more activist. Europe's institutional investors, which typically manage private or public retirement funds, tend to be risk-averse by nature, but there are signs some have begun to learn from the aggressive tactics of their US counterparts, the most vocal of which is CalPERS, the California Public Employees Retirement Scheme. Even before the collapse of Enron, institutional investors for example blocked plans by Abbey National to take over a Scottish bank and halted Telecom Italia's plans for a financial restructuring that was expected to cost holders of non-voting shares dearly in 2001.

An increasing number of large non-institutional investment funds now specifically target underperforming European companies. Among them are UK Hermes Lens Asset Management, which led a shareholder revolt over strategy at UK media company Mirror Group; the funds run by billionaire Swiss investor Martin Ebner of BZ Bank, who relocated operations of his $16 billion in investment funds to London to concentrate on UK and other EU companies vulnerable to activist investors; and UK Active Advisors, which handles $200 million of CalPERS' resources – an example of how US institutional investors are now using private funds based in Europe to export their brand of shareholder activism to the EU.

Case study 6.5

Mattel settles shareholder litigation

Toy maker Mattel Inc. (MAT) announced in December 2002 that it agreed to pay $25.5 million toward a $122 million settlement and to negotiate 'certain corporate governance procedures', in lawsuits that began in October 1999. The lawsuits alleged that Mattel and its then subsidiary The Learning Company made false and/or misleading statements in joint proxy statements that artificially inflated Mattel's stock price and compelled shareholders to approve the merger between the two companies. Mattel dumped The Learning Company a mere 16 months after the merger, all but giving it to Gores Technology Group, citing that The Learning Company was losing nearly $1.5 million a day. Mattel bought the company for $3.5 billion but had taken a $430 million after-tax loss by September 2000.

Small shareholder coalitions have grown in importance. In 2001, several thousand small shareholders in German steel group ThyssenKrupp forced a hasty management restructuring. In some cases small-shareholder coalitions are led by a larger investor: in 2000 US arbitrage specialist Guy Wyser-Pratte mobilized small investors to remove the senior management team at French retailer Groupe Andre. Organized public affairs activism on the part of small shareholders is of course not new; what is new is activism by shareholders primarily interested in profit.

The costs of not responding to the new shareholder activism can be high. Companies that are listed or operate in the US are also liable to 'class action' suits that group disaffected small shareholders. Such cases are not confined to the US; in 2001, German shareholders in Munich media company EM.TV launched an action demanding $12 million in damages after its share price collapsed. Such cases can prove highly expensive, especially when launched against the growing number of European companies that have a US dimension. Institutional investors in 1999 sued Cendant, the US parent of UK motor garaging company NCP, after the company was forced to restate its profits (a common motive for class action suits). The damages were a record $2.83 billion.

An investigation in the summer of 2002 by the FT in the US found that 50 top executives have extracted $3.3 billion from companies they led into bankruptcy so there is fertile ground on which activism can thrive. In fact shareholder activism is clearly on the rise – and can no longer be viewed as a niche interest of a vocal minority. As Gordon Brown said in a TUC policy document in 2003, 'one of the key recommendations, now adopted in a voluntary code by the Institutional Shareholders' Committee, is that investors should intervene early in underperforming companies, to safeguard the long-term future of their investments. Such constructive engagement by investors is better for UK companies and it is better for the individuals who are the beneficiaries of pension funds'. A rare joint TUC/CBI statement on productivity published in December 2001 raised the same points. It stated:

In discharging their fiduciary duty to be active shareholders, it is appropriate for fund managers to consider issues such as company training, workplace practices or business processes more generally – to the extent that they are judged to affect company financial performance, and providing that the intervention has the objective of maximizing long-run financial performance while safeguarding the assets of the pension fund.

TUC, 2003.

As with corporate governance, the UK seems to be taking a clear lead. On 24 February 2003, the TUC called for trade unions to embrace shareholder activism. It is specifically targeting the 900 members of its Member Trustee Network. These pension fund trustees have responsibility for invested funds amounting to around £260 billion, representing one-third of total UK pension fund assets.

The same day two events occurred which will only encourage the TUC's new area of work with the investment community:

■ Royal Ahold, the world's third largest supermarket operator, disclosed a number of accounting irregularities in what is being seen as Europe's worst ever accounting scandal. Its CEO and CFO were ousted after discovering earnings were inflated by at least $500 million during the past two years.

■ Eight former and current executives of Qwest Communications were charged with helping to inflate the company's financial results by nearly $150 million. The US Justice Department filed criminal charges that group revenues were improperly boosted by $33 million. Arthur Andersen was Qwest's auditor.

How will the TUC's shareholder activism operate in practice?

1 'The TUC intends to pursue working with analysts to include employment practices in company analysis. Discussions with staff at mainstream financial institutions suggests that ... the following template, [seen in Figure 6.3], could be developed.

2 The TUC suggests a number of 'issues that unions might want to push'. These are set out in Figure 6.4. Companies should read them carefully and feel confident in how they will explain their position to people who are, ultimately, the owners of the business.

3 Two of the 'action points' identified are set out in Table 6.5, i.e. these are priorities within the 2003/04 reporting season.

The key question is, therefore, are companies – and their Investor Relations teams – prepared for what can only mean more probing and scrutiny of corporate behaviour?

The other question is probably how many CEOs are really aware of the TUC's increasing access and influence with the institutional investment community?

Fig. 6.3 TUC template

Issue	e.g. Staff representation, training, equal pay policy.
Questions	Three to five questions to get the right information on company policy and implementation.
Best practice	Industry standards or benchmarks against which a company could be judged.
Business case	Why the issue highlighted is important to shareholders.
More information	Sources where the analysts could go to get more background information.

Fig. 6.4 TUC issues for trustees

Governance issues	■ A recent study by Institutional Design found that on a number of key issues some fund management firms were actually asking for less than compliance with the Combined Code from investee companies and even in some cases asking for less than the governance standards many FTSE companies operate to. ■ Research carried out in conjunction with Just Pensions shows that trustees are already convinced that good governance has a financial impact, and that the importance of it will increase over time. It is important, therefore, that pressure is still exerted on both companies and the fund managers to fully embrace the Combined Code and look at what further governance reforms may be required.
Non-executive directors	■ The TUC has a long-standing position that the number of non-executive directorships held by an individual should be limited and that NEDs should be drawn from a wider pool (including employees, public sector management, etc.). ■ Some investors have indicated a willingness to work with the TUC in order to push for more radical changes to the current NED system. Working with other investors could enable these ideas to gain wider acceptance.
Directors' pay	■ The Government has introduced new regulations to give shareholders an annual vote on directors' pay. A number of large institutional investors such as Hermes and CIS have already signalled their willingness to use this vote to crack down on unjustifiable or unchallenging pay policies. ■ It may be possible to argue to investors that companies which do not provide a decent pension for their staff risk higher staff turnover, lower morale and, as a result, lower productivity. This should be a legitimate concern for investors. It is unlikely that such pressure could reverse the drift away from defined benefit provision, but it could at least be a valuable weapon to use to help slow the process.

Fig. 6.4 *continued*

	■ We have seen that investors may be putting pressure on insurance companies not to build up too much 'exposure' to the stakeholder market, which may be contributing to the lack of take-up so far. It could be argued that in fact the best strategy for investors in insurance companies to take is to encourage insurers to lobby for compulsory pension contributions, since this would boost their revenues.
Company reporting	■ Companies are increasingly expected to produce statements on the social and environmental impacts of their operations and the policies that they have on such issues. The French government has recently legislated for companies to also report on employment practices and this is an idea that institutional investors could also push UK companies to adhere to. ■ The advantage of companies reporting on such practices is two-fold. First it makes it easier for investors to gauge the performance of a company – particularly if the reporting is done with reference to accepted benchmarks. But secondly it could give investors something to vote for or against. Investors are more willing to vote against, or abstain, when it comes to company reporting as the reports are put forward by the company itself rather than being raised by an outside special interest group. ■ Already some investors vote on companies' environmental reporting. Some are even willing to vote against management where it is felt that the reporting is not sufficient or of a decent standard. It is likely that they would also be willing to vote against management on employment-related company reporting.

Source: TUC, 2003.

Table 6.5 TUC action points

Getting employment practices into investment analysis.	There is clear developing interest among some investors in the impact on employment practices on organizations both socially (from activist investors) and financially (from the mainstream investors). By developing guidance that promotes good employment practices, particularly if this is done with other investors, there is a real opportunity to influence corporate attitudes.
Talking to the investors.	Initial work on institutional investment this year has revealed a strong appetite from some investors for what the unions have to say. The TUC should build this rapport with institutional investors by providing them with regular information on union activity worldwide in this field and by arranging briefings for

investors on TUC policy and intentions on issues of interest to
investors. Investors have already asked to talk to the TUC
about issues such as NEDs and directors' pay, health and
safety and equal rights. The TUC should set up investor
briefings on such issues.

The drive for activism looks set to come from the US. In 2003, the Securities and
Exchange Commission (SEC) voted 4–1 to require mutual funds[3] and investment
advisers to disclose their proxy voting policies and voting records. The SEC's two
new rules require funds and advisers to disclose their proxy voting guidelines and
procedures as well as their voting records. The result will be more openness and
accountability in the way funds and advisers cast their votes, more support for
shareholder resolutions on important social and environmental issues, and more
confidence in corporate governance and the financial markets.

A record number of governance-relation motions were submitted by
shareholders in the 2003 proxy season in the US. The counts as of 25 February
were 659 compared with 527 during the whole of 2002. Even if some 85 per cent
of all proxy votes take place in the first four months of the year, this is still a large
amount. The range of issues under consideration has also shifted – and who is
filing them. Labour unions and their pension funds account for 45 per cent of all
the activity, up from 30 per cent in 2002 and less than 10 per cent a decade ago.

It is not certain whether or not proxy voting disclosure can prevent any more
Enron-style corporate meltdowns but it is likely that mutual fund managers will
now consider more carefully whether they should vote to approve a company's
auditors, to require reports on non-financial areas such as social and environmental
policy and practice or to pay a hefty severance package to an outgoing CEO.

The rating agencies are – belatedly – beginning to address the fact that issues
such as lazy boards of directors, dominant chief executives or bloated pay
structures can threaten companies' success – and investor wealth – as seriously as
excess debt or flawed business plans. For a fee of $50,000 to $150,000, US
companies can hire Standard & Poors to come in and perform an extensive review
of their corporate governance practices, from director independence, to executive
pay and benefits, to shareholders rights and takeover defence mechanisms.

The other two dominant national rating agencies, Moody's and Fitch have also
strengthened their corporate governance units. Moody's is focusing on board
structure, particularly the quality and independence of audit committees and
executive pay. It says that corporate governance questions come up most often at
two critical points in the debt-rating process: when a company is first classified as
'investment grade', or safe for the average investor and when it is upgraded to
Aaa, the top rating.

Two developments in October 2002 reinforce the fact that shareholder activism
is a growing trend that companies ignore at their peril:

1   Attorney William Lerach and corporate governance activist Bob Monks joined forces to advance a radical shareholder rights agenda through the US judicial system. Lerach is currently preparing cases against several prominent US corporates – including Sprint, Qwest Communications and AT&T to force them to revise their board compositions, executive compensation packages, and other governance related policies. Lerach said the planned litigation was best described as 'corporate governance at the point of a gun'. Monks added that 'we have tried to persuade corporate America to change through traditional shareholder actions but are we getting anywhere with this? The answer is, we're not. So now we're going to try, not as shareholders, but as plaintiffs.'

2   A group of Britain's most prominent pension funds and institutional investors agreed on a new industry code to limit corporate governance abuses and remedy underperforming companies. Members of the group, called the Institutional Shareholders Committee (ISC), included the Association of British Insurers (ABI), the National Association of Pension Funds (NAPF), the Association of Investment Trust Companies (AITC) and the Investment Management Association (IMA).

The new code aims to pressure powerful institutional investors to take a more proactive stance on shareholder activism. While voting against measures at corporate annual meetings that violate best governance practices will not be mandatory, institutional investors will be required to publish a concise statement detailing their policy on shareholder activism as well as how they monitor firms they invest in, voting policies, and the ways in which they intervene in errant corporate behaviour. Institutions will also be expected to evaluate companies' internal controls, such as the skills and abilities of independent directors to provide adequate oversight. Investors will have to publish evaluations of their own effectiveness in how they engage companies and report their findings back to their clients.

In May 2003, the NAPF announced that it is to radically expand its voting advice service on boardroom pay and corporate governance in response to the growing shareholder rebellion over executive pay. The NAPF, which represents £600 billion of institutional investment, is setting up a new company that will give corporate governance analysis and voting recommendations on the FTSE All Share index, rather than just the top 350 companies it currently covers. It will be a joint venture with the US-based shareholder lobbyist company, Institutional Shareholder Services. This means that UK companies will now face new pressure from American investors who will be given advice in line with the NAPF corporate governance guidelines. This marks a huge potential change in shareholder behaviour, as the UK is the second largest place of investment choice for US investors after Canada where they hold around 30 per cent of UK stocks.

The ISS and the NAPF are working together to design and harmonize a set of principles to recommendations and research on companies outside the UK.

Companies can manage their reputational risk by being alert to the pressure points among shareholder activists. For instance CalPERS said in November 2002 that it would support shareholder effort to force three companies to reincorporate in the US. CalPERS wants Tyco International and Ingersoll-Rand both currently incorporated in Bermuda to abandon their offshore incorporations. CalPERS said offshore incorporations not only allow companies to avoid US taxation, but also make it difficult for shareholders to hold executives and directors accountable for corporate malfeasance. Companies with weak reputations with investors should not be surprised if investor scrutiny sharpens on areas where transparency is opaque.

Many US companies are behind on corporate governance rules. In a recent survey of the Standard & Poor's Super Composite 1500, only 51 per cent of the companies were found to have formed governance committees with only 13 per cent meeting the NYSE requirement that corporate boards have a majority of independent directors. 29 per cent of audit committees, 25 per cent of compensation committees and 48 per cent of nominating committees still failed the NYSE's independence test.

However, there are real signs of change. A 12-member panel led by US Treasury Secretary John Snow[4] has recommended that public companies consider splitting the roles of chairman and chief executive – or, alternately, that they name a lead independent director to their boards. Convened by the Conference Board, the influential Blue Ribbon Commission on Public Trust and Private Enterprise said that US investors trust CEOs only slightly more than they do used car dealers. It argued that 'a primary concern in a significant number of the scandals is that strong CEOs appear to have exerted a dominant influence over their boards, often stifling the efforts of director to play the central oversight role'. To restore public confidence in corporate America, it suggested that:

- boards should hire outside legal experts to investigate ethics violations

- outside accountants should evaluate audits

- companies should rotate audit firms periodically

- executives should emphasize workplace ethics and establish a system for employees to report violations.

More than 300 shareholder resolutions on executive pay were introduced before the start of the annual meetings season in April 2003, triple last year's figure, according to the Investor Responsibility Research Centre. Of all resolutions submitted to companies for this year's annual meetings 30 per cent related to executive pay. The strong votes recorded in 2003 suggest that a growing number of private sector fund managers – who normally prefer to vote with management

– are beginning to throw their weight behind activists such as the union and state pension funds.

The New York Stock Exchange, under pressure for corporate governance reform and possible malpractice on its trading floor, is to undertake the biggest review of its boardroom structure since the 1970s which will include how compensation is set and disclosed. Its chairman and chief executive Richard Grasso was paid more than $10 million for 2002 despite a third successive year of declining share prices while at the same time the exchange stiffened governance requirements for its listed companies after a series of corporate scandals last year.

In May 2003 a shareholder resolution calling for the annual directors of Avon Products to be subject to annual elections won an overwhelming 85 per cent majority approval vote. This ranked as one of the top ten votes ever in US corporate history, where the resolution was opposed by the board and is a sign that shareowners are taking their rights and responsibilities seriously.

Shareholder activism is also growing in Germany. There are 12 million private investors in Germany – invested directly or indirectly in equities. That is double the number five years ago, in spite of the three-year stock market downturn. Their attendance at annual general meetings is rising so fast that large companies are being forced to seek out ever bigger venues. Ron Sommer, then chief executive of Deutsche Telekom, was ousted after shareholders attacked him for amassing €67bn. of debt and presiding over a 90 per cent collapse in the group's share price. Much of the criticism came from Deutsche Telekom's 3 million individual shareholders, who had helped kickstart a mass market for private equity investment when the group was privatized in 1996 and were now feeling let down.

In 2003 new corporate governance rules stated that the terms of stock option plans will now have to based on 'comparative parameters'. This shifts the focus away from plans based only on absolute performance targets (where, for example, options can be exercised if a company's share exceeds a target price within a given period) to relative parameters (such as a share price's movement relative to that of a broader index). However, several of Germany's largest blue chips have recently introduced stock option plans governed only by absolute hurdles – for example at Deutsche Telekom which two years ago abandoned the combined relative and absolute targets of its 2000 option plan to introduce a single, performance target. Are these companies leading or lagging? Reputational risks will increase for the laggards.

In a move that will greatly impact German boards, the EU will apply more pressure to meet the standard of what is expected of them in terms of their behaviour with companies now needing to publish individual compensation figures for executive directors, including a breakdown of performance-related pay.

Deutsche Asset Management has indicated that it will use its leverage to invest sizeable amounts in a handful of companies and then seek a board role to influence performance. DaimlerChrysler has refused to publish individual salaries and not reveal the compensation for individual board members – contrary to a recommendation by the German government. The carmaker will instead continue to publish the sum total of pay for all 13 of its directors together, which is all that is required under current German law. Like Canute, this is arguably swimming against the tide, especially as their institutional investor base broadens and in the light of government proposals that boardroom pay should be made public. Disclosure is an international issue – and, aided by the Internet, activists are becoming more coordinated in exerting the pressure points.

Case study 6.6

GSK's defeat over exective pay at its AGM in May 2003

Shareholder activists scored a landmark victory in May 2003 against spiralling executive pay by voting down a plan by GlaxoSmithKline, to give its chief executive, Jean-Pierre Garnier, £22 million ($35 million) if he were to lose his job. The resolution on boardroom pay was voted down by 50.72 per cent to 49.28 per cent. After stripping out abstentions, less than 40 per cent of shareholders backed the board.

The depth of the protest at GSK was masked by the number of abstentions with GSK criticized for failing to reveal the number of shareholders who failed to vote. In a rare development, Schroders, a leading institutional investor which manages part of the GSK pension fund and owns 1.09 per cent of the company, wrote to GSK to complain about being denied the opportunity to ask questions when the meeting was curtailed and that it effectively ignored abstentions at the AGM.

Although only advisory, the vote marked one of the first times in the UK that shareholders rejected a company's proposals over executive pay – and this in the country's third-largest company. It was an unprecedented example of shareholder activism, the most significant defeat of a big company's board at its annual meeting and the first time in British corporate history that a major company had lost a shareholder vote on remuneration. Adrian Cadbury, who called the historic defeat of the GSK board over pay and rewards 'a major step forward and absolutely right' noted that it would have been 'inconceivable five years ago'. Ironically GSK chairman Christopher Hogg acted as adviser to the committee that drew up the Cadbury Code.

The GSK annual meeting was the biggest protest over executive pay after companies such as Barclays, Shell, Reuters and Royal & Sun Alliance had come under attack from investors.

The vote – and the campaign that preceded it – brought together union leaders; some of the biggest names in British fund management (such as M&G and Standard Life); industry groups (such as the National Association of Pension Funds and the Association of British Insurers); the California Public Employees' Retirement System (CalPERS), the largest pension fund in the world; and private shareholders.

UK law now requires publicly traded companies to have an annual vote on executive pay. Although GSK is not required to alter its executive remuneration packages by law, it is now on notice to redraw its pay policies.

The vote further damaged the credibility of several GSK directors:

- Paul Allaire, head of the remuneration committee, is the former chairman of Xerox Corporation. As well as having direct responsibility for Mr Garnier's contract, Mr Allaire is also still under investigation by the SEC over allegations of accounting irregularities at Xerox and had to resign from the GSK board several days later.

- The deputy chairman is Sir Roger Hurn who was chairman of Marconi during its near-disintegration. He was one of the subjects of a 20-month investigation by the FSA into allegations that Marconi directors withheld information from shareholders. The investigation found that important information was not disclosed in a timely basis.

- Sir Peter Job, former chief executive of Reuters, the media group that has seen its share price collapse and in 2003 reported its first loss since flotation (and also a member of Shell's remuneration committee which had also recently come in for criticism over top-level pay).

- Though chairman Christopher Hogg (also chairman at Reuters which had also been criticized over rewarding underperformance) acknowledged that 'the major reason for this negative vote has been the fact that there are elements of our senior level remuneration package which do not accord with what is regarded as best practice by shareholders' he failed to recognize that it was incumbent on the board to anticipate the reputational risk implicit in ignoring such clearly expressed investor opinion. This led the board to avoid at least watering down its proposals.

Key lesson

The GSK vote represents a landmark in the willingness of institutional investors to confront management. Companies need to be very clear with what they are doing on their remuneration policy and have to have a policy that they can defend – with credibility and integrity – in public.

The key point is that this has raised the bar on what is seen as best practice – whether to do with board structure, disclosure, transparency or accountability. On executive pay, whether or not regulatory reform follows, the opinion of policy-makers is clear:

> *My quarrel is with 'rewards for failure'. Directors receiving extraordinary pay-offs for delivering falling profits, dwindling investment, redundant workers and out of date skills. Are the performance conditions testing enough? Are directors' pockets being filled at the expense of the business or investors?*
>
> Patricia Hewitt, Trade and Industry Secretary, 2003.

Boards – and their Renumeration Committees in particular – need to be absolutely clear that payment for failure is unacceptable. In a number of cases this year, shareholder protests centred on contracts that provided for excessive severance.

While these contracts may have been written long ago and cannot easily be changed, the fact that two major institutional investor groups – the Association of British Insurers and the National Association of Pension Funds – had warned explicitly in December 2003 that companies should not in future write contracts that overpay on severance, should have been a warning shot across the bows. Companies that insisted on doing so should have recognized the way in which their decision could become a dangerous reputational risk by ignoring expectations expressed by powerful shareholders who would be – and, as events at GSK proved, in fact were – increasingly prepared to punish remuneration committees and boards for ignoring how key stakeholders expected them to behave.

Boards need to recognize the way in which investors assess pay has changed as a result of legislation that requires greater disclosure of directors' remuneration and gives shareholders the right, for the first time, to vote on the overall package. Hitherto the only aspects subject to a vote have been share-based remuneration schemes. Investors have had no direct say over bonuses, pensions, base pay or severance payments.

Companies increase their reputational risks, as some are doing, by inserting into the small print of their remuneration report an increase in the maximum bonus payable in future. This could lead some in 12 months to raise their bonuses and argue that this has already been approved by shareholders.

Companies can build their reputations by being in the first wave to take a more holistic look at corporate governance in general and executive remuneration in particular. Failing to do so, leaves them as potential laggards, the target of increasingly coordinated shareholder activists (especially if, for whatever reason, total shareholder return is low) and so increase reputational risk over the long term.

As Alistair Ross Goobey (2003), former CEO of activist investor Hermes and chairman of the International Corporate Governance Network, has noted, 'unfortunately a lot of companies with more introverted cultures are simply unaware of the reputational risks they face going into an AGM with a large number of shareholders opposed to parts of their remuneration packages'.

RESPONSIBLE SHAREHOLDING AND LONG-TERM FIDUCIARY DUTY

Linking values with value creation/value(s)-based management

An essential component of value-based management is an emphasis on communication – in style, tone as well as content – both internally and externally. Investors are not just looking for short-term rewards in the form of dividends and an increasing share price: they want long-term prospects for growth. There is now a great deal of evidence that the market evaluates management decisions according to their impact on long-term discounted cash flow.

Three pervasive misconceptions exist in connection with the investment community and their correctives are included in Figure 6.5.

Fig. 6.5

Market belief	Market reality
The market is short-term.	The market takes the long view.
Earnings per share dictate value.	Earnings tell us little about value.
Price-earnings multiples determine value.	Price-earnings multiples are a function of value.

Source: Rappaport and Mauboussin, 2001.

The market value drivers of public corporations have been clearly set out by Bob Monks who the *Economist* described in 2003 as 'perhaps America's most distinguished corporate governance activist'.[5] These distinguish between those that are company and country specific.

Fig. 6.6 Market value drivers of public corporations

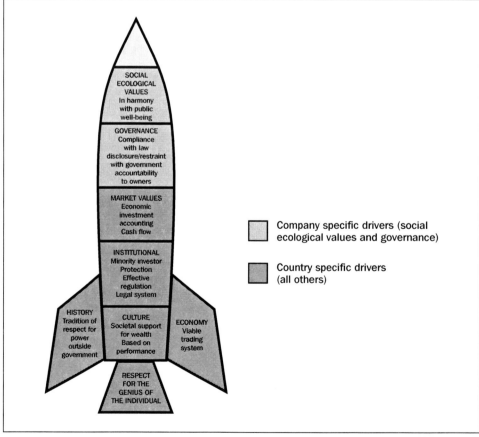

Source: Monks, 2003.

The competition for capital and the competitive environment are becoming increasingly:

- global – investors can shift funds anywhere
- demanding – investors' expectations keenly account for risk

Demand for improved corporate governance is increasing sharply around the world and managing for shareowner value can no longer take a back seat to other business priorities. A high degree of shareowner alignment has many benefits:

- it satisfies fiduciary responsibilities of the board to investors
- it increases investor and lender confidence
- it attracts more capital, hires top talent, allows companies to innovate and grow faster
- it enables companies to acquire and accelerate value-generation from under-performing and undervalued companies
- it reduces the risk of an unwanted takeover
- it minimizes the risk of painful restructuring and adverse publicity
- it rewards managers and employees with reasonable equity gains
- it creates a financial surplus to support community and environmental goals
- it obtains a higher share price.

In a major international industry survey Stern Stewart (originators of EVA) and Hackett Benchmarking and Research (2001) identified (*see* Figure 6.7) what the emerging best practices in shareowner alignment were.

Fig. 6.7 **Key best practices in shareowner alignment**

Leadership	■ Board focuses on long-term shareowner value and viability. ■ Management makes value-adding decisions.
Culture and organization	■ Middle managers have sound financial acumen. ■ Leaders communicate success consistently.
Decision making	■ Projects are funded solely on the basis of value.
Management reporting	■ A consistent focus on value metrics.

Fig. 6.8 Leadership: best practices and findings

Best practice	Actual findings
The board is primarily focused on shareowner value	Fewer than half of boards rank shareowner value or long-term viability of the firm as the number-one priority.
Management decisions focus on long-term value over short-term earnings impact.	Board members and management at value-aligned companies have a more material stake in the firm than at unaligned companies.
Board members and management have a material stake in the firm.	Many firms make value-destroying decisions to preserve short-term earnings; even value-aligned companies find short-term earnings tradeoffs difficult.
The firm communicates a wide range of information to the markets.	Over 80 per cent of firms communicate more information than required to the markets.

Fig. 6.9 Culture and organization: best practices and findings

Best practice	Actual findings
All levels of the organization are focused on shareowner value, are literate in finance and business elements, and have an understanding of key firm stakeholders.	Value focus, literacy and stakeholder understanding drop off drastically below the senior management level.
Firms have strong internal communication and share information with partners.	Internal and external communication are limited in most firms.
The structure of the firm establishes clear lines of sight.	Firms are mixed in the degree to which they encourage and manage new businesses.
The firm actively encourages the creation of new business and establishes mechanisms and cultures to do so.	The complexity of organization and profit recognition in many firms limits line of sight.

Fig. 6.10 Decision making: best practices and findings

Best practice	Actual findings
Planning processes are tightly integrated.	Only 25 per cent of companies consider their processes tightly integrated.
Measures are used consistently across processes to ensure continuity and measures are matched to strategic focus.	Measure overlap is under 50 per cent at best, and measures often do not match with strategy.
Managers proactively manage risk.	Risk management is generally informal.
Functional managers make decisions that consider impact on other functions.	In 30–70 per cent of companies, managers make functional decisions without considering impact across functions.
Managers understand the cost of capital, and it is readily available to value-adding projects.	At about two-thirds of companies, managers understand the cost of capital, but the capital process is still tightly controlled.

Fig. 6.11 Management reporting: best practices and findings

Best practice	Actual findings
Management reporting focuses on indicators that track value and its drivers and have continuity with planning processes.	Only 20 per cent of companies focus primarily on value metrics; most reporting is traditional financial; and continuity with the planning process is minimal.
Accounting practices are adjusted to match expenses with the value they generate.	Most scorecards are unbalanced and often misused for purposes such as incentive compensation.
Scorecards reflect a true balance of indicators and are used for operating guidance.	Most companies benchmark frequently within their industries; few benchmark outside.
The best companies benchmark frequently within and outside their industries to identify best practices.	Few companies consistently capitalize expenses that generate long-term value.

Source: Stern Stewart and Hackett Benchmarking and Research, 2001.

The key message for boards in the quest for value is that we are seeing every buy-seller exchange increasingly coloured by values – which may be economic, informational, emotional, and/or ethical. This can be traced back to Adam Smith at least who suggested that 'the health of corporate capitalism comes down to the exercise of virtue'. As the interplay between values and value creation moves further into the spotlight and as the economic winds blow hard, companies aspiring to world class ethical behaviour must get a grip on what their key shareholders (as well as their most valued customers and most talented employees) think, perceive and believe. Such attitudes and behaviours will increasingly be fundamental for any company wanting to sustain value.

This in fact calls for 'an inclusive approach' which specifically links risk management and reputation.

Fig. 6.12 An inclusive approach

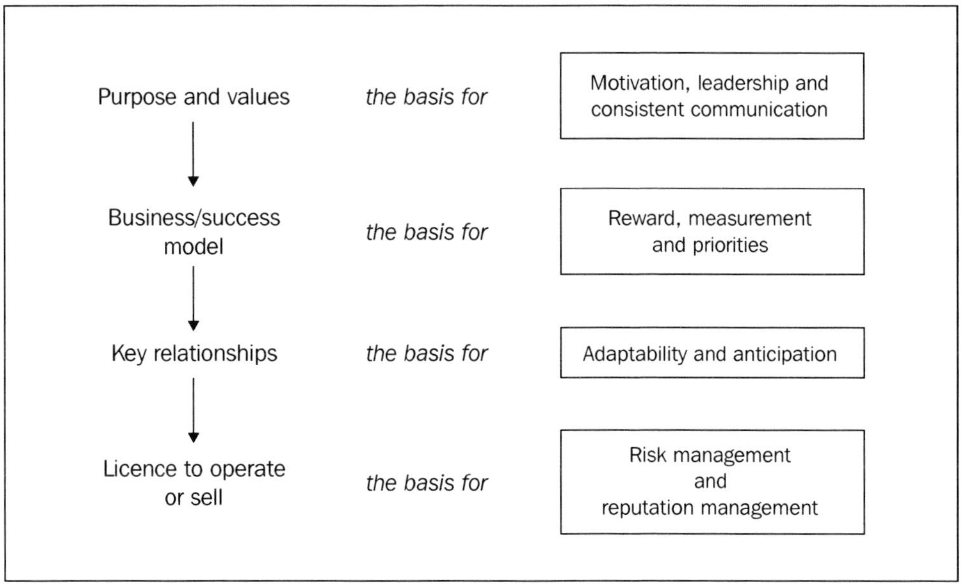

Purpose and values	*the basis for*	Motivation, leadership and consistent communication
↓		
Business/success model	*the basis for*	Reward, measurement and priorities
↓		
Key relationships	*the basis for*	Adaptability and anticipation
↓		
Licence to operate or sell	*the basis for*	Risk management and reputation management

Source: Goyder and Desmond, 2001 (adapted).

THE EMERGENCE OF PENSION FUNDS

In the late twentieth century, a new type of shareholder emerged: the global investor. Whether based in New York, Boston or London, global investors (often pension funds for government employees) are buying significant amounts of corporate equity. More importantly, in an increasing number of cases, they are showing signs of responsible ownership as historically significant as investment in early trading companies. There are several key areas of evidence and trends:

- the size of US outbound investment – both direct investment (in assets and entire companies) and portfolio investments (in stock)

- foreign issuers have made more of their equity available in US markets, sparking a dramatic growth in American Depository Receipts (ADRs) traded on US stock exchanges. The number of US exchange listed ADR programmes more than doubled between 1992 and 1998 (from 215 to 484) and the volume of listed ADRs nearly quadrupled (from $125 billion to $555 billion)

- a global market-place for ownership has emerged. With few exceptions, all equity markets, large and small, are to some degree now foreign owned.

The significance of the global equity movement becomes even greater when we focus on how the modern investment process works. The companies that sell shares to investors use the funds from their sale of equity, along with funds derived from internal cash flow and borrowing, to buy plant and equipment or to invest in research and development – in fact in the whole range of assets, tangible and intangible, that help grow their business. This process of corporate investment literally creates the future of society. Here decisions are made that shape the future, determining which regions will prosper, what technologies will be advanced, which jobs will be created and what educational requirements will be set.

Half of the shares in the US and 80 per cent of the shares in the UK, are held by institutions that manage money for the benefit of pension holders. As more and more final salary schemes are phased out, people have a direct interest in the share price of the companies that their pension funds have invested in.

It used to make perfect sense to distinguish sharply between 'portfolio investment' and 'direct investment'. Portfolio investment suggested the absence of power; direct investment, the presence of power. Today, however, these two types of investment – portfolio and direct – are beginning to converge.

Fig. 6.13 The new global investors: who are they?

Rank	Fund	Country	Assets (US$ bn.)
1	Stichting Pensioenfonds ABP	Netherlands	159.7
2	California Public Employees' Retirement	US	133.5
3	Association of Local Public Service Personnel	Japan	101.3
4	New York State Common Retirement Fund	US	99.7
5	General Motors Investment Management Corporation	US	87
6	California State Teachers' Retirement	US	82.6
7	Alimanna Pensionsfonden (Board 1, 2 & 3)	Sweden	80.1
8	Florida State Board of Administration	US	77.5
9	National Public Service Personnel	Japan	75.6
10	New York State Teachers' Retirement System	US	71.1
11	Texas Teacher Retirement	US	69.5
12	Public School Personnel	Japan	67.1
13	Federal Retirement Thrift Investment Board	US	64.5
14	New Jersey Division of Investment	US	63.3
15	General Electric	US	58.7

Source: Monks, 2001.

NB Asset values will be lower as a result of falling equity prices (though many will have exposure through other asset classes) but this is also true for other investors.

The rise of the global investor pressure is happening at the same time that the clamour for regulatory change is growing.

The Myners report (2001)

In the UK, the Myners Report (HM Treasury 2001), the landmark review on institutional investment led by Paul Myners, former chief executive of Gartmore, argued persuasively that for too long, regulators and trustees have allowed the interests of fund managers or pension plan sponsors to take precedence over the need for the sole benefit of pension plan participants. Myners warned of the destruction of value suffered by shareholders if they adopted a passive approach to underperforming companies. The government subsequently issued threats to introduce legislation to compel shareholders to become more activist. In response, leading fund managers drew up an industry code for tackling underperforming companies. The trustee boards of pension schemes have also been putting increasing pressure on fund managers to act.

The government is assessing pension funds' compliance with a code of best practice, devised by Myners. This has been partly fuelled by news that UK pension funds lost about £100 billion in 2002, continuing to invest heavily in equities, even as the markets plunged deeper into trouble, arguably taking excessive risks and increasing the likelihood of a collapse of a big corporate pension scheme. Paul Myners himself is now an NED at Marks & Spencer which has one of the top ten pension funds in the UK in terms of asset size.

The Government intends to legislate to require trustees and fund managers to use shareholder powers to intervene in companies, where this is in the interests of shareholders and beneficiaries. This principle will therefore differ from the other Myners principles in that compliance will be mandatory. However, a key point is that it is the trustees who will retain the overall responsibility for corporate governance, as this is required by their fiduciary duties. Trustees will not be able to delegate their responsibility for ensuring that the duty of active shareholding is carried out. In order to enforce the new legislation, the Government is proposing to make a breach of the new statutory duty the subject of civil proceedings. Funds will also have to disclose their approach to activism in the Statement of Investment Principles or trustees' report and accounts.

Long-term fiduciary duty also extends to being clear about behaviour with specialist advisers. One area where companies are increasingly vulnerable is in their relationships with remuneration consultants, who have a vested interest in designing ever more lucrative pay schemes for companies. Often they are hired directly by the management benefiting from such schemes rather than by independent board remuneration committees. One major consultancy, Towers

Perrin, advises nine out of the top ten companies and is lead adviser to seven of them. Towers Perrin provides other services to all except one of these nine companies. Only BP and Diageo have appointed consultants who do not also advise the management. As well as advising GSK, Towers Perrin also acted for Barclays, Reckitt Benckiser, BG, Reuters and ICI, whose boardroom deals were all greeted with significant shareholder revolts in 2003. At a cost of up to £5,000 an hour, it is the biggest of the boutique operators providing such advice.

Research by Derek Higgs for his report on non-executive directors (DTI/Higgs, 2003) indicated that consultants were 'too ready to encourage firms to position their remuneration policy in the "upper quartile", or top 25 per cent of their peer group'. This view is also shared in the US. The Conference Board Commission on Public Trust and Private Enterprise, set up in the wake of Enron and WorldCom and chaired by John Snow (The Conference Board, 2003), just before his appointment as US Treasury Secretary, suggested that 'the balance in the relationship between board, management and compensation consultants has, in too many cases, been skewed to produce an overly close relationship between consultants and management'.

Under new regulations in 2003, 180 of the FTSE 350 companies have been obliged to disclose which remuneration consultants they use in their annual reports so consultants such as Towers Perrin are increasingly falling under scrutiny. Never having been involved in accountancy, it has benefited from the post-Enron laws in the US banning accountants from performing non-audit consultancy work for their audit clients.

THE RISE AND RISE OF SOCIALLY RESPONSIBLE INVESTMENT (SRI)

If there is a social values underway the retail opportunity has not been missed by fund management groups who have launched a growing number of ethical funds. The drivers actually vary by region (*see* Table 6.6).

While an explosion in institutional interest may be some way off, a modest number of SRI mandates suggest a steady trickle of demand. One recent survey found that 73 per cent of asset managers believe that SRI mandates will increase in 2003 in the UK while 75 per cent believe they are on the increase in continental Europe. However, at just 1 to 2 per cent of overall pension fund money, SRI investment in the UK is still dwarfed by developments in the US. A recent study by Calvert (*http://www.calvert.com*), a US consultancy, estimated that, in ten years' time, SRI will represent 10 per cent of all US mutual fund assets.

In 2002 the socially responsible investment (SRI) market came of age in Europe, with the Nordic countries leading the way, and Germany and France close behind.

However, UK institutions, apart from some local authority schemes, have resisted putting their money in the sector for fear it would constrain their returns.

Table 6.6 **Market trends and drivers**

UK	■ Pensions disclosure regulation requires pension fund trustees to state 'how (if at all) social, environmental and ethical considerations are taken into account in the selection, retention and realization of investments'. ■ £4 billion under management in over 50 retail SRI funds.
EU	■ Government support in Germany, France and Scandinavia. ■ Retail and institutional demand both growing.
North America	■ $2 trillion invested in a socially responsible manner. ■ 82 per cent growth between 1997 and 1999.
Asia	■ Rapidly growing investor interest in Japan and legislative support in Australia.

Source: HSBC, 2002.

Continental Europe has seen the launch of several products as well as a number of partnerships between fund managers and SRI consultants. Institutions, including the Swedish national pension funds and Dutch giants ABP and PGGM, have allocated assets to funds or adopted an SRI overlay for entire portfolios. Sweden, Norway, Denmark and Finland are blazing the SRI trail with more investors demanding transparency on environmental and ethical issues.

In 2002 assets committed to SRI funds in Sweden increased tenfold to more than €6 billion ($6 billion), representing pledges from public funds, trade unions and foundations to invest 10 per cent of funds into the asset class. Following new legislation reforming Germany's pension system, certified private and occupational pension schemes have to report whether ethical, ecological and social aspects are taken into account when investing paid-in contributions.

A pan-Europe accreditation standard for SRI funds aims to filter out 'ethics-lite' fund managers. Pressure for such a standard has grown during the past year amid SRI industry concerns that new entrants to SRI fund management claim stringent social and environmental criteria but practise otherwise.

The European Commission has commissioned the Netherlands-based European Sustainable and Responsible Investment Forum (Eurosif) to create a voluntary standard. The standard, planned for introduction in 2003, is to be developed along the lines of a 14-point code launched the same year by the Dutch Association of Investors for Sustainable Development. It encourages SRI fund managers to disclose how they choose their investments and what methods they use to assess companies. With the shake-up in corporate governance after the Ahold scandal (described by the EU as Europe's Enron) it remains to be seen how credible a Netherlands-driven approach can be.

Two developments in mid-2003 which will encourage increased shareholder interest in CSR issues are:

■ The SEC's new regulations on proxy voting which will require more than 6,000 registered investment advisers with authority to vote clients' shares, provide procedures for evaluating and voting proxies, and Proxy voting guidelines to clients on request. The SEC states that 'the duty of care requires an adviser with proxy voting authority to monitor corporate events and to vote the proxies' on areas such as 'corporate governance matters' and 'social and corporate responsibility issues'.

■ The Australian Securities and Investments Commission ruling that financial advisers providing personal financial advice should enquire whether environmental, social or ethical considerations are important to their clients.

Fig. 6.14 Largest funds in Europe (on 31 December 2001)

Ranking December 2001	Ranking June 2001	Asset management company	Name of the fund	Country of the mother company	Asset (million Euro)
1	2	Friends Ivory & Sime Plc (now ISI Asset Management)	Friends Provident Stewardship Unit Trust	United Kingdom	919
2	1	Sanpaolo-IMI Asset Management SGR	Sanpaolo Azionario Internazionale Etico	Italy	775
3	3	Framlington	Health Fund	United Kingdom	700
4	5	ABN AMRO Asset Management	ABN AMRO Groen Fonds	Netherlands	463
5	4	Sanpaolo-IMI Asset Management SGR	Sanpaolo Obbligazionario Etico	Italy	462
6	new entry	UBS Asset Management	UBS (Lux) EF Eco Performance	Switzerland	445
7	7	Dexia Asset Management	Stimulus Invest Stimulus European Balanced Medium	Belgium	410
8	9	SNS Asset Management	ASN Aandelen fonds N.V.	Netherlands	292
9	6	Henderson Global Investors	NPI Global Care Growth	United Kingdom	274
10	new entry	ING Fund Management B.V. and ING Bank Fondsen Beheer B.V.	ING Bank Duurzaam Rendement Fonds	Netherlands	254

Source: SiRi Group/Avanzi in cooperation with CSR Europe 2002.

Table 6.7 SRI market size

Worldwide	Total value of SRI portfolios is between US$1.4 trillion and US$1.5 trillion. SRI mutual funds represent approximately US$33 billion, far less than 1 per cent of the global collective investment scheme market-place. NB Cerrulli only count mutual funds that declare socially responsible objectives in their annual reviews. Cerrulli predict that worldwide, SRI mutual funds could hold US$150 billion by 2005.
UK	■ the UK is the leading provider of ethical pension funds in Europe. ■ 32 ethical pension funds are based in the UK with UK funds most likely to employ strategies of ethical screening and engagement when investing. ■ 101 retail ethical funds under management in the UK.
Europe	SRI funds available to private investors increased by 58 per cent to 251 funds between January 2000 and June 2001. Total assets under SRI management increased by 36 per cent, from €11.1 billion at the end of 1999 to €15.1 billion in mid-2001. However, despite the impressive increase in SRI funds across Europe, the sector represents only a very limited portion – just 0.43 per cent of total assets managed by European funds, although in the UK alone it amounted to 1.03 per cent.
USA	SRI assets in the US topped a record $2 trillion in assets in 2001, capping two years of outsized growth despite a market turndown. Assets in socially screened investment portfolios rose by 36 per cent from the second half of 1999 to the middle of 2001. There are now 230 SRI mutual funds in the US, up from 168 socially screened funds identified in 1999. Nearly two-thirds of all socially screened funds tracked by the Forum earned one of the two highest rankings for performance from either Lipper or Morningstar or both.

In the UK, total SRI assets grew from £22.7 billion in 1997 to £224.5 billion at the end of 2001. Currently assets in SRI funds are relatively small in the UK – about £3.7 billion of retail and over £50 billion of institutional money. Whatever the importance of environmental, human rights and corporate governance concerns, performance of SRI portfolios is likely to be the overriding factor influencing investment decisions. Unfortunately, performance so far gives no strong indication either way. In 2002, the DJSI (Sustainability) Stoxx Index on average slightly underperformed the MSCI Europe Index, while over the same period, the FTSE4Good Index marginally outperformed the FTSE All-World Developed Index.

However, take-up of SRI has been slow. Heavy investment losses suffered by most funds have overridden any ethical concerns trustees may have and SRI remains patchily supported at best by UK institutional investors. Weak fund flows have forced several providers to close retail SRI funds as asset management firms consolidate their investment range in a bid to cut high cost-bases. Some of the growth will probably come from local authority funds, especially when combined with the TUC's new-found enthusiasm for shareholder activism. The £18 billion University Superannuation Scheme (USS), view SRI as part of an overall programme of corporate governance. Those active in marketing SRI funds include Morley, Henderson Global Investors, Isis Asset Management and HBOS's Insight Investment, and in Japan, Nikko Securities.

Pension funds, which control around £720 billion of assets own around 20 per cent of the UK stock market. Since July 2000, UK pension funds must state whether they take into account social and environmental matters in investment decision making as part of their mandatory statement of investment principles. There is no compunction by Government if they fail to do so and, unsurprisingly, it has not sparked off a flood of investor money into the sector.

The pace quickened in 2001 when the Association of British Insurers, which control another 20 per cent of that market, issued voluntary guidelines for members raising awareness of the potential risk to bottom lines from social and environmental issues. These guidelines are being steadily adopted by more than a dozen of the UK's largest investment institutions, with combined assets of more than £1 trillion so they could give substantial impetus to corporate activity in this area.

The creation of the FTSE4Good in July 2001 as an ethical index which operates an exclusion policy on certain stocks, has also given the profile of the SRI market in the UK a boost. The new index raises awareness in all parts of the market and has caught the attention of many companies. The FTSE4Good index is the first attempt at identifying companies that implement good ethics across a range of issues and has attracted about $25 billion of institutional and retail funds. The hurdle is that the level of disclosure by companies is varied. That is improving but there are not any set criteria on which it is possible to measure companies with companies using different methods of reporting or different types of data – an issue which Ken Rushton, Director of Listing at the FSA, recently indicated his increasing impatience.

Both the Dow Jones Sustainability and the FTSE4Good indices evaluate companies that place importance on issues such as strategic planning, corporate governance, environmental reporting, environmental product design, human rights and policies on corruption. The Dow Jones index, which started in 1999, has a policy of including all sectors and picking the best SRI practitioners in each. However, FTSE International claims that since the Dow Jones index compilers invite companies to apply, it looks at a much smaller universe than FTSE. FTSE4Good by comparison looks at about 2,200 companies. However, it contains only those that meet FTSE's criteria on social, environmental and human rights issues. It specifically excludes certain sectors – tobacco, arms manufacturers and nuclear power or uranium producers. As a result, about 55 per cent of companies in the FTSE All-Share are excluded from the FTSE4Good index.

Cynics from customers to NGOs, remain to be convinced that ethical indices are anything other than subjective, politically expedient, economically naïve and over complicated. Indices exclude Tesco while including the likes of BP and Shell or companies such as WorldCom and Global Crossing. When launched, some high profile FTSE 100 names such as Tesco and Royal Bank of Scotland were excluded from FTSE4Good, largely because they had failed to publicize adequately the SRI initiatives they were taking (both companies have since been added).

Fig. 6.15 The most frequent stocks in SRI funds portfolios (on 31 December 2001)

Ranking December 2001	Ranking June 2001	Most common stock
1	2	Nokia
2	4	Johnson & Johnson
3	1	Vodafone
4	3	GlaxoSmithKline
5	8	ING
5	new entry	Vivendi
7	16	Royal Dutch Shell
8	6	Pfizer
9	11	BP
10	new entry	Home Depot
11	14	Intel
12	17	Lloyds TSB
13	20	Fannie Mae
14	new entry	Ericsson
15	new entry	Aventis
16	new entry	Sanofi Synthelabo
17	5	Royal Bank of Scotland
18	13	Microsoft
19	new entry	BNP Paribas
20	new entry	L'Oreal

Source: SiRi Group/Avanzi in cooperation with CSR Europe 2002.

Most providers prefer engaging with poorly managed and underperforming companies rather than excluding them. They argue that as shareholders it is possible to drive through reforms that will improve share performance in the long term. Engagement is 'active and sustained dialogue with companies to deepen our analysis and use our position as a shareholder to exercise influence for improvement'.[6] Hermes, the corporate governance investment manager owned by the BT pension scheme, adopts this approach through its Focus funds. There are important legal reasons why engagement is better than exclusion. A seminal judgment made in 1984 following the coal miners' dispute ruled it was not permissible to exclude stocks from portfolios purely on ethical grounds. Perhaps this is just as well, as some sectors often excluded on ethical grounds, including US oil stocks and tobacco, have been some of the best performers in the last 12 months and have even encouraged the launch of 'sin' funds in the US.

Table 6.8   SRI Methodologies

Negative screening	Excluding business which do not meet certain defined social responsibility standards (e.g. get involved in tobacco industry gambling).	41 per cent
Positive screening	Actively selecting businesses at the forefront of social responsibility.	22 per cent
Active engagement	Working with portfolio businesses to develop practices which meet defined social responsibility criteria.	22 per cent

NB

1 There seems to be a greater acceptance of screening as an option.
2 A small percentage of fund managers would use a combination of screening and active engagement with others leaving it to their clients to lead on the methodology to be employed or indeed to undertake their own screening.

Source: Deloitte & Touche, 2002.

SRI's continued growth (albeit from a low base) should not obscure the fact that it actually has its own share of reputational risks – that, unless addressed soon, threaten the credibility of a nascent movement. The single biggest issue is survey fatigue which even Stephen Timms, the UK Government's Minister for CSR, has acknowledged. In 2003, the Investor Relations Society found that 68 per cent of in-house investor relations practitioners agreed or agreed strongly that CSR questionnaire fatigue 'is a real problem'. This problem is compounded by the sheer number and apparent lack of accountability of many CSR interest groups with companies not aware that many of the lobby groups in question do not merit serious attention. One logical response – to publish the results of a key questionnaire from major mainstream investor(s) or industry groups such as the ABI or NAPF seems to be overlooked – and yet could save time, cost and build reputation if companies have the courage to be more open about their responses. Minor CSR lobby groups (or even some SRI fund managers) sending questionnaires could then be directed to the corporate website where answers to major stakeholders (shareholders?) appear. There are other issues:

1 Fund performance – while 'vicars' indices' which exclude tobacco, alcohol, gambling and defence have fallen 20 per cent tobacco has outperformed them by 40 per cent and defence and beverages by more than 25 per cent in 2002.

2 The quality of SRI analysts and training – this is a real issue and threatens to undermine engagement with companies. There is no formal qualification required to be an SRI analyst and very few have hard commercial experience with most from the not-for-profit sector or from academia. Despite ostensible concern with diversity issues, almost all SRI analysts are themselves white.

3 Weak links to primary research – often links between SRI analysts are poorly developed with sector analysts in mainstream funds. It is still not clear if and when the SRI analysts communicate internally and how they are directly involved in corporate assessment. As one FTSE 100 CSR Manager retorted to a question from one leading SRI analyst to what the CSR Manager was doing to encourage CSR, 'what are *you* doing' [in sharing knowledge with your sector analyst colleagues to achieve a better understanding of corporate behaviour]?

4 No clear definition of what constitutes SRI – in the US one of the leading funds still excludes corporate governance because the area is 'too complex'.

5 No consistent methodology – that makes it very difficult for companies, let alone investors, to use, evaluate and compare analytical approaches.

6 Lack of rigour in analysis – country analysis is often too superficial (e.g. China) and sector distinctions are seldom made (putting a consumer corporate brand like an M&S in the same bracket as a BP).

7 Silence prior to Enron – as the Global Head of CSR with Zurich Financial Services put it to a meeting of the Conference Board days after Enron's CEO appeared before Congress, 'how did the analysts (including the SRI analysts) miss the warning signs regarding Enron?'

8 Finance sector turmoil – leading SRI players have suffered from their parents' weak reputations with customers (Insight Investment's parent, HBOS, was fined £750,000 by the Financial Services Authority in February 2003 for putting 30,000 customers at risk of losing money from their PEP and ISA investments) and shareholders (Henderson's parent AMP lost half of its board the same month on the eve of handing down its yearly profit results with the chairman bringing forward his retirement by five months and four other board members agreeing to leave over the next six months). This has arguably become a credibility with some investors who have shouted loudest about SRI and governance and then attacked by their own shareholders. Shareholders at Aviva, parent of Morley Fund Management, called the directors 'fat cats' and 'incompetent' at their 2003 AGM. Of the shareholders 14 per cent voted against the group's executive remuneration policy, which allowed the CEO a pay increase last year to more than £1 million. The more than 40 per cent rise was granted in a year when

Aviva's operating profits dropped by £200 million, shares in the merged Norwich Union group halved and Aviva cut its dividend substantially.

That said, although the market in SRI investment funds is well under 10 per cent of the global asset management market, SRI considerations *are* beginning to have a much broader effect on investment decisions. While definitions of what constitutes socially responsible investment vary, the influence on portfolio selection of ethical criteria is growing in importance. Indeed BA chairman Lord Marshall and Unilever's chairman and CEO, Niall Fitzgerald, together stressed exactly this point at a meeting at Chatham House in October 2002. Even traditional broking houses such as Cazenove, Dresdner, HSBC, UBS and Goldman Sachs have appointed SRI analysts. One leading corporate governance institutional investor, for instance, published its own Socially Responsible Investment Statement of Principles and Policies at the end of 2002 and made a clear link with reputational risk:

> *Standard Life Investments believes that a company run in the long-term interests of its shareholders should manage its relationships with its employees, suppliers and customers, and behave responsibly towards the environment and society as a whole. Companies that demonstrate a commitment to environmental and social responsibility are likely to enjoy comparative advantage in the long run. Increasingly, companies that fail to maintain adequate processes to manage these issues risk damage to their reputation and consequent negative effects on their brand and image that can directly affect their financial performance.*
>
> *Because we take our responsibility as a shareholder seriously, we seek to use our influence to encourage the achievement of best practice standards of environmental and social management at the companies in which we invest with a view to protecting and enhancing the value of the investments held on behalf of our customers.*
>
> Standard Life, 2002.

The key message for companies is to watch and proactively address the increasing influence of SRI-type thinking on mainstream investors. Even mainstream investors and asset managers need to latch onto perceived 'best of class' companies, not least to drive perception of their own leadership in asset allocation and stock selection decisions to secure more business themselves, e.g. from pension funds.

EXECUTIVE SUMMARY

1   Market behaviour often diverges from what we would expect in a rational efficient market. Psychology matters, people are irrational, markets do not

always work. This is seen for example in the manipulation of corporate earnings and managers' financial reporting behaviour.

2   People want to invest in companies they trust, understand and believe in. Financial analysts are no different. In financial markets credibility is a function of three things: corporate performance, consistent truth and a clear willingness to deal forthrightly with the public and those who analyse securities on their behalf.

3   Sell-side and buy-side investors alike make their own decisions about non-financial performance and then act upon these evaluations.

4   Reputational risk in financial markets is driven in large part by market sentiment (the central mood that drives individual share prices, sectors and the equity market as a whole). It is made worse where there is the slightest doubt about a company's credibility, honesty or the opacity of its accounts.

5   CEOs may do better in managing expectations than managing the company.

6   The value of a company is the present value of the expected cash flows on the company and implicit in this are investors' views about the company, the behaviour and credibility of its management and the potential for excess returns.

7   Superior corporate governance can both significantly increase corporate value and substantially reduce the risk of corporate failure. However, it remains a great concern for institutional investors worldwide and on a par with financial indicators when evaluating investment decisions. At its core it is about creating value from the quality of decision making. It is concerned with value, accountability, consensus, action and quality.

8   A critical area which ties together the work of the NEDs set out by Higgs and the Audit Committee set by Smith is the Operating and Financial Review (OFR).

9   Institutional investors were growing more activist, even before Enron. An increasing number of large non-institutional investment funds now specifically target underperforming European companies. Small shareholder coalitions have also grown in importance.

10 The influence on portfolio selection of ethical criteria is a more important trend and has been recognized as such by the FSA, several FTSE 100 boards and traditional broking houses. Companies need to watch and proactively address the increasing influence of SRI-type thinking on mainstream investors.

Key message

Internal ethics – corporate governance and clear accounting – are also a social responsibility and corporate behaviour matters to every investor.

What you must ask of your team/staff/consultants

1   Who are our top three shareholders?

2   How are we perceived in terms of our corporate governance by our executive team, our most powerful shareholders and our own pension fund managers?

3   Is our institutional investor base changing in terms of geographic profile?

4   What does our board expect from the employees?

5   What do we expect from our board?

6   Do we have an engagement policy with shareholder activists and SRI analysts?

7   If we do, how do we know it is effective?

8   If not, do we need one?

What you must do today

1   Set aside 60 minutes in the next seven days to read, reflect and react as necessary to Higgs and Smith (using this Chapter as a guide).

2   Try and identify the similarities and differences between what our key shareholders expect of us.

3   Track our share price over ten years and see if we can explain key high/low points.

4   Retrieve the board profile for the company you admire most.

5   Reflect on what would appeal most to a SRI investor in our company.

6   Look at how we describe our risk exposure and processes in our Annual Report.

Related websites

DTI post Enron initiatives
http://www.dti.gov.uk/cld/post_enron.htm

The Corporate Library
http://www.thecorporatelibrary.com

Henley Management College Centre for Board Effectiveness
www.henleymc.ac.uk/henleymc02.nsf/pages/cbe

CalPERS' corporate governance
www.calpers-governance.org/forumhome.asp

Insight Investment (HBOS)
www.insightinvestment.com/Responsibility

Notes

1 The rankings were based upon 57 separate questions, of which approximately 70 per cent were strictly quantitative (i.e. 'is the chairman of the board an independent, non-executive director?') and approximately 30 per cent involved subjective judgement by the CLSA analyst (i.e. 'is it true that there have been no controversies or questions raised over whether the board and senior management have made decisions in the past five years that benefit them, at the expense of shareholders?').

2 Alan Buchanan, Company Secretary, British Airways in evidence to the Higgs Review, 16 September 2002.

3 About 95 million Americans invest in mutual funds, either directly or as an option in their 401(k) or other employer-provided retirement plans. More than $6.6 trillion is invested in the thousands of funds now on the market, and mutual fund money accounts for about 21 per cent of the ownership of American companies.

4 Members of the panel included former Federal Reserve Chairman Paul Volcker, former SEC Chairman Arthur Levitt, Intel Chairman Andrew Grove and former TIAA-CREF President John Biggs.

5 Monks has been a pioneer in the shareholder activist movement though his views are now very much at the heart of mainstream thinking in terms of best practice. He is more than just a thinker. He led campaigns to reform Sears Roebuck, Eastman Kodak and Westinghouse and now acts as deputy Chairman of the activist Focus funds run by Hermes, one of the largest UK fund managers. He is also President of Henley Management College's Centre for Board Effectiveness.

6 Rob Lake, Head of SRI Engagement and Corporate Governance at Henderson Global Investors, 2003.

References

All Europe Research Team (2002) in Golding, Tony (2003) *The City: Inside the Great Expectations Machine*. London: Financial Times Prentice Hall.

Deloitte & Touche (2002) *Socially Responsible Investment Survey*. http://www.deloitte.co.uk.

DTI (2002) Modernizing Company Law: Draft Clauses (Companies Bill, Cm 5553–11). HMSO. July.

DTI/Higgs, Derek (2003) *Review of the Role and Effectiveness of Non-Executive Directors*. London: DTI. http://www.dti.gov.uk/cld/non_exec_review/pdfs/higgsreport.pdf.

Financial Reporting Council (2003) Audit Committees Combined Code Guidance: a Report and Proposed Guidance by an FRC-appointed group chaired by Sir Robert Smith. London: Financial Reporting Council.

Financial Times (2003) 'Study Criticizes Companies for Poor Reports', 6 February.

Fitzgerald, Niall (2003) Birmingham Post. 8 May.

Goobey, Ross (2003) 'Shareholders Seize Their Power'. Financial Times, 26 April.

Goyder, Mark and Desmond, Peter (2001) 'The Role of Leadership' in Business Ethics. London: Economist and Profile Books.

Hewitt, Patricia, Trade and Industry Secretary (2003) Financial Times, 10 April.

Higgs Report (2003) Review of the Role and Effectiveness of Non-Executive Directors. London: DTI. http://www.dti.gov.uk/cld/non_exec_review/pdfs/higgsreport.pdf.

HM Treasury (2001) Myners Review of Institutional Investment. London: HM Treasury.

HSBC (2002) Presentation by Mike Tyrell, HSBC to a joint meeting of the Conference Board's European Council on Corporate Governance and Board Effectiveness and European Research Working Group on Corporate Citizenship. March, Brussels.

King, Mervyn (2003) Presentation to conference at the Royal Institute of International Affairs Good Profits: Rebuilding Trust in Corporations. 11 February, Chatham House, London.

KPMG Survey (2002) http://www/kpmg.com.

Larsen, Dennis (2002) Determining the Relationship Between Investor Relations and Reputation. 6th International Conference on Corporate Reputation. Boston, May 23–5.

McKinsey (2002) Global Investor Opinion Survey. http://www.mckinsey.com/practices/corporategovernance/research/.

Monks, Robert (2001) The New Global Investors – How Shareholders Can Unlock Sustainable Prosperity Worldwide. Oxford: Capstone.

Monks, Robert (2003) The Market Value Drivers of Public Corporations. http://www.raqm.com/rocket/index.html.

Rappaport, Alfred and Mauboussin, Michael (2001) Expectations Investing. Boston, MA: Harvard Business School Press.

Rogers, Jonathan and Stocken, Phillip (2002) Credibility of Management Forecasts. Philadelphia: The Wharton School, University of Pennsylvania.

SiRi Group (2002) Green, Social and Ethical Funds. http://www.sirigroup.com/pdf/SRI-Funds-Report2002.pdf.

Standard Life (2002) *Socially Responsible Investment Statement of Principles and Policies*. Edinburgh: Standard Life. *http://www.standardlife.com/page.php?id_link=675*.

Stern Stewart and Hackett Benchmarking and Research (2001) Emerging Best Practices in Shareholder Alignment. *http://www.saisurvey.com*.

Thaler, Richard (1999) 'The End of Behavioural Finance'. *Financial Analysts Journal*. November.

The Conference Board (2003) *The Commission on Public Trust and Private Enterprise*. NY: The Conference Board.

TUC (2003) *Working Capital: Institutional Investment Strategy*. London: TUC. *http://www.tuc.org.uk/pensions/tuc-6269-fo.pdf*.

Zaman, Arif (2003) Unpublished MBA dissertation. Henley Management College.

7

Globalization, international relationships and responsibilities

WHAT YOU MUST KNOW BEFORE YOU START

1 What do we mean by political risk?

2 How does this connect to reputational risk in emerging markets?

3 How does reputational risk affect alliances, joint ventures and strategic relationships?

4 Should we focus on corporate responsibility or corporate social responsibility (CSR)?

5 Is there a relationship between reputational risk and sustainable development?

6 What is the link between corporate governance and global governance?

GLOBALIZATION AND POLITICAL RISK – WHAT HAS CHANGED?

Political risk is usually understood to be something to do with regulatory risk, country instability, security consultancy (often provided by an organization like Control Risks Group) and insurance (often provided by a major broker such as Marsh).

This is of limited value in the context of companies and reputational risk as described in this book. It also ignores the fact that as a result of globalization (and the backlash to it), political risk is becoming defined in broader ways. These include societal drivers and the actions of non-governmental players (though not necessarily campaigning mainly western NGOs but also trade unions, independent think tanks and academia). Moreover political risk needs to be seen as both the actions of legitimate government authorities but also as events caused by factors outside the control of government. This definition recognizes clearly that companies' political risks are increasingly subject to societal conditions and societal expectations.

Case study 7.1

Changed identities – the new generation in Saudi Arabia

No question will be more decisive for the Middle East and the Islamic world, as for the stability of the global energy market, than the future of Saudi Arabia. Yet in understanding the regional or wider dynamics (e.g. implications for US companies of the new-found tension between the US and Saudi Arabia post 9/11 or the unusually open criticism by Muslim artists, politicians and commentators of some religious leaders in Saudi Arabia and across the Islamic world) one level of analysis is often missing – understanding Saudi expectations and fears.

To investigate what Saudis really think, the outlook, expectations and frustrations of the younger generation need to come under focus. Saudis are struggling to come to terms with economic and social uncertainty, globalization and freedom of political and intellectual expression. There has been a marked shift away from the relatively open and relaxed view of the US in the past. A strongly articulated sense of moral decline expressed by contemporary youth is frequently voiced alongside criticism of the relations between Saudi Arabia and western powers, especially the US. Sometimes this is couched in terms of cultural values and fears of a weakening of cultural integrity.

This is not the stuff of conventional market research but such an analysis (political and social) is needed to understand how western companies especially can build relationships with local customers, suppliers and policy-makers whether BA flying in to Jeddah or Sony exporting the latest Playstation there (important markets for both companies).

It became clear after 9/11 that conventional analysis of country political risk was not enough. The terrorists behind the World Trade Center attack were distinctive in various ways:

- a loose-knit network without even a cell structure across dozens of countries
- not easily infiltrated
- important communications were in Internet code or by hand
- they adapt simple solutions
- suicide bombers need no escape route
- they take the long view and undergo laborious training
- they probably have ambitious plans unimaginable to opponents.

There are two ways companies can respond:

1   The first – and more obvious – is more internally-driven and deals with the areas over which companies can still exert some control even at times of increased geopolitical risk. This takes a more transaction and quantitative-based approach: increase investment in security, ensure meticulous compliance to corporate and government safety and security measures in place. In fact the more effective approaches will be those where this is seen simply as part of the culture and the way that people behave.

    Two examples of how companies need to respond to supply chain risk – in goods and services – show this in action.

    An example for manufacturing companies is where US Customs are now expecting companies that import and export products to be aware not only of their own means of security, but also that of their clients. The logic is that should there be another attack on the US, only certified companies would be able to move cargo across the borders or through US ports.

    An example in the service sector is anti-money laundering. Over the past two years, there have been a great many changes in the anti-money laundering laws and regulations in the UK, the US and many other jurisdictions. While some of these changes are a response to the corporate governance crisis, others owe more to the events of 9/11 or merely the natural evolution of anti-money laundering laws.[1] Money laundering law now encompasses the proceeds of any crime, no matter how insignificant the crime or the proceeds and no matter where the crime was committed so long as it would have been a crime if it was committed in the UK. Moreover money laundering regulation is being expanded to encompass the insurance industry, law and accounting, property and dealers in luxury goods.

2   The second response is more externally-driven and takes more of a qualitative and relationship-based perspective. It also implies that this is not something companies can solve on their own (or even should) but that, through working with others, there is more chance of success than failure. This recognizes that action in Afghanistan may have dealt with the symptoms of terrorism but it does not reduce the need to tackle the causes of that outrage. This has been well put by two people who also speak from a valued perspective: Nobel Peace Prizewinner, Aung San Suu Kyi and Maleeha Lodhi, twice Pakistan's Ambassador to the US (last during 9/11), currently the Ambassador in the UK and the first woman editor of an Asian English language daily newspaper:

> *At this time when the world is preoccupied with the menace of terrorism, it is worth considering that people who feel deprived of control over their lives – necessary for a dignified life – are liable to search for fulfilment along the path of violence. Merely providing them with a certain material sufficiency is not enough to win them over to peace and unity.*
>
> Aung San Suu Kyi, 2002.

> *We must ensure that the root causes of terrorism are also addressed and ultimately for this war against terrorism to be sustainable, we must win the hearts and minds of people.*
>
> Maleeha Lodhi, 2002.

The second response asks 'how can society respond – and what part can business play in this process?'

It is naïve to believe that global trade relationships – such as giving local farmers access to international markets – will of itself reduce terrorism but it is similarly simplistic not to acknowledge that economic relationships can help to undermine an ideological message built on ignorance, fear and hate. Rising levels of foreign direct investment, poverty reduction and minimizing political risk are increasingly becoming connected for example in China, India, Vietnam and Pakistan. As Vietnam's Deputy Prime Minister recently said, his Government is not just expecting the country's poverty challenges to be taken up by international financial institutions, development agencies and NGOs but, increasingly, it wants to know from foreign companies using Vietnam as a pool of low cost labour, how they can help too (and this need not be financial 'philanthropy').[2]

The coincidence of an increase in acts of terrorism, international tension, economic weakness and a backlash against globalization has raised unprecedented challenges for business in global markets. However, the trend towards global manufacturing will not reverse. The inevitable increase in freight costs from increased security requirements is not going to wipe out the benefits of manufacturing in low-cost countries abroad. The cost advantages for a Ford sourcing parts from Hungary or China versus some US location remain compelling. The semiconductor industry is not about to retrench to California. People will continue to drink coke, consume fruit and vegetables and wear jeans.

However, companies are going to have to think long and hard about how they are perceived outside of their home market and the extent to which they are positive symbols of global capitalism. Distrust of the foreign company and national in some emerging markets has increased as 'think global, act local' and cultural sensitivity assumes a new urgency after 9/11. The war against Iraq has increased the political risks for US and UK corporate brands whether in the Middle East or Africa – and provided opportunities for German companies, for instance, in their wake.

Case study 7.2

The clerical error that rocked an economy

CalPERS, the largest and most powerful public pension fund in the US, divested in four emerging stock markets in Asia in early 2002 – Indonesia, Malaysia, the Philippines and Thailand – because they failed to meet its standards for investment. CalPERS rates the countries it invests in under two broad categories: country factors such as political stability, transparency and labour practices; and market factors that include market liquidity, volatility, capitalization, openness, settlement proficiency and transaction costs. In 2001, it began to consider civil liberties, press freedom and political risk in making investment decisions after board members argued that investing in more stable countries with liberal practices would yield better long-term returns.

Within months CalPERS had to admit that the Philippines was excluded by mistake (*Financial Times*, 2002). CalPERS cited an error in data collected by Wilshire Associates, a consulting firm it used to rate emerging markets. Wilshire wrongly recorded that the Manila Stock Exchange used a manual trading system. Under the CalPERS grading system, that dragged the Philippines below the average or better grade required for investments in a country. In fact, Manila had had computerized trading from 1997. When the mistake was discovered, CalPERS recalculated the country's score in its new pass/fail rating system and the country passed.

CalPERS is still a relatively small investor in emerging markets with just $15.7 million invested in the Manila market, a small fraction of its overall assets. Nevertheless, the effect of its announcement was substantial. Manila's PSE index, which had risen 25 per cent in US dollar terms from January to February 2002, slid 3.2 per cent in the three days after the CalPERS announcement. With CalPERS moves closely watched by other investors, the decision also surprised investors, coming as the emerging Asian markets were posting world-leading performances.

After a meeting in early 2003 between Philippines' Finance Secretary, their US Ambassador and CalPERS board members in California, CalPERS upgraded its score on the Philippines, allowing it to qualify as a permissible site for investments. CalPERS also said it would consider adding countries to a 'watchlist' before it sold off holdings in those markets.

Lessons

1 The original announcement came within months of 9/11 when a key priority of the US Federal Reserve was sustaining business and consumer confidence and financial stability in an uncertain economic climate. The exit of major Asian markets by the largest pension fund in the US cannot have helped international relations, especially when there is not always a distinction made in the popular mind in the economies affected between US public and private policy.

2 The original decision put CalPERS in an awkward situation. It actually caused damage to a market that was legitimately moving forward in terms of corporate governance (and at a time when Enron's collapse could not have validated the supremacy of US models). This was precisely the opposite effect of what CalPERS' process was intended to do.

3 CalPERS own processes were highlighted when the error was acknowledged. In fact Argentina had been ranked as the top-rated emerging market even though it was in the midst of financial and political crises. The recommendation of a CalPERS consultant to drop the Philippines from its list of preferred investments was based on third party data that was not validated.

4 It exposed critical weaknesses of CalPERS approach to country risk assessment. As a Philippines government official, noted 'the problem with Wilshire is that when they gather data, they do it as if they were doing a thesis. They get it from third party sources, which is so archaic. Analysts are supposed to be gathering data on a primary basis ... The sad thing is it is affecting the impression of investors of the Philippines because investors do not know what kind of data gathering process Wilshire is doing' (Guidote, 2003). Kathleen Connell, California's state controller and a CalPERS board member (who opposed the new rating system but abstained from the board's vote to approve it) admitted that 'there are many disturbing instances where the model doesn't equate to economic or political reality. My concern is that you can't look singularly at an entire country and determine if it's going to be suitable' (2002).

5 It gave rise to a feeling of cultural arrogance by the US even from surprising sources such as the chair of the Philippine Stock Exchange, Vivian Yuchengco, who said 'I was shocked when I found out they didn't think we were computerized. They probably thought we all live in trees' (2002).

6 Although CalPERS holding was small in the Phillipines, it suffered from reputational risk over its weak processes (ultimately it was accountable for the decisions it took) but this was also the key risk locally. Indeed the 'reputational risks' that the country would be subjected to if CalPERS removed it from its list of preferred investments were cited as a key factor by the Finance Secretary in lobbying for a reconsideration of CalPERS' 2002 decision. This may have also been because the Manila Stock Exchange was still trying to shake off a stock manipulation scandal that helped topple the country's ex-President (Joseph Estrada) the previous year. Thus reputational risks can increase if it inadvertently combines with perceptions hungover (and not tackled) from previous – unrelated – events.

Case study 7.3

Sainsbury's in Egypt

In September 1999, Sainsbury's launched its first shop outside the UK and the US. The store was one of a hundred that the company opened in and around Cairo in less than two years. At the time the move was widely seen as one of the UK's leading companies exporting mass retail consumerism into the heart of what previously appeared to be a very different culture. Within two years Sainsbury's had sold its 81.1 per cent stake back to local partners with an estimated loss of £100million–150 million (*Financial Times*, 2001). Its chairman cited the 'hostile environment' of Egypt's retail sector along with the 'deterioration of the trading environment in the Middle East' as aggravating factors.

Lessons

1 Sainsbury's had run into unforeseen political obstacles in Cairo and across the wider Middle East. Initially the supermarket's policy of aggressive pricing caused resentment among owners of small shops. The small traders enlisted the help of local mosques in their battle with the multinational giant. The result was preaching that equated shopping with Sainsbury's with adultery and drug-trafficking (no matter how incredible this may seem to the British suburban shopper).

2 The problems for Sainsbury's became much more serious when there was renewed violence between Palestinians and Israelis in the autumn of 2000. Although not connected to the conflict, Sainsbury's – as a potent symbol of western consumerism – suffered from the general rise in the political temperature. A major boycott was organized and some of its stores suffered violent attacks.

3 The real lesson was in what has been called 'glocalization' – the cultural and historical sensibilities specific to a region that are amplified and disseminated by global technology but that often act in opposition to the universalizing forces of globalization.

ALLIANCES, JOINT VENTURES AND STRATEGIC RELATIONSHIPS

There are a range of ways in which companies can develop their strategic relationships from marketing agreements to alliances and joint ventures and merger. How long alliances last and how successful they are depends on the time view adopted. The longer companies engage in an alliance, the more trust accrues with repeated interactions – provided that the relationship is strengthened by the interactions.

Even so the failure rate among alliances is high and is often cited as more than 60 per cent. One survey collected from a survey of CEOs suggested reasons why alliances fail. To some extent, failure can be attributed to a lack of alliance experience and the inability to appreciate that alliance management differs from traditional management. BP's Lord Browne has identified the following as critical success factors:

■ working towards joint goals

■ delivering on promises

■ being (and visibly acting) open and flexible

■ being (and visibly acting) humble

■ thinking long-term.

Fig. 7.1 Why alliances fail

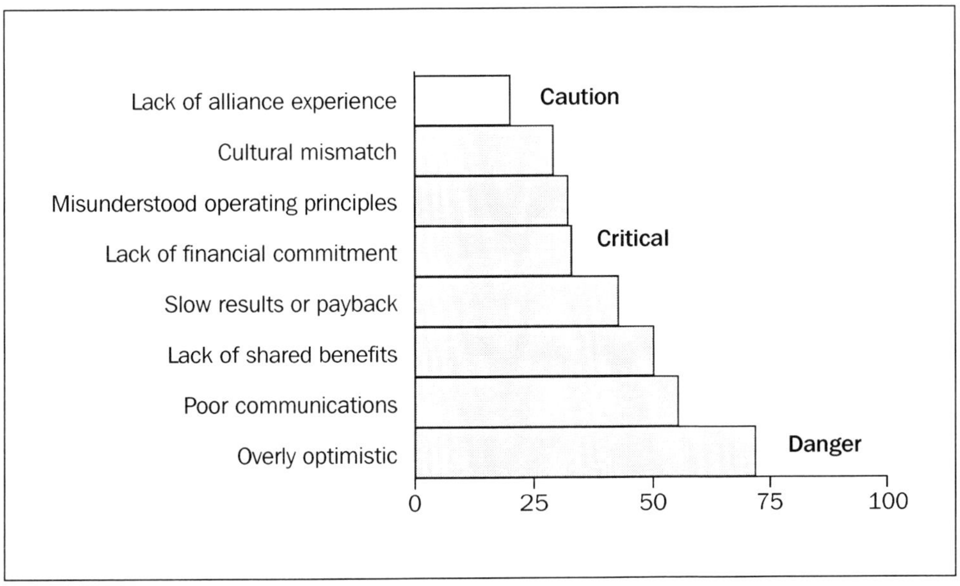

Source: Speckman and Isabella, 2000.

Lord Marshall's key learning from his involvement in alliances and joint ventures – whether at BA, BT or HSBC – was to invest more time upfront in getting to know people from the other side.

The nature of the relationship is perhaps best seen as being both cooperative and competitive. This can be placed in the context of what is actually achievable or realizable in the alliance partnership.

Fig. 7.2 Cooperative/competitive realizability matrix

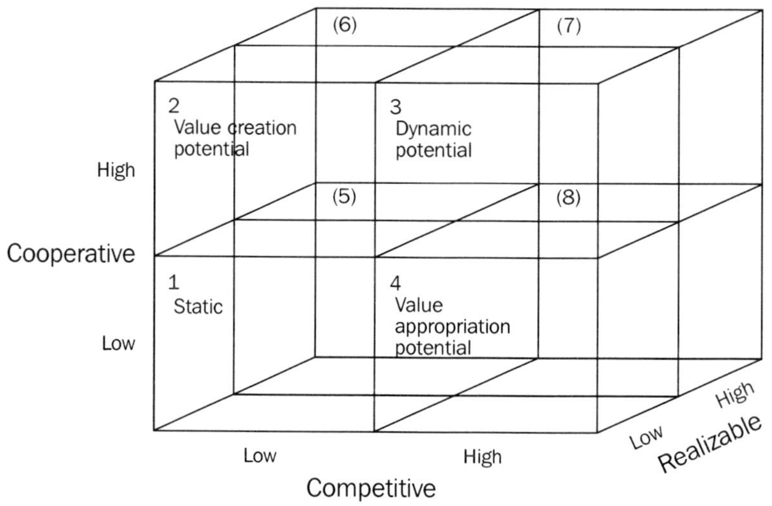

NB Numbers in brackets refer to boxes at rear of matrix.
Source: Stiles, 2001.

Where the intentions of an entrant into an alliance are only slightly cooperative and competitive, regardless of whether the partnership is realizable in other ways, the relationship is likely to prove static with little value added or gained and at worst the entrant firm is at risk of being taken over (boxes 1 and 5). Where the partner firm encourages a highly cooperative approach to the relationship with few competitive elements present (boxes 2 and 6), there is a high level of value creation potential by the entrant firm. This will be more likely to occur, however, if realizability is high (box 6) while, in box 2, the potential for value creation could remain largely unrealized. This could be due to factors such as the partner firm's reluctance to communicate or be open with the entrant firm, lack of experience or cultural incompatibility, i.e. because of how the firm behaves.

If a firm enters a relationship where it becomes strongly competitive and mildly cooperative (boxes 4 and 8), what will result will be value appropriation. Where there is a low level of realizability this means a dormant risk to the other partner. However, where realizability is high, the other partner will risk loss of skills, markets and possibly ultimate extinction or acquisition of the firm (box 8).

Where the entrant firm's intentions are both cooperative and competitive, the relationship is likely to reflect strong complex, dynamic and volatile characteristics (boxes 3 and 7). In this situation the entrant firm will actively work with the partner firm to generate growth and synergy. Under these circumstances, changes in the development of the alliance are potentially most likely and the dynamics of the relationship will probably push the alliance towards increasing emphasis on value creation or value appropriation.

A key question to ask in determining a potential partner's value-adding capabilities is how is the partner perceived in the market-place? What is their reputation? Potential partners should be sought out because they are seen as a valued company with which to partner.

CORPORATE SOCIAL RESPONSIBILITY OR CORPORATE RESPONSIBILITY?

CSR is about companies taking into account their complete impact on society and the environment, not just their impact on the economy.

Fig. 7.3 The business in society

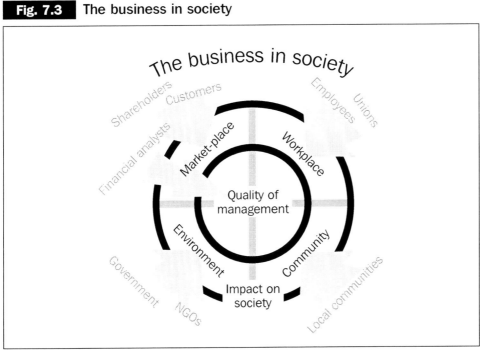

Source: Mallen Baker, 2003.

There are at least seven reasons to bother with CSR:

1 Moral and ethical reasons – to 'do the right thing'.

2 Sustainability of the markets companies rely upon for income.

3 Brand image/reputation.

4 Employee/stakeholder motivation.

5 To enable the company to respond proactively to changing stakeholder agendas and be able to operate effectively under a range of business conditions.

6 To account positively on its performance to stakeholders in a way that will enhance the company's reputation.

7 To provide managers with a framework for managing the business in a more holistic manner.

Case study 7.4

Enron: a corporate citizenship examplar?

In December 2001 the Centre for Corporate Citizenship at Boston College was closing a two-year project researching community and business development in the US. This looked at six companies 'that brought economic opportunities – and hope – to low-income communities'. One of those six companies was Enron with the party involved, 'Enron Investment Partners, among its complicated web of partnerships and subsidiaries' (Googins, 2002). One leading figure in the energy sector later acknowledged that such activities, as with Enron's financial transactions, were deliberately used to mislead others. As one senior Enron employee said in the opening 2002 BBC Reith Lecture on trust, 'what was really shocking was that it *appeared* to be a very morally run company in which not just I, but many others, trusted'. Indeed Enron's CEO gave speeches at business ethics conferences and CEO retreats and put together a statement of values emphasizing 'communication, respect and integrity'.

Henderson Global Investors was one of the few major institutional investors to avoid Enron. It did so on the basis of how Enron was alienating local communities and generating popular protests in India. As Rob Lake, their Director of Governance and Strategy, said 'it was not hard to find out how weak Enron's reputation was in India – a simple search in Google using India "and" Enron as the search terms – produced a string of negative articles. We avoided Enron because of unease about what this inability to handle community relations signalled about management's ability to handle risk' (Lake, 2003).

The growth of corporate social responsibility is such that it has now entered the corporate consciousness to the point where CSR is an accepted acronym, social reports are becoming more common and CSR managers are beginning to appear in service (and not just extractive) sector companies as diverse as Reuters, Standard Chartered Bank and the BBC. The UK has even has a government minister who was responsible for CSR, and in 2001 the European Union published a CSR Green Paper.

Reputational risk is one of the key drivers of increased corporate investment in more socially responsible behaviour. As the EU has said:

> *Many aspects of the business case are intuitive and relate to increased employee retention and motivation, better productivity, better relations with local communities and key stakeholders such as customers, business partners, and consumers. A business model integrating CSR can also be a source of innovation driven by quality, new commercial opportunities, competitive advantage, and a better brand image. But one of the most important drivers of CSR is the management and prevention of risk. Issues that were once considered 'soft' by investors and managers (i.e. human rights, community relations, environment, health and safety) are now hard. Hard to manage, hard to ignore and very hard if you get them wrong. And potentially very costly, not only in financial terms but also because they may influence the company's licence to operate and its acceptance by society at large.*
>
> Commission of the European Communities, 2002.

This is something which FTSE chairmen are increasingly acknowledging:

> *As business becomes more free to respond to market forces, we are also being reminded – in some cases, forcibly – that we do not operate in a political vacuum. The protests at last year's trade talks and international meetings may reflect the views and actions of extremists. But they are a reminder of the pressures that could build on politicians to reverse the recent trend towards liberal markets and less government intervention in business activity. To avoid such a reversal, business needs to operate in a framework in which it is seen to carry out its responsibilities to the wider society.*
>
> Lord Marshall, Chairman, British Airways, 2001.

Areas where reality, perceptions and expectations are misaligned can lead to significant reputational problems in the future. Priorities for action can be established using risk management techniques, including assessing whether issues are likely to lead to damaging headlines and boycotts. It is important to frequently update the analysis, as stakeholder expectations and perceptions change over time. But what makes an issue campaign-friendly?

> **Is the issue:**
>
> Plausible?
>
> Emotional?
>
> Media-friendly?
>
> Backed by a credible and strong NGO?
>
> Faced primarily by you by virtue of scale of issue and
> your natural high profile?
>
> **If yes – then your company's issue could be campaign friendly**

Activists and NGOs can be seen as the spin doctors on behalf of society (though they always have their own agenda too, e.g. competing for a share of voice with other NGOs). There are typically two dominant groups which activists tap as reputational agents which they consider to be their most effective allies: customers and legislators.

Fig. 7.4 Direct and indirect outside pressure

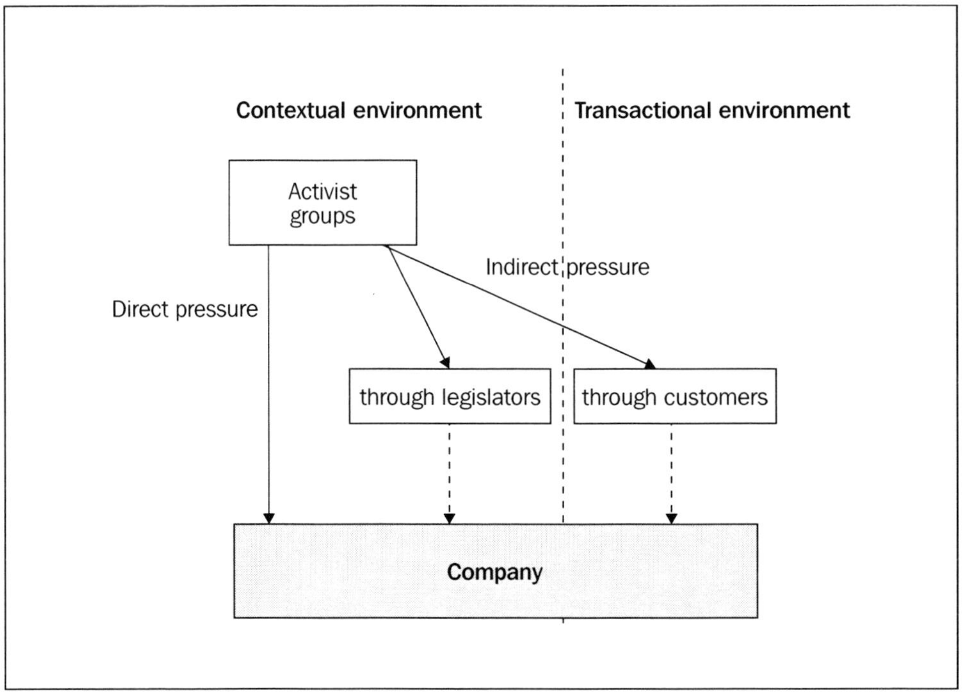

Source: Winter and Steger, 2001.

Some activists are even becoming as, or more adept than, professional marketers. *Adbusters* is a magazine and part of what has been called a 'culture-jamming network'. It trivializes the original marketing message using spoof ads. For example, in a spoof of ads for the fragrance 'Obsession' where the slogan 'Obsession for

Women' is placed over the back of a naked, lithe woman who can be made out clutching her stomach and leaning over a toilet bowl, vomiting to maintain her advertiser-defined body.[3]

However, even among NGOs there is scepticism of supposed bedfellows such as SRI analysts (in the campaign against Balfour Beatty and its infrastructure projects in Turkey, Friends of the Earth spent £30,000 buying shares to try and influence the company decision at the AGM only to be let down, it felt, by SRI firms who it felt accepted the company's arguments). NGOs have their own legitimacy and reputation problems (Friends of the Earth web address somewhat embarrassingly has a .com suffix) – but this does not stick as much as with companies. People do not remember Greenpeace accepting that its arguments on Shell over Brent Spar were flawed on economic and commercial grounds but do associate this as the point at which Shell's reputation plummeted.

CSR RISKS

Corporate *irresponsibility* is '*when a gap opens up between society's expectations and company business behaviour*'. What are the issues? They are what society says they are. This is not to say that a list of risks, a risk map, should not be developed. However, it is likely that these risks would come under headings similar to the following:

- corporate governance
- health and safety
- employee rights
- supply chain issues and ethical sourcing
- marketing and communications
- environmental issues
- community/society impact
- animal rights
- investment issues
- technology and data privacy
- government intervention
- ethical failures.

Most often CSR risks do not look like traditional risks. Are there any particular characteristics which allow easier identification and prioritization.

1   They are of concern to a company's stakeholders ...

- sometimes they are out of a company's arc of vision but important to its stakeholders
- often based on cherished ideals (not necessarily acted on by promoter)
- stimulated by a distrust of business and its practices
- resonate with personal experience and concerns.

2   ... they are volatile ...

- subject to shifts in nature and perception
- emotive in nature, stimulating passionate responses
- move quickly from fringe to mainstream
- can also arise from well-intentioned initiatives – i.e. it's not just 'the bad stuff' you do, it's the impact of 'the good stuff' also.

3   ... easy to communicate ...

- relatively simple to communicate and media friendly
- supported by vocal or influential champions or opinion formers
- topical issues are particularly powerful
- clear call to action – e.g. 'Don't buy Brand X'.

4   ... and they do not exist in isolation

- risks can also be compounded by other events, some of which may be similar in nature but others which are not at all linked.
- 'creeping catastrophe' identifies how initially an event may have no impact, but that as additional problems occur they can tip the balance to create a catastrophe. This can be seen in the problems which beset Barclays Bank, Shell and Monsanto in the late 1990s.

CSR risks:

are old risks ...

Companies have always been at risk for misunderstanding the expectations of stakeholders and there have always been business behaviours which have been considered unacceptable. A company may have failed to understood what their customers really wanted; fell foul of government opinion, or misjudged the importance that shareholders placed on certain issues. So in this way, companies have always had strategic risks associated with misunderstanding certain influential groups in society.

... but the issues are new

However, the issues involved in CSR are often new. Shifts in public opinion and the increased power of external stakeholders to influence that opinion, have stimulated new issues to become important, new thresholds of acceptable behaviour created and therefore different levels of performance expected. For example only ten years ago companies were not expected to 'interfere' in the countries in which they operated, it was called imperialism and was frowned upon. In the main because of Shell's experience in Nigeria, today a company which does not use its influence to improve conditions or inequalities is often accused of a serious social failure risking significant damage to its reputation.

Child labour, concern about the impact of large companies on indigenous populations, the belief that companies have a responsibility for issues such as social exclusion which were previously the sole domain of governments, are new issues and result in new risks to the company.

Society has decided that it minds about these issues, where previously it did not. The issues are new because they are based on opinions of a larger group of stakeholders, who have a much more powerful influence on the success of the organization than in the past. Customers, employees, pressure groups, government, media and the public in general each use this influence more proactively than ever before. The solution to understanding and anticipating CSR risks is to understand the opinions, perceptions and emotions of this larger group of stakeholders and reflect their views in your behaviour.

But companies have always had to listen to the sometimes contrary opinions of external stakeholders. A company's relationships with the City, which are reflected in its share price, rely on the personal opinions of powerful individuals; a fashion retailer will hold its breath until the editor of a national newspaper pronounces on its latest collection and building relationships with government in order to put one's point across for one's own advantage is as old as government itself.

Just like the new breed of stakeholder, they could not be bought, they would not change their minds based on what you want them to do, they made their own judgements based on their perceptions of how much your behaviour reflects their view and their expectation. Poor handling of these relationships in the past could build or shatter any company.

Nothing new about this, just new people whose opinions matter. If the issues are new, how do we see them coming?

It is possible for a company which is sensitive to the shifts in people's expectations to anticipate most CSR risks. Expectations are usually raised by the demands of opinion formers, which are expressed through the media and the Internet. A company which notices and listens to these voices and responds quickly and positively is likely to head off major catastrophe. A company which has a reputation for responsiveness and responsible behaviour will almost certainly do so.

Morals are rarely mentioned in business but morals are at the heart of what CSR and CSR risk is all about.

Ethical risks arise from the fact that people have a wide range of often rather demanding expectations about the ethical behaviour of individuals and corporations. When these moral expectations are breached, people typically react strongly and emotionally, and will frequently change their behaviour with regard to the individual or company concerned.

MANAGING CSR RISK

The focus is on the processes of *identification, prioritization and implementation* of CSR risk and reflects on how these can be integrated into current risk management frameworks.

Governance

CSR risks and ethical risk management systems should be reviewed regularly by the board or a relevant board committee. Sensitization of the board to such issues and the importance of incorporating the views of external stakeholders is often the first stage of an effective CSR risk management process.

Risk identification

As a result of regulatory pressures and incentives to report on risk, many organizations have become familiar with formal risk identification as a regular discipline, whether by facilitated cross-functional workshop or by an equivalent round of internal interviews or questionnaires.

The identification of social and ethical risks can only have value if it leads to a practical programme of actions to mitigate those risks or create new opportunities for performance improvement. But considerations of social and ethical risk can be complex. This complexity may arise from the diversity of an organization's activities as well as the intangible and evolving character of some social and ethical issues.

The exercise has two aims: first, to provide senior management with a manageable overview of identified threats to the organization's performance; secondly, to create a framework for prioritized action planning.

The risk map

The identification process is likely to result in a 'risk map' – a list of issues which the company believes could become barriers to achieving its commercial objectives. The single page risk map or matrix tends to perform well as a starting point and focus attention on the scope of the risks and allow categorization and allocation according to business area, commercial objective or other criteria. It may be necessary to provide an agreed glossary of CSR terms to ensure a common basis of understanding.

In some companies a cross functional team may be able to assess all the risks in a one day session. However, with larger companies this needs to be done in a more focused way to begin the process of 'ownership' of the issues. This entails operational teams spending time to assess their own risks. This can be facilitated by the Risk and CSR departments, but it is a very important process – not just to sensitize the organization to the issues and risks, but to begin to prepare operational units for the need to integrate stakeholder thinking into their business planning.

This can be an unnerving process, the list of potential issues, and therefore risks can be extensive though it is essential to understanding the nature and scope of the potential risks. However, without an understanding of stakeholder perceptions and opinion and because of the often insular nature of many organizations, particularly one which has not completed this sort of process before, it is unlikely that the process will unveil a relatively complete portfolio of the risks.

The stakeholder map

An important part of the risk assessment process is the mapping of key stakeholders to gain a detailed understanding of their current perceptions of the organization and their expectations of its behaviour. This is critical in assessing how important and likely a given issue is to pose a significant risk. This can occur before or after the risk mapping exercise, though it is usual that different issues suggest different stakeholders.

In many cases it may also be helpful to demystify the identities of significant stakeholders and their priorities. Where appropriate this can be achieved by supplementing conventional text-based research with short photo stories or thumbnail sketches of representative stakeholders as individuals.

All this needs to be supplemented by stakeholder sensitivity. An integrated programme of social and ethical risk management really begins when the entire risk assessment process is consciously supplemented by sensitivity to the attitudes of all significant stakeholders and their expectations of corporate conduct in any situation.

However, it is difficult, probably impossible, for a group unused to this process of 'outside in' thinking to anticipate the perceptions of stakeholders while stuck in a conference room for a short period of time. The need to understand the perspectives of unfamiliar pressure groups, trade unions or the media may call for a different approach to the process of identification. The contribution of stakeholders through their representatives or external specialists can significantly enhance effectiveness.

As organizations begin to formalize and embed their CSR policies, there will be a need for at least one influential participant in any risk identification exercise who is fully briefed on the nature of social and ethical risk and on the status of stakeholder issues potentially relevant to the organization. However, it is through the sensitivity of all participants that effective risk management occurs.

It is worth bearing in mind that knowledge of a single industry context may be insufficient. Stakeholders' expectations evolve in society at large or internationally. The same activists and opinion formers may focus on different categories at different times.

Learning from the experiences of apparently unrelated industries may also prove to be as important as assessing issues arising in one's own. Some 'left-field' risks will always prove impossible to anticipate. This does not diminish the value of a systematic process to identify all other known or predictable risks to reputation and performance.

In implementing effective CSR programmes to mitigate the damage of social and ethical risk then, a sensitivity to the opinions and expectations of stakeholders is essential. However, embedding a sensitivity, particular external stakeholders, has a number of 'components'.

Fig. 7.5 Six components of stakeholder sensitivity

No. 1 – Listen

Listen to their views and what they feel and want.

No. 6 – Feedback

Keep listening. Continuous improvement comes from feedback and response.

No. 2 – Consider

Consider their views when making decisions about how you do business, your products and services.

Stakeholder sensitivity

No. 3 – Involve

Involve them in the development of solutions, not just to your CSR problems, but in all aspects of your business.

No. 5 – Communicate

Communicate in appropriate ways with all your stakeholders – keep them in the loop, keep them involved.

No. 4 – Respect

When your business interacts with any stakeholder treat them well and respect them as individuals or groups.

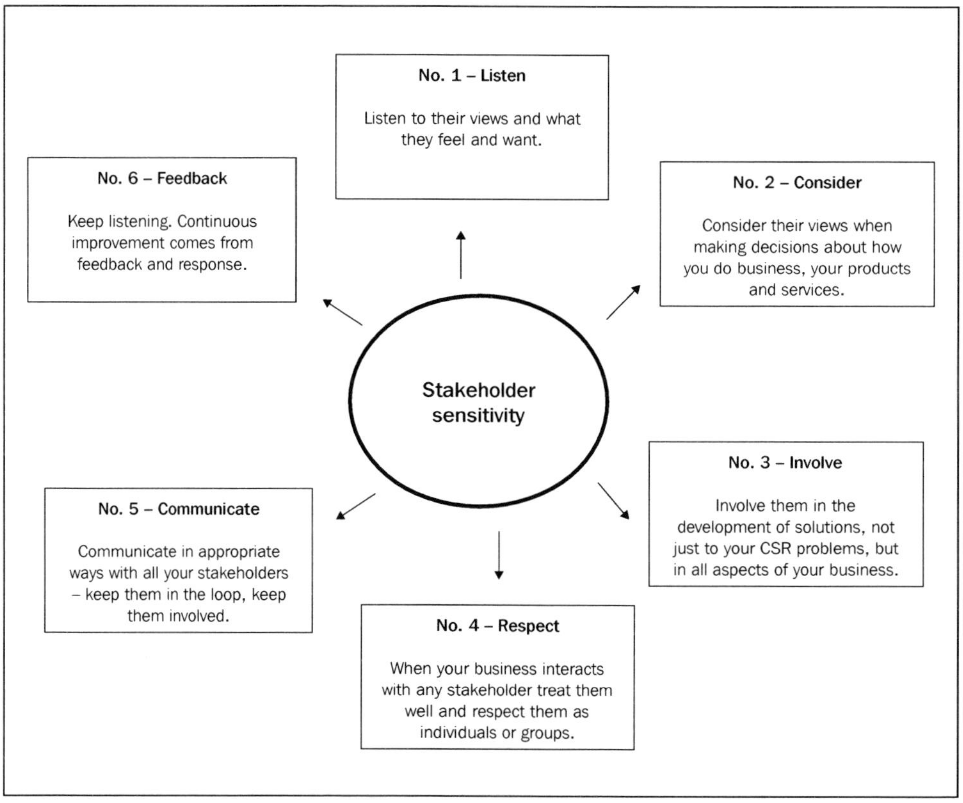

Source: Social and Ethical Risk Group, 2001.

The key point about it is that companies should, as BT have noted, 'always consult stakeholders in an open-minded way. Listen to their agenda – do not listen to them in terms of your own agenda. Many companies do a lot of stakeholder consultation but a lot of them get it wrong because they are looking at the stakeholders to validate what they are already thinking. This is a real pitfall and an easy danger to fall into. A far more effective consultation is to ask the stakeholders to actually set the agenda, in other words – what are your concerns about society or business or our company?' This is also more likely to flag issues in a reputational risk radar which companies can then use in, for example, their risk mapping.

Case study 7.5

Duke of Edinburgh on the value of NGOs

In 2003 the Royal Society of Arts chose as its annual discussion theme with its major corporate supporters 'Globalization and corporate values'. The Duke of Edinburgh hosted a meeting at Buckingham Palace in which this was explored. He took the group of heavyweight corporates by surprise when he pointed out that the term 'CSR' was not new and was one he had in fact suggested at a meeting of Commonwealth industrialists in 1956 when he was encouraging them to consider their social impacts. At the time the phrase was not used because it was considered too radical. He then surprised the audience even more by arguing for the value of NGOs (he had chaired a major one, the World Wildlife Fund for many years). Multinational companies need peace and stability and NGOs need to know the wider impacts of their activities. This calls for not a confrontation but an honest explanation of what the problems are. This builds trust. In addition, companies can inadvertently damage the environment which creates another need for NGOs, especially where legislation is weak.

As CSR has grown there has been a proliferation of social reports, voluntary standards (often developed by unaccountable and mainly western NGOs) and an industry of consultants trying, though seldom succeeding, in helping companies make sense of it all. This has now reached a point where there is a backlash as social reports are produced of varying value (in terms of comprehensiveness, clarity and convenience with people beginning to ask why not just put an edited version in the Annual Report?) and there are many award schemes for environment performance and sustainable development (at least 200 in the UK arguably defeating their own aims, which in most cases, are to promote best practice and reward high performers).

Anna Diamantopoulou, the EU's Commissioner for employment and social affairs has said that 'corporate social responsibility and corporate governance are two sides of the same coin: "greenwashing" your social and environmental performance is as bad as "whitewashing" your profits. CSR is no longer just a job for marketing departments' (Commission of the European Communities, 2002). However, a more robust framing of CSR is needed at a time when doubt is beginning to be cast on the genuineness and efficacy of the concept.

A more useful approach is to focus on *corporate responsibility*. This more naturally links to corporate behaviour. As Reuters (2003) has put it: 'corporate responsibility is both an individual and a collective undertaking'. Mars, still a privately-owned company, has the following credo: 'as individuals, we demand total responsibility from ourselves; as associates, we support the responsibilities of others' (*http://mars.com/home/responsibility/asp*) which more clearly links its translation into practice through its supply chain activities. Telefonica is another example which has found 'corporate responsibility' a more useful term.

This also opens up a natural tie-in to corporate governance at a time when 'corporate collapses have highlighted the need for improved disclosure and transparency in corporate reporting in the Operating and Financial Review or as Management's Discussion and Analysis'.[4]

The UK's Finance Minister, Gordon Brown, MP for Dunfermline, clearly set out the context and focus in a major speech at Chatham House at the beginning of 2003, which coincided with a £50 billion commitment to the UK's overseas aid budget.

In recent years corporate social responsibility which started, for many companies, as something akin to philanthropic engagement has evolved into a far deeper understanding of what benefits business and benefits our economy – corporate citizenship now understood to be something very broad indeed:

- *A recognition that business activities have a wider impact on the society in which you operate.*

- *An attempt to advance economic, social and environmental goods together.*

- *The good economy and the good society pursued together by businesses working as part of the communities around them.*

- *And the good economy and good society seen not as irreconcilable opposites but dependent on each other – enterprise and fairness marching forward together.*

- *And in these last few decades – as socially responsible business behaviour has come to mean not just charity philanthropy but also greater transparency, environmental care, direct engagement in community involvement ... the emphasis no longer just on external giving but now internal business processes, the focus less on how companies give money away to focusing on how companies make money.*

Corporate social responsibility broadening all the time into a belief that economic, social and environmental objectives can be pursued together and in harmony. And in particular that corporate self-interest and corporate social responsibility are not irreconcilable opposites but can progress together.

The new understanding of corporate social responsibility is a recognition, in part, that in business trust is critical to success; that reputation management is essential; that a brand must enjoy people's confidence; that long-termism matters; and that there is something in corporate responsibility that is the smart solution for business and for long-term economic growth.

A recognition that when business loses trust and then legitimacy – either through lack of transparency or social engagement or irresponsibility, whether it be Enron or WorldCom – it is at its most vulnerable.

And so there is a growing recognition that corporate social responsibility does not just relate to your own competitiveness as a business but defines it; that social responsibility is not an optional extra but a necessity – not a part of the business of a company but at its heart, not a sideshow but a centrepiece, not incidental but integral to what you do.

Brown went on to argue for a higher and deeper approach to corporate responsibility – and one which saw trade liberalization as increasingly important.

Progress being made at Doha and beyond on the trade round can show that extending trade can be a benefit to all, especially developing countries, and not a threat. Trade can be a powerful engine for growth. Research suggests that reducing or removing remaining restrictions on world trade would produce anywhere from $250 billion to upwards of $400 billion annually for the world economy, of which over a third would go to developing countries.

We must ensure that all countries have the opportunity to reap these benefits and so must deliver on the commitments made at Doha:

- *We must ensure that poor countries have access to the medicines they need to tackle the diseases crippling their societies – AIDS, tuberculosis, malaria – and protect public health and we must urgently rectify last year's failure to reach agreement in the WTO on this issue.*

- *We must continue to press for other developed countries who have not yet done so to follow the European Union's lead by offering duty and quota free access to all products except arms from the forty-nine least developed countries.*

- *And since three-quarters of the world's poor live in rural areas, urgent action is needed to reduce agricultural protectionism and open up trade.*

This is also something which a number of business leaders[5] subscribed to at Davos in 2003 who argued that 'bringing down barriers to trade and investment – at the right pace – can be a vital part of a country's strategy to reduce poverty'. This is what Japan's Prime Minister Koizumi termed 'trade-related capacity-building' at the Johannesburg Earth summit in 2002, e.g. providing international air cargo services to Tanzania and Ghana so giving local producers access to international markets.[6]

Key facts

- The total external debt of developing countries rose from $90 billion in 1970 to almost $2,000 billion in 1998.

- 2.8 billion of the world's 6 billion people live on less than $2 a day; 1.2 billion on less than $1 a day.

- Between 30,000 and 35,000 children under five die every day of preventable diseases.

- The gap between the richest 20 per cent and the poorest 20 per cent of the world's population has doubled over the past 40 years, with the assets of the world's top three billionaires exceeding the GNP of all the 48 least developed countries (population: 600 million).

RISK AND SUSTAINABLE DEVELOPMENT

'The pressure for sustainable development comes from the premise that, now and for the future, everyone – not just employees, customers and shareholders – has a stake in international commerce and industry.'[7] Sustainable development can be summarized as 'future viability'. As Duncan Brack, Head of the Sustainable Development Programme at the Royal Institute of International Affairs has noted, 'All *environmental problems*, when it comes down to it, can be defined as:

- pollution
- depletion of natural resources
- loss of biodiversity.

Environmental problems can cause threats to national security.' In climate change this is seen through emissions of 'greenhouse gases', the 'greenhouse effect' – where carbon dioxide is the main source for warming the surface of the earth.

Temperature trends since 1850 also underline the importance of global warming as an issue of risk.

Fig. 7.6 Climate change

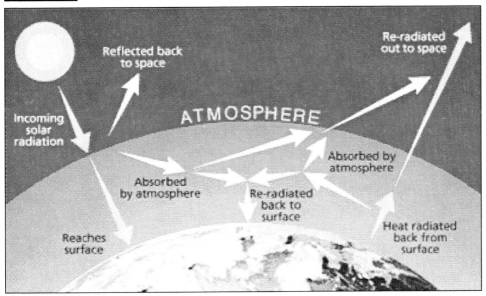

Source: Brack, Royal Institute of International Affairs, 2002.

Fig. 7.7 Temperature risks

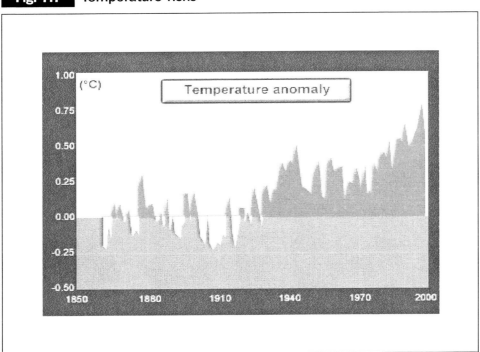

Source: Brack, Royal Institute of International Affairs, 2002.

This also affects national security – but how?

Territorial integrity.	■ Sea level rise. ■ Island and coastal states particularly affected – note problem with refugees.
Economic prosperity.	■ Costs of adaptation to rising sea levels, storm surges. ■ Changing weather patterns – impacts on agriculture, built areas (note house insurance in UK).
Human health and well-being.	■ High temperatures (though fewer cold-related). ■ Disease vectors.

Source: Brack, Royal Institute of International Affairs (2002).

However, a major survey, released in early 2003, of the 500 largest global companies by market capitalization, highlighted the fact that 'investors are failing to take account of climate change in their asset allocations and equity valuations face serious investment repercussions over time'. The survey was the largest ever to assess and provide hard data on a company's exposure to climate change through impacts of both extreme weather events and regulation of greenhouse gas emissions, presenting these factors in terms of the value of shareholdings in corporations worldwide. It found that while 80 per cent of respondents acknowledge the importance of climate change as a financial risk, only 35 to 40 per cent were actually taking action to address the risks and opportunities.

Risk exposure varies widely. Those at greatest risk were not necessarily those with the strongest risk management architecture. For example:

■ Auto: FT500 manufacturers vary by a factor of 35 in terms of carbon dioxide (CO_2) emissions per vehicle sold/produced.

■ Electric Utilities: In the US, estimated total costs of reducing greenhouse gas emissions intensity by 10 per cent, range from over \$1.7 to below \$0.2 per MWh.

■ Oil and Gas: Total costs of reducing 2001 CO_2e emissions by 10 per cent, assuming a uniform €20/tonne marginal abatement cost, range between 0.7 per cent and 5.1 per cent of 2001 Net Income.

■ Banks: Share price valuations could fall as much as 29 per cent for banks without adequate carbon risk management strategies. Inadequate preparation will also have a profound impact on supply chains.

The survey showed that the additional costs associated with climate change would alter the economics of supply chains, especially in the commodity and manufacturing businesses.

The key point from all this, as Tony Blair said when the report was released, is that 'the answer to reducing greenhouse gas emissions lies as much with companies and investors as it does with governments, international agencies and the public' (Carbon Disclosure Project, 2003).

Managing the financial risks of climate change does not necessarily impose a net cost on companies. Companies that are quick to reduce gas emissions stand to gain competitive advantage, in terms of both cost and market risk management. For example BP has cut annual CO_2 emissions at their plants by 10 million tonnes, saving some \$650 million.

Another key challenge is reducing poverty. The links with terrorism are implicit in the comments by Aung San Suu Kyi and Maleeha Lodhi earlier in this section. But what can business practically do to impact change on the ground? In what Gordon Brown called a 'pioneering event' an unprecedented cross-section of companies (led by Pfizer and British Airways), policy-makers, investors, the UN, development agencies, international financial institutions and NGOs participated in a conference at Chatham House followed by intensive breakout sessions at the Treasury to address that very question. They produced the 'London Principle on Partnerships for Poverty Reduction'.

This argued that 'encouraging a strong business sector is essential for sustainable development and poverty reduction'. Although 'different actors may have different responsibilities, all actors should be transparent and accountable'. Moreover

tri-sector partnerships for development and poverty reduction can yield significant mutual benefits. All partners have different roles to play, including public and private sectors and civil society:

- Governments *as part of their wider strategy for poverty reduction and development, must work to create a good business climate; through institutions and infrastructure, investing in human development, striving to eliminate corruption, and providing an environment to promote consultation and participation by all stakeholders.*

- Businesses *are primarily wealth creators, but they recognize the benefits to be gained in working with others to drive forward wider economic, social and environmental progress. They must also play an active role in wider efforts to stamp out corruption.*

It also outlined what the roles of others should be:

- Civil society *can play an important part in monitoring the activities of both public and private sectors, facilitating representation and strengthening capacity for communities, and in offering a bridge for communication between the different parties involved.*

253

■ International Financing Institutions (IFIs) *and donors play an important part in poverty reduction and also in macroeconomic surveillance. Their activities need to be in line with both the aims and poverty reduction strategies in the recipient countries, and with global efforts to improve aid effectiveness.*

The London Principle on Poverty Reduction then set out a ten-point action plan where these groups could add mutual value by working together:

1   Encouraging investment in developing countries *We need to find ways to improve the investment climate and reduce risks to investors, e.g. through overcoming political risk and through workable and specific measures which will be additional to those already in existence.*

2   Engaging with governments *Multinational companies (MNCs) should promote and participate in dialogues along the lines of cross-sectoral discussions on trade and trade policy, to identify barriers to investment and economic development. Ideally these discussions should take account of the interests and priorities of poor people, and should where possible take place within the context of national poverty reduction strategies.*

3   Sound corporate governance *With a view to improving corporate practice and stabilizing investment environments, we emphasize the need to upgrade capacity and practice of companies in developed and developing countries to publicly and transparently report on financial and non-financial issues.*

4   Corporate payments to governments *We support tighter standards on financial reporting of corporate payments to governments, with governments in turn making public how revenue and investments are used to enhance development.*

5   Contributing to economic development *While companies should concentrate on their core competences, there are many areas of public policy where multinational companies could work with others to help close skills gaps and build human capital (e.g. through secondments, scholarships and training). For many countries the development of policies, frameworks and capacity at the regional level could help provide greater scale and consistency.*

6   Fostering local entrepreneurship *Multinational companies can help identify opportunities to develop skills and capacity in both local SMEs and their own businesses by working with and learning from local*

business partners. This could include training partnerships, technology transfer and supply chain integration.

7 Joint advocacy *There is much scope for joint advocacy by companies and NGOs to promote economic growth and poverty reduction, for example by working together to reduce barriers to trade which are harmful to producers in developing countries. Such joint advocacy must be coherent and consistent with country-owned poverty reduction goals.*

8 Knowledge exchange and capacity building *Internationally and locally, MNCs should take every opportunity to facilitate wider learning and capacity building with companies, governments and civil society. This will include using the experience of civil society, company and government contacts for examples and case studies in third countries.*

9 Codes of conduct for socially responsible business behaviour *We support voluntary social, environmental and ethical codes that build on already agreed national and international principles. We encourage all parties to adopt codes of conduct – their spread encourages new ideas. Such codes should capture local concerns, and be developed with local business associations and stakeholders. Codes should also take account of existing international agreements, and should be constructed to avoid trade protectionism.*

10 Measuring impact *Lessons learnt and comparisons of best practices should be systematized to create benchmarking and metrics which will assist in measuring the development impact of partnership activities.*

Case study 7.6

Companies decrease social risk and increase reputation in local markets

Three examples show how diverse company activity can be.

Housing – Dell vs. Fedex and UPS in China

For Dell, China is a strategically important market. However there are plenty of examples of how companies have come unstuck or struggle to make any profits out of their activites partly due to weak relationships with national or local policy-makers. The private sector in China is still largely a myth with 95 per cent of the companies trading on the Shanghai Stock Exchange owned by the Government.

A lot of research homework was done before we went into China, practical homework, talking to ministers of the government in the area of trade, the area of resourcing and so on to understand what would fit right for them. It's very easy to go in and pay lots of money so that you can get people coming to you but even that is going to make the local economy unstable, so even detail of what levels of pay should we be offering [were needed]. We built dormitories. You might be thinking 'build dormitories? – that's a bit awful' but actually that's their culture and that's something if we didn't do it they'd think we're an awful company. But we wouldn't have known that if we hadn't gone there and spoken to the government and actually understood what we needed to do, so very much a collaborative effort there. We've done a similar sort of thing with our facility in Mexico, really gone into the government and said 'we'd like to work in your country, tell us what we need to know to get it right for you'.

Zaman, 2003a.

Since entering China five years ago, Dell has aggressively built up its local network and is now China's number 3 seller with about 5 per cent of the market. With China's PC market expected to grow about 17 per cent in 2003, Dell believes it can grow its revenue by some 50 per cent, boosting its market share to about 7.7 per cent. Dell gained the number 3 spot in China in 2002 after finishing fourth in 2001 behind IBM. In 4Q 2002, its unit sales jumped 72 per cent from a year earlier.

This is a story with many lessons:

1 This was not just a bit of altruism for local employees but a carefully targeted outcome from extensive market research. For a company not used to reinventing its business model and for a reputation for ruthless cost controls, Dell knew that to succeed in China it had to invest in infrastructure, in this case housing for its workers. This was necessary to build trust with local stakeholders (national and local government, employees, community) and meet the expectations of how these groups expected a large foreign company to behave. As Dell itself acknowledged 'we recognized the importance of getting understanding and empathy with the people who run China'. Moreover in a culture where relationships are so important it recognized at an early stage that their challenge in China was fundamentally different to 'other countries where you can just go in, set up your factory and away you go, e.g. in Hungary'.

2 Dell's market environment had been characterized by fierce pricing eroding margins. One consequence is an increase in the importance of reliable low cost manufacturing bases in their supply chain. How they handle relationships in, e.g. China, therefore directly plays back into their ability to successfully compete and deliver value to customers and shareholders.

3 The existence of a strong local competitor, Legend could have complicated matters for Dell. However, it identified what was necessary and, unlike some companies with labyrinth decision-making processes, quickly moved to implementation to signal another way in which it was committed to the local economy. In contrast, during the same period, FedEx and UPS were engaged in a very public dispute with the Chinese Government over the interpretation of rulings from different ministries over what they could or could not do. The question is did they invest as much care, attention and time in understanding what was expected of them, by whom, when and how? The irony is that Dell is a major FedEx customer in China.

Education – Toyota in Pakistan

A programme jointly administered by Indus Motors (Toyota's 50 per cent joint venture in Pakistan) and a local government technical college in northern Pakistan provides opportunity for young people to acquire industry oriented training in automotive engineering and develops their skills base. Financial support of £30,000 over two and a half years in training materials may seem modest but is seen as valuable by local policy-makers who at the end of 2002 said they feel that 'more companies like Toyota should support industry focused education'.[8]

In 2003 Toyota announced that it will begin a double shift at its Pakistan plant in order to meet rising demand. Vehicle production has grown by some 4 per cent, spurred on by new leasing deals and favourable car-financing loans.

Health – BA in Zambia

The Change for Good programme was launched in 1994, collecting foreign currency donated by customers on board British Airways flights. Since its launch, over £15 million has been raised for UNICEF which has helped projects in over 50 countries around the world. BA works very closely with UNICEF in managing the programme and joint decisions determine which countries will be the recipients of the donations. In July 2002, BA helped to launch a National Immunization programme in Zambia. Change for Good money supplied all the polio vaccines to 1.2 million children inoculated in the July campaign in efforts to remove Zambia from the list of the few countries still afflicted with polio. It enabled social risk to be reduced for a large pool of unprotected children.

Zambia remains a key BA market for the movement of people and cargo. In March 2002, it launched direct flights between Lusaka and London using new Boeing 777 aircraft in a year which marked the 70th anniversary of BA's operations in Zambia – underlining the generational connections for a corporate brand.

This legitimately raises the question of where private sector responsibility ends and public responsibility begins. Indeed three elite global business groups – the World Economic Forum, International Chamber of Commerce and World Business Council for Sustainable Development – have recently launched governance initiatives, intended to clarify exactly that. Even so, the business case for caring is also connected to the realization, in Gordon Brown's words (2003), that 'since the tragic events of September 11 we have recognized a profound and pervasive truth: that what happens to the poorest citizen in the poorest country can directly affect the richest citizen in the richest country and as individuals and nations we are dependent upon each other for our security and prosperity'. Terrorist bombings in locations such as Morocco, Riyadh and Mumbai (Bombay) within months of these words being delivered at Chatham House suggest that time is not on our side.

Business case for caring

It is worth re-stating the business imperative for social investment. That this can build reputation is not a reason to pursue it; in fact supporting initiatives and not submitting cases to award schemes of questionable value for companies with global reach and presence such as the UK's Business in the Community annual awards arguably has more credibility. Ingredients for a progressive society are self-evident and they are ones in which values-based businesses will recognize a shared stake:

- access to affordable health
- political stability
- the rule of law
- economic prudence
- a commitment to educational opportunity
- a buoyant consumer market.

The clearest common denominator between business and wider society interests is that of economic progress. Business has a key role to play in economic development and in raising the living standards of the poorest sections of the world population. Lack of political stability and poor education are probably the biggest deterrents to development – and key sources of social alienation and, yes, increase the risks and sow seeds of terrorism. The scope for companies to address these issues directly is limited but where the right conditions and leadership exists, a responsible business should be looking for opportunities outside the confines of the major western economies. As businesses reflect the social and environmental challenges of their activities, a constructive relationship (partnership) with governments can also help. One simple idea, rarely sized upon, would be to align CSR in poor countries like Vietnam and Tanzania with national strategies to reduce poverty. This makes sense for economic development and for business itself. It is simply a fact that tomorrow's markets – and global security – depends on it.

CORPORATE GOVERNANCE AND GLOBAL GOVERNANCE

As Scott McNealy, Chairman, President and CEO of Sun Microsystems told a CBI meeting in the summer of 2002, 'investor and corporate responsibility is converging – and rightly so'.

This is how. The increased focus on qualitative descriptors in the Operating and Financial Review (OFR) under changes to UK company law or in Management's Discussion and Analysis elsewhere calls for a different kind of narrative explanation.

According to the DTI (2003),

information that is material to the OFR may be quantitative or qualitative; and may relate to facts or probabilities, and to past, present or future events and decisions ... The information in the OFR may be a description of an important issue or the expression of a probable future event as often as a past event or a matter of fact. These should be judged in the context of the risks, opportunities and threats facing the business, including an assessment of non-financial issues, such as environmental, ethical or reputational risk. So facts and events, probabilities, risks and opportunities may all be material and qualify for inclusion in the OFR if it is to meet its objectives.

Case study 7.7

CSR committee at Marks & Spencer

Marks & Spencer is one of a small number of companies that has put in place a sub-committee of its board called the CSR committee. This 'guides the board on the social, ethical and environmental impact of company activities, and is supported by the CSR team (part of Corporate Communications) and the CSR forum – a representative group from all business units and areas, chaired by the Head of Food Technology'.

Key lessons

1 The biggest risk if and when companies set up such a process is that it is used as a 'feelgood forum' with little bite and hardly anyone of real interest involved. As another FTSE 100 chairman noted in M&S's case, 'this has people with real credibility and a strong internal and external reputation'.[9] It includes Paul Myners who joined the Board as a NED in 2002 and chaired the Government-commissioned Myners Committee which called for a more activist policy by institutional investors. Internally the committee includes Yasmin Yusuf, Creative Director for Clothing from 2001 (the company's most senior woman and ethnic minority employee) who has been a key figure in the M&S revival and reconnection to its customers. She joined M&S from Warehouse where she had turned a loss-making business into a profitable one. Both are by no means evangelicals for CSR (though supportive of its thrust) which itself should help to improve the quality of discussion and decision.

2 It is chaired by the non-executive chairman, Luc Vandevelde, signalling its importance as a mainstream issue (whether to operational managers or institutional investors) by someone who was personally involved in developing M&S's Global Sourcing Principles when chairman and CEO.

3 M&S recognizes the importance of awareness of wider social issues as a matter of business competence for its NEDs. It was one of the very few, if only FTSE 100 company, with the fore/insight to say in its evidence to the Higgs Report, that

increasingly [NEDs need] an awareness of social, environmental and ethical issues including:

- *ability to recognize emerging values and reconcile conflicting interests*
- *getting the best out of people to pursue corporate strategy*
- *being sensitive to the company's impact on society.*

Pressure is directed at companies through such global instruments as the UN's Global Compact, the Global Reporting Initiative (GRI), SA8000, the EU's European Action Framework for CSR, AA1000 and the Ethical Trading Initiative of the UK Government to name but a few. Despite the plethora of voluntary standards and noises by NGOs and the occasional politician of the necessity for regulatory reform to mandate a stronger commitment to CSR (e.g. by making social reporting or pension fund disclosure on CSR issues mandatory), legal CSR compliance is unlikely to be a powerful driver.

One regulatory area which companies need to watch carefully are Listing requirements. Sarbanes-Oxley has not served the interests of the US as a market in which foreign companies can list and has underlined the attraction of the UK as the other major English-speaking market. Interestingly in Australia, two parallel developments, hardly noticed in Europe, could point the way for London and even Hong Kong within, say, the next three years.

Fig. 7.8 Listing requirements of the Australian Stock Exchange: risk oversight and management

Issue	Content	Comment/subtext
Statement of objectives of the best practice guidelines.	■ Risk is good – if it is commensurate with an adequate level of return. ■ Risk oversight and management is not just about accountability and the mitigation of hazards but about identifying and optimizing opportunities to create value. ■ A board policy on risk oversight and management is recommended.	■ Risk is not necessarily a bad thing and not just about hazards (a key argument in Chapter 3). ■ The policy needs to be agreed, monitored and developed at board level.
Policy.	■ It is important that management defines how the company is identifying, evaluating and managing risk. ■ Disclosure of the mechanism for assessing risk promotes confidence in the accuracy of the profile.	■ Focus in not just on risk management – but also on identification and assessment, possibly part of overall evaluation. ■ Risk disclosure builds trust.

Issue	Content	Comment/subtext
Content of policy.	■ There are two main categories of risk relevant to the strategic, operational and financial objectives of listed entities – business risk and financial risk. ■ Reputation risk, an example of business risk, is the potential for gain or loss from changes in community expectations of corporate behaviour. ■ It is the responsibility of company management to formulate their risk profile within a management framework and update it as the dynamics of the business change. Where possible, the broad categorizations suggested should be adopted.	■ A simple but powerful risk categorization at the top level. ■ The definition is close to the one used here but, as this book argues, the potential to manage reputational risk for value creation lies in not confining this to any one stakeholder (and certainly not community who can with difficulty claim to be a more key stakeholder than customers, employees and shareholders). ■ Risk profiles need to be living, breathing efforts and should be subject to periodic review (maybe twice yearly).
Monitoring and assessment.	■ There is limited value in a company identifying and disclosing its risk profile and risk management policies if there is also no corresponding measure of what their actual 'practice' has been during the reporting season. Many companies put a lot of information in their annual reports regarding corporate governance policy but little information as to how they are backing up with action. ■ It is advisable that there is dual sign-off of the reporting against risk management policy implementation by both internal audit (management) and the board.	■ Risk reporting needs to much more content-specific. Readers are not likely to give boards the benefit of the doubt. ■ Accountability and internal responsibility lies with audit. Though logical, companies are likely to *increase* risk if this is not accompanied with training – as much in behavioural skills than the application of process mechanisms.

Source: Australian Stock Exchange (2003) – with final column added

This does not, however, mean that expectations of a clearer focus on CSR as a mainstream priority for companies will grow. Customers, employees and investors could – and should – collectively do more for value creation than compliance with government policy, however enlightened. What is more likely is the integration of CSR into mainstream (voluntary) standards. Of these, two in particular stand out:

1 *Movement towards ISO (International Organization for Standardization) standardization of CSR*: A multi-stakeholder advisory group has begun an analysis of whether eventual work by ISO to assist organizations in meeting their 'social responsibilities' would represent an added value to programmes already existing with a decision on standardization of CSR being taken in March 2003. The ISO has already indicated that it was 'feasible to develop international standards benchmarking corporate responsibility' (Zaman, 2003). This 'indicated that (1) the type of standards desirable would be management system standards and (2) that firms should be able to self-declare compliance or seek certificates from authorized third parties. It was suggested that key components of the standards are likely to include such issues as compliance with laws and regulations, consumer protection, environmental conservation, fair labour practices, health and safety protection, prevention of corporate corruption, human rights and contributions to the local community.'

   As one influential view, the Keidanren, the Japan Business Federation, feels that 'if the ISO decides to proceed with CSR standardization, the impact on Japanese industry will presumably be great' (Zaman, 2003) even if some cultural customization may be necessary; given the Japanese manufacturing presence in low cost markets this could be a significant driver especially if major companies like Toyota, Sony, Daiwa and Mitsui build on their progress to date.

2 *OECD Guidelines for Multinational Enterprises*: The only multilaterally endorsed comprehensive framework of rules governing the activities of multinational enterprises. Though not binding on companies, they are binding on the signatory governments and are of potential relevance. They run in parallel to the ILO (Tripartite Declaration of Principles concerning Multinational Enterprises) but go beyond employment and industrial relations issues to cover general policies for good corporate behaviour. It operates internationally through nominated government departments.

All these are pieces of a global jigsaw that can best be termed 'global governance' – not because CSR will be subject to the whims of international bureaucrats or an international political body be it the EU or the UN but because the companies that will build reputation as an effect (rather than as is too often the case, the cause) of their commitment to CSR will be those that can innovate in two ways:

- a continuing awareness of what CSR means for them
- an unrelenting resolve to align this with what the company is doing to create value.

Case study 7.8

Mars and global governance

In 2001, Cadburys publicly committed to end child slavery on cocoa plantations in Africa and elsewhere after a ship bound for the Ivory Coast was found to contain at least 43 children. As it said at the time, 'this is not an issue confined to cocoa. We believe the same thing happens with rice, maize and coffee. We do not want to sort one problem out to create another.'

Mars is a private company but, like Cadbury and Rowntrees (before the latter was acquired by Nestlé) still with strong Quaker roots. It found that in many cases there was local knowledge and skills lacking to effectively help to reduce the kind of social – and reputational – risks that it found unacceptable. It realized that to ensure it behaved responsibly it had to be far more proactive than it might wish. By formulating policies and guidelines and helping to build local capacity and alternatives to child labour with development agencies, the UN and African national governments among others, it began to reduce the social risk and increase its reputation. As Amnesty International said in 2003, it was getting involved in global governance even if it did not realize it. From AI's perspective this was a good thing and could even act as a lever to encourage other companies with similar exposure to do more of the same.

EXECUTIVE SUMMARY

1   Political risk needs to be seen as both the actions of legitimate government authorities but also as events caused by factors outside the control of government. This definition recognizes clearly that companies' political risks are increasingly subject to societal expectations. Political risk is also about the quality of relationships between companies and policy-makers.

2   In developing alliances, joint ventures and strategic relationships a key priority, often overlooked, is to invest more time upfront in getting to know people from the other side.

3   A key question to ask in determining a potential partner's value-adding capabilities is how is the partner perceived in the market-place? What is their reputation?

4   Corporate irresponsibility is when a gap opens up between society's expectations and company business behaviour.

5   Morals are rarely mentioned in business but morals are at the heart of what CSR risk is all about. Ethical risks arise from the fact that people have a wide range of often rather demanding expectations about the ethical behaviour of individuals and corporations. When these moral expectations are breached, people typically react strongly and emotionally, and will frequently change their behaviour with regard to the individual or company concerned.

6 Companies should always consult their stakeholders in an open-minded way. Listen to their agenda – do not listen to them in terms of your own agenda.

7 There has been a backlash to social reports as many produced are of varying value (in terms of comprehensiveness, clarity and convenience). 'Greenwashing' your social and environmental performance is as bad as 'whitewashing' your profits.

8 A more useful approach is to focus on *corporate responsibility*. This more naturally links to corporate behaviour. This also opens up a natural tie-in to corporate governance at a time when there is a need for improved disclosure and transparency in corporate reporting through the Operating and Financial Review or Management's Discussion and Analysis. Corporate responsibility does not just relate to your own competitiveness as a business – it defines it.

9 Reducing poverty is a key challenge in which business has a stake. A strong business sector is essential for sustainable development and poverty reduction.

10 The companies that will build reputation as an effect (rather than as the cause) of their commitment to CSR will be those that can innovate in two ways – a continuing awareness of what CSR means for them and an unrelenting resolve to align this with what the company is doing to create value.

Key message

Corporate responsibility is about how a company manages its global relationships and responsibilities.

What you must ask of your team/staff/consultants

1 Who manages our political risk? – and is their understanding of the term the same as mine?

2 How do we evaluate the effectiveness of our key strategic relationships?

3 Do we produce a social report – and who are we really producing this for?

4 What is stopping us from having two pages each on evaluating our customer, employee, shareholder and community relationships in the next annual report – one page of text, one of graphics?

5 Do we ever look at our community activities and key stakeholder relationships through the lens of social investment and the impact on making people employable (sustainable livelihoods)?

6 Ask your CFO where your company could list outside its primary market – and then ask your Head of Investor Relations whether your company has relationships with local institutional investors and how strong/weak they are.

7   Do we know what the latest developments in ISO and the OECD are in CSR and are we fully engaged in integrating/aligning with these directly or via intermediaries?

What you must do today

1   Join the charitable organization, the Royal Institute of International Affairs (a modest investment in political risk perspective of £2,000 p.a.) and participate in its events and research to sharpen the connection to the markets in which you operate.

2   Make an appointment with your local MP/MEP and discuss your top three business concerns.

3   Download a copy of your competitor's social or environmental report.

4   Ask your Head of Internal Audit how s/he addresses social and ethical risk – then ask the same of your senior NED.

5   Buy a bar of chocolate and look at the ingredients and country of origin on the wrapper. Then reflect on what you know/would like to know about the labour conditions in the market identified (if any).

Related websites

The Royal Institute of International Affairs
www.riia.org

The Institute of Social and Ethical AccountAbility
www.accountability.org.uk

Sustainability
www.sustainability.com

CSR news
www.mallenbaker.net/csr/

EU
http://europa.eu.int/comm/employment_social/soc-dial/csr/csr_index.htm

OECD
www.oecd.org/EN/home/0,,EN-home-93-3-no-no-no,00.html

UN Industrial Development Organization
www.unido.org

Notes

1 These include UK's Financial Services & Markets Act (FSMA), USA Patriot Act 2001, EC's Second Directive on Money Laundering, UK's Anti-Terrorism Act 2001, UK's Proceeds of Crime Act 2002.

2 Conversation with author (Hanoi, March 2003).

3 *http://www.adbusters.org/creativeresistance/spoofads/fashion/*

4 'General Principles Regarding Disclosure of Management's Discussion and Analysis of Financial Condition and Results of Operations.' Report of the Technical Committee of the International Organization of Securities Commissions (February 2003).

5 The list includes Lord Browne, CEO, BP; Niall FitzGerald, Chairman, Unilever; Digby Jones, Director General, CBI; Lord Marshall, Chairman, British Airways; Sir Mark Moody-Stuart, Chairman, AngloAmerican; Sir Nick Scheele, Chief Operating Officer & President, Ford Motor Company; Sir Martin Sorrell, CEO, WPP Group; Adair Turner, Vice Chairman, Merrill Lynch Europe; Sir Philip Watts, Chairman, Shell; and Sir Robert Wilson, Chairman, Rio Tinto.

6 Conversation with Hassan Kibelloh, Tanzanian High Commissioner and Kwamena Bartels, Ghana's Minister for Private Sector Development, Chatham House, January 2003.

7 Lord Marshall, Chairman, British Airways and the Conference Board.

8 Pakistan Press International Information Services, 29 October 2002.

9 Another example – and an earlier one – was Cadburys which includes Baroness Wilcox as one of the NEDs (conversation with John Sunderland, CEO, 2001). She is President of both the National Federation of Consumer Groups and the Institute of Trading Standards and a Member of the Governing Body of the Institute of Food Research. Wilcox made her reputation as Chairman of the National Consumer Council from 1990 to 1995.

References

Aung San Suu Kyi, Winner of the 1991 Nobel Peace Prize (2002) The Human Development Report. UNDP.

Australian Stock Exchange (2003) http://www.asx.com.au/about/13/proposed listingruleamendments_aa3.shtm/

Brack, Duncan, Head, Sustainable Development Programme (2002) Royal Institute of International Affairs speech to Royal Institute of International Affairs Members' Conference.

Carbon Disclosure Project (2003) Statement issued at the launch of project, 17 February 2003. *http://194.242.156.103/cdproject/downloads/lettersforCDPfromthe PrimeMinister.doc.*

Commission of the European Communities (2002) Corporate Social Responsibility: A Business Contribution to Sustainable Development. COM 347 final Brussels. July.

Connell, Kathleen (2002) *Wall Street Journal*, 13 May.

Conversation with Rob Lake, Head of Engagement and Corporate Governance Henderson Global Investors at Chatham House, February 2003.

DTI (2003) http://www.dti.gov.uk/cld/ofrwqcon.pdf/

Financial Times (2001) 'Sell-off sees Sainsbury's on the Rise'. 10 April.

Financial Times (2001) 'CalPERS reverses Philippines pull-out: clerical error blamed for pension fund's u-turn on Manila stocks'. 14 May.

Googins, Bradley (2002) 'Even good works fell in the Enron scandal', Newsday, 2 February.

Gordon Brown speech at Royal Institute of International Affairs (2003) 'Financing Sustainable Development, Poverty Reduction and the Private Sector', Funding Common Ground on the Ground conference, Chatham House, London. 22 January. *http://www.hm-treasury.gov.uk/newsroomandspeeches/press/2003/ press0803.cfm.*

Guidote, Cora, executive director of the Philippines Government Investor Relations Office (2003) *Business World*, 19 February.

Lodhi, Maleeha (2002) 'Root Causes of Terrorism Should Be Addressed – Ambassador'. Business Recorder Financial Times Information – Asia Africa – Intelligence Wire. 21 August.

Lord Marshall of Knightsbridge (2001) Speech at the Royal Institute of International Affairs. 17 January.

Reuters (2003) Corporate Responsibility Report. London: Reuters.

Royal Institute of International Affairs (2002) Carbon Disclosure Project. *Carbon Finance and Global Equity Markets*. London.

Social and Ethical Risk Group (2001) Unpublished Report.

Speckman, Robert and Isabella, Lynn (2000) *Alliance Competence*. NY: John Wiley.

Stiles, Janine (2001) 'Strategic Alliances' in *Rethinking Strategy*. London: Sage Publications.

Winter, Matthias and Steger, Ulrich (2001) *Strategies for Preventing Corporate Disasters*. Chichester: John Wiley.

Yuchengco, Vivian (2002) 'CalPERS to reverse position on investing in Philippine Market. *Wall Street Journal.* 13 May.

Zaman, Arif (2003a) *Made in Japan: Converging Trends in Corporate Responsibility and Corporate Governance.* London: Royal Institute of International Affairs.

Zaman, Arif (2003b) Unpublished MBA dissertation Henley Management College.

8

Differential advantage, value creation and reputational risk

Managing risk has always been a natural part of day-to-day business, but the increasing complexity and internationalization of business, coupled with a greater focus of corporate responsibility, has now made reputation risk an explicit component of corporate governance. Reputation risks emanate from perceptions of company behaviours which threaten to impair the level of trust and support from the firm's stakeholders. If this support is reduced or withdrawn, then the performance or even the viability of the business is at risk.

The management of reputation risk is therefore imperative. However, the very way we think about companies needs to be challenged.

Investor relations. Customer relations. Human resources. The labels companies use to categorize functions and departments can obscure them from two central points in managing reputational risk:

1 Reputational risk is about relationships – and these need to be managed beyond people in the areas operating in functional silos. This comes together at the executive leadership and board level.

2 Reputational risk is a much more powerful creator of corporate value if seen in relation to an organization's key stakeholders – customers, employees and shareholders.

Table 8.1 Intangible assets and reputational risk

Intangible asset	Why relevant for reputational risk
Reputation and trust.	Reputation and trust are at the heart of expectations by stakeholders of corporate behaviour.
Relationships.	Effective relationships are key to identifying, assessing as well as managing reputational risk whether at the executive team level or at the front-line customer interface.
Culture and values.	■ Reputational risk is not managed because consultants are brought in or because the CEO says it is important. ■ Reputational risks relate to behaviour – both individual (values) and corporate (culture).
Leadership and communication.	Reputational risk is a board issue but ensuring it is understood relies on communication that is both clear and honest.
Knowledge.	■ External awareness of how employees, customers and shareholders perceive the organization is key to reputational risk. ■ Knowledge derives both from the application of tools and techniques (e.g. being developed at Henley) but also effective market insight/intelligence (i.e. environmental scanning, filtering, analysis and communication to decision makers).

Reputational risk needs to be managed on three levels.

A: **Strategy** – the foundations on which sustainable business is built.

B: **Structure** – alignment and inter-linkages (A + C).

C: **Process** – how the dynamics work.

Fig. 8.1 Strategy – the foundations on which sustainable business is built (A)

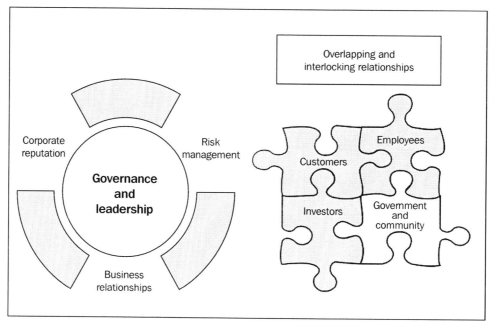

Corporate identify is a reflection of corporate strategy – and this includes a strategy for your people. What is often overlooked – and perhaps was in the case of BA with its tailfins saga in 1998 – is that corporate identity is also about organizations' social context. Corporate reputation is also about organizational as well as corporate identity. If corporate identity is about the logo, slogan or livery, organizational identify consists of the many ways in which members of an organization perceive, feel and think of themselves as an organization. Stories and corporate folklore are all part of this, especially in a service-based company where people have such a central role and word of mouth is a key way in which news is spread.

Key points in understanding how to manage reputational risk for differential advantage are:

1 Reputation and risk must be prioritized together, though this requires a deeper understanding of both concepts.

2 Reputational risk needs ongoing board monitoring and executive management.

3 It depends on managing *key* stakeholders' expectations of corporate behaviour such as customers, employees and shareholders.

4 It is arguably becoming more important for a CEO than managing the company.

5 Emotional factors affect perception and expectations and cut across all key stakeholder groups so that attitudes, feelings and experiences bind customers, shareholders and employees who have overlapping identities.

6 It is greater for companies competing in dynamic environments and/or established corporate brands, i.e. those that have resonance with three or more generations.

7 It needs to have a clear line of sight to the board for two reasons. First because it is integrally linked to value creation and risk identification, assessment and management. Second, because of the need for corporate accountability – with the non-executives playing a key role.

8 The executive management team needs to understand what it is and how it can be aligned.

9 Key elements of reputational risk can be defined for international service companies but the priorities, degree of focus and impact varies.

10 Reputational risk and reputational opportunity need to be managed together to drive value creation.

Key points in understanding how to manage reputational risk for value creation are:

1 Reputational risk is directly related to trust and commitment (for customers, employees and shareholders) and is crystallized when this is broken.

2 It *depends* on the *expectations* of key stakeholders, the *behaviour* (perceived and actual) of the organization and the *trust* to sustain the relationship. It is leadership that moves it from reputational risk to reputational opportunity.

3 *At its core* is the attitude, feeling and experience from the stakeholder to the organization *and* vice-versa. This is an increasingly important determinant of commitment and trust and it can be manifested in the tolerance levels for corporate behaviour.

4 Managing *reputational risk is an integral element in managing relationships* with customers, employees and shareholders. In that respect it is an increasingly critical determinant of cash flow and other measures of business success. This is increasingly characterized by a stronger expectation of transparency in corporate governance, pricing, competition and reporting/communication.

5 *Strong internal cultures minimize reputational risk.* Cross-functional working can be used to embed it in the corporate culture and stress-test organizational response. However, this requires a climate of trust, openness and a willingness to accept criticism, where founded.

6 The current focus from risk professionals, auditors and communications consultants is on protection or superficial enhancement. Reputational risk is much more than this and needs to be seen as an intangible asset and an integral part of corporate governance to ensure the top level focus for it to be monitored. It can then be converted into an opportunity to create value.

7 Value creation has hard and soft components which is being increasingly recognized by financial regulators.

8 The shareholders vs. stakeholder debate is a distraction: stakeholders increasingly have multiple identities (employees are shareholders; investors are consumers, consumers are activists, employees are consumers) which influence their expectations of corporate behaviour. This is being accelerated by generational change and people's awareness of their power in this context. Stakeholders' interests are converging.

9 Social and ethical risk is a subset of reputational risk and boards need to see it through the reputational risk lens.

10 Corporate accountability needs to be seen as part of a company's international relationships and responsibilities and not as an optional add-on for global players. Increasingly it must be framed in a context to which host communities and their policy-makers and companies can relate which itself can mitigate relationship/reputation risk.

11 Political risk is connected to reputational risk and applies to public and private sectors.

12 The performing arts can be key to communicating reputational risk especially when there is a need to instil wider perspectives quickly, for example, through training.

Fig. 8.2 Process – how the dynamics of reputational risk works (C)

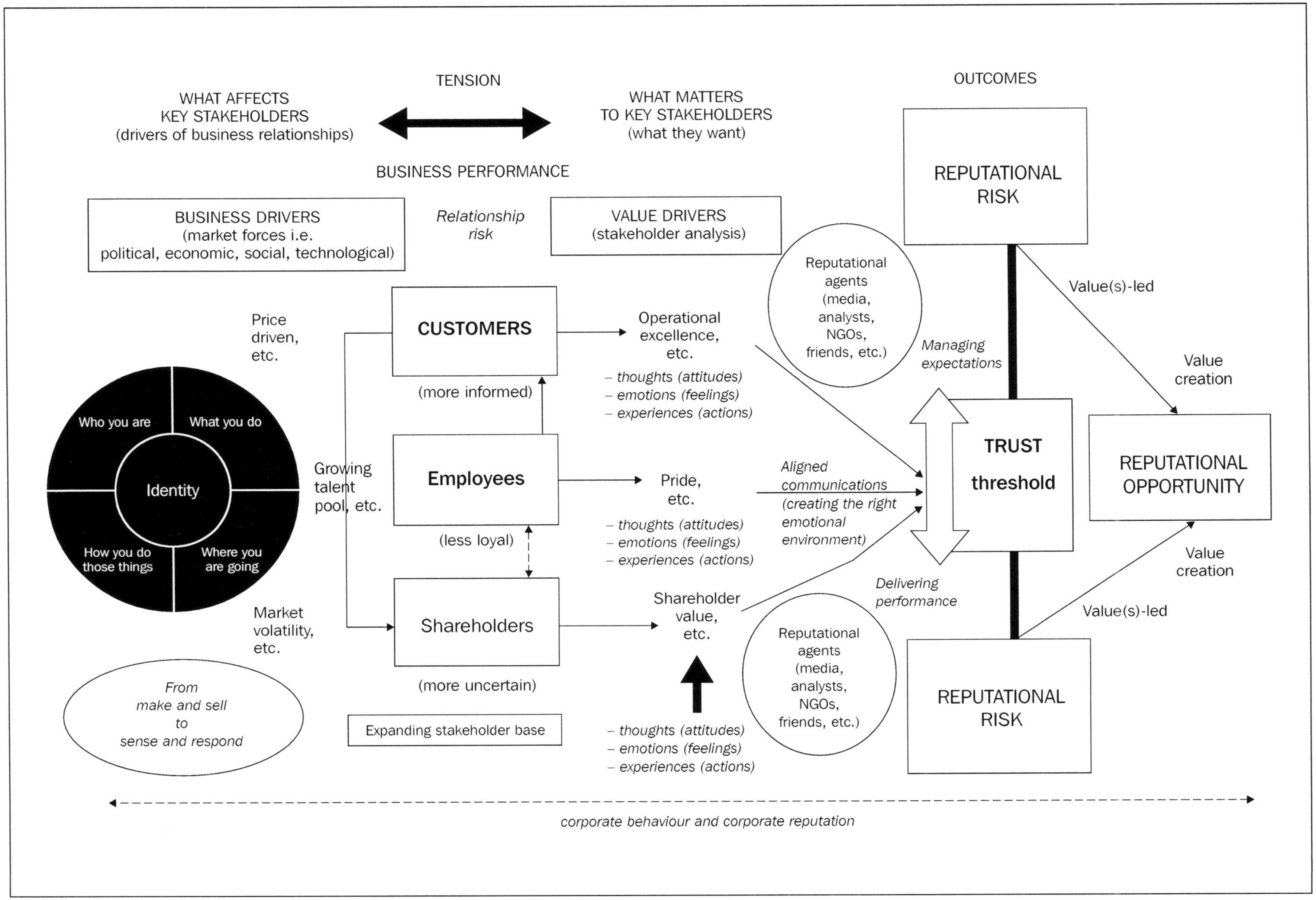

Appendices

Assessing the effectiveness of risk and control processes: appendix to the Turnbull Report (1999)

Some questions which the board may wish to consider and discuss with management when regularly reviewing reports on internal control and carrying out its annual assessment are set out below. The questions are not intended to be exhaustive and will need to be tailored to the particular circumstances of the company.

This Appendix should be read in conjunction with the guidance set out in this document.

1. Risk assessment

Does the company have clear objectives and have they been communicated so as to provide effective direction to employees on risk assessment and control issues? For example, do objectives and related plans include measurable performance targets and indicators?

Are the significant internal and external operational, financial, compliance and other risks identified and assessed on an ongoing basis? (Significant risks may, for example, include those related to market, credit, liquidity, technological, legal, health, safety and environmental, reputation, and business probity issues.)

Is there a clear understanding by management and others within the company of what risks are acceptable to the board?

2. Control environment and control activities

Does the board have clear strategies for dealing with the significant risks that have been identified? Is there a policy on how to manage these risks?

Do the company's culture, code of conduct, human resource policies and performance reward systems support the business objectives and risk management and internal control system?

Does senior management demonstrate, through its actions as well as its policies, the necessary commitment to competence, integrity and fostering a climate of trust within the company?

Are authority, responsibility and accountability defined clearly such that decisions are made and actions taken by the appropriate people? Are the decisions and actions of different parts of the company appropriately coordinated?

Does the company communicate to its employees what is expected of them and the scope of their freedom to act? This may apply to areas such as customer relations; service levels for both internal and outsourced activities; health, safety and environmental protection; security of tangible and intangible assets; business continuity issues; expenditure matters; accounting; and financial and other reporting.

Do people in the company (and in its providers of outsourced services) have the knowledge, skills and tools to support the achievement of the company's objectives and to manage effectively risks to their achievement?

How are processes/controls adjusted to reflect new or changing risks, or operational deficiencies?

3. Information and communication

Do management and the board receive timely, relevant and reliable reports on progress against business objectives and the related risks that provide them with the information, from inside and outside the company, needed for decision-making and management review purposes? This could include performance reports and indicators of change, together with qualitative information such as on customer satisfaction, employee attitudes, etc.

Are information needs and related information systems reassessed as objectives and related risks change or as reporting deficiencies are identified?

Are periodic reporting procedures, including half-yearly and annual reporting, effective in communicating a balanced and understandable account of the company's position and prospects?

Are there established channels of communication for individuals to report suspected breaches of laws or regulations or other improprieties?

4. Monitoring

Are there ongoing processes embedded within the company's overall business operations, and addressed by senior management, which monitor the effective application of the policies, processes and activities related to internal control and risk management? (Such processes may include control self-assessment, confirmation by personnel of compliance with policies and codes of conduct, internal audit reviews or other management reviews).

Do these processes monitor the company's ability to re-evaluate risks and adjust controls effectively in response to changes in its objectives, its business, and its external environment?

Are there effective follow-up procedures to ensure that appropriate change or action occurs in response to changes in risk and control assessments?

Is there appropriate communication to the board (or board committees) on the effectiveness of the ongoing monitoring processes on risk and control matters? This should include reporting any significant failings or weaknesses on a timely basis.

Are there specific arrangements for management monitoring and reporting to the board on risk and control matters of particular importance? These could include, for example, actual or suspected fraud and other illegal or irregular acts, or matters that could adversely affect the company's reputation or financial position.

Lord Marshall: speech to British Airways managers, 10 March 2000

Welcome everyone. A rather traumatic day I guess in the history of our great company. And obviously with a considerable degree of sadness to see Bob Ayling after almost 15 years taking off. And I obviously owe it to you to give you some explanation and background to this. And we have to also recognize that the media will put its own various spin and reach its own conclusions. No doubt we will have a considerable degree of buffeting from certain elements of the press and perhaps from the television and radio. I suspect that that is going to go on for a few days. Almost certainly it's going to have a life of its own tonight, in the Saturday press and for sure in the Sunday press, with all those inside jobs where they will be probing and delving and basically reach their own conclusions and ending where they choose to write those un-named sources to confirm the particular conclusions that they will have drawn in advance. So we'll have to weather that storm.

But I'll start if I may by saying that Bob has made a very major contribution indeed over the entire time that he was here. He and I have worked together very closely throughout those 15 years. And I think in the last four years, which have certainly not been easy by any stretch of the imagination, a lot of tough decisions have been taken and have been implemented. And they have been, certainly in an overall sense, for the benefit of this company. The board came to a viewpoint very recently – and when I say very recently I'm talking specifically in the last two to three weeks and certainly since our last board meeting in early February – that perhaps the time was approaching when it would be appropriate to have a new face at the helm. Recognizing all of those achievements, all of those tough decisions that had been taken over these four years but, and also agreeing unanimously with the strategy that we have in place is the right one. However, we had a growing sense and feeling that we still had quite a bit to do in terms of morale in the organization and that also would have an effect, because it inevitably does, on the levels of service that we provide to our customers. And it was that which resulted in my sitting down with Bob earlier this week and in the process of several discussions during the course of the week led to the conclusion last night that it would be appropriate for Bob to resign and for us to seek a replacement who would be able to fulfil those objectives of taking the present strategy, taking the tough decisions of the last few years and adding to it what I hope is going to be over time a significant increase, a significant improvement in the morale of the company. And that of course requires us to ensure that our people do feel motivated, and that in turn we believe – and certainly has been the case in the past – will lead to high levels of customer service and more approbation out there for the job that is done by all of the people of our company.

So as we look to the future, we are going to be searching both inside and outside to select the very best person possible, that we can possibly get to provide in a way a new focus, to take the helm and lead the company forward in the immediate years ahead. I've already said to you that the strategy has full approval of the board of directors. And we believe that that is absolutely right as we go forward. Certainly in terms of the complete plan, certainly in terms of the root structure and the changes that have been made, some changes that are in mind for the immediate future, certainly in terms of the product and service enhancements that have been announced and are in process of being introduced recently. Just as an aside, when I spoke to the editor of the *Financial Times* about an hour ago he said, gee I'm really feeling great today, I'm able to talk with you because I flew in your new club world seat-bed last night back from New York, he said I had a great night's sleep, I really feel very rested indeed. So I said Richard that's absolutely what we want to hear in terms of all of the investment that we're making, just spread the good word around all of your colleagues particularly in the *Financial Times*. So I can't tell you how long it's going to take, how long you're going to have to put up with me in this pro tem role. It will take as long as is necessary for us to reach the final decision on who is the best person to ensure the future success of the company, as I say building on the existing strategies.

... So if anybody's got any questions I would love to respond to them ... anybody want to raise any particular points ... all stunned, well these things do happen, they always happen and I guess when they happen they come as a surprise, there is always a shock element, there's always some degree of emotion attached to them. We are big enough to cope I'm sure with that situation and to give as much encouragement as we can throughout the organization. So I look forward to working more closely with you than I have over the last four years and see what we can do to really enhance what has been done during that period of time. Thank you very much, good luck.

Fostering growth and promoting a responsible market economy. A G8 declaration, Evian, June 2003

Efficient capital markets are critical to achieving and maintaining economic growth. To support growth, economies need sound legal systems, effective regulation and transparent corporate governance practices. These factors underpin effective disclosure that is fundamental to well-functioning markets. Sound social frameworks and attention to the long-term impacts, including on the environment, of investment decisions and business processes are also important for sustainable growth. Timely and accurate information assists shareholders in exercising control and investors in allocating funds to their most productive uses. In support, governmental authorities should ensure that corporate reporting assists them in monitoring markets and in identifying vulnerabilities.

Trust and confidence are key ingredients of a well-functioning market economy. Restoring investor confidence through sound corporate governance, as well as corporate structures and market intermediaries that are more accountable, is essential to promoting growth in our economies. We encourage the many initiatives underway, in national capitals, international financial institutions and by international standard-setting bodies, to strengthen governance standards and disclosure regimes.

Corporate integrity, strengthened market discipline, increased transparency through improved disclosure, effective regulation and corporate social responsibility are common principles that are the foundations for sound macro-economic growth.

COMMON VALUES AND PRINCIPLES

1. Corporate governance

1.1. Market integrity

We commit to pursue with strong resolve our fight to further improve the integrity of the international economy (including efforts against money laundering, financial crime and terrorist financing), which is essential for its efficiency, fairness and transparency. We will continue to work towards investor protection, enhanced regulatory compliance and vigorous law enforcement, including through comprehensive cross-border assistance.

1.2. Strengthened market discipline and effective regulation

We re-affirm our support of sound regulatory regimes that encourage and promote market dynamism and foster fair and effective competition among market participants. In order to support the beneficial process of globalization, we aim in particular to enhance international cooperation and to foster a sound level playing field. We strongly support the work undertaken by the Financial Stability Forum (FSF).

1.3. Accountability and enhanced corporate governance

We reaffirm that companies must be accountable to their shareholders. As underscored in the OECD Principles of Corporate Governance, other stakeholders also have strong interests in these issues. To this end, we call for continued efforts globally to enhance corporate governance.

We also strongly support the ongoing review of the OECD Principles and the implementation of the International Organization of Securities Commission (IOSCO) principles relating to corporate governance.

1.4. Increased transparency and quality of financial information

Integrity, quality and accessibility are the cornerstones of reliable financial information. We call on all information providers – first and foremost companies and their auditors, as well as financial analysts, investment banks and rating agencies – to abide by these principles.

Recognizing the need for financial stability, we commit to promoting high quality, internationally recognized accounting standards that are capable of consistent application, interpretation and enforcement, especially for listed companies.

2. Corporate social responsibility

Consistent with the outcomes of the World Summit on Sustainable Development, we support voluntary efforts to enhance corporate social and environmental responsibility.

We will work with all interested countries on initiatives that support sustainable economic growth, including the creation of an environment in which business can act responsibly. We also welcome voluntary initiatives by companies that promote corporate social and environmental responsibility, such as the OECD Guidelines for Multinational Enterprises and the UN Global Compact principles consistent with their economic interest. We encourage companies to work with other parties to complement and foster the implementation of existing instruments, such as the OECD guidelines and the ILO 1998 Declarations on Fundamental Principles and Rights at work.

3. Corruption and transparency

We emphasize our determination to fight corruption, one of the key obstacles to economic and social development, and mismanagement of public revenue and expenditure.

Significant and lasting progress in these areas can only be achieved through the concerted efforts of all governments, international institutions, the private sector and civil society. To this end we set out the attached G8 action plan.

We will jointly ask UN bodies, the IFIs, FSF, standard-setting bodies and other relevant international organizations to work with us on these issues and to further integrate them in their programmes and actions.